JOHN DEWEY:
HIS THOUGHT AND INFLUENCE

THE ORESTES BROWNSON SERIES
ON CONTEMPORARY THOUGHT AND AFFAIRS

No. 2   1960

John Dewey:

His Thought and Influence

Edited by
JOHN BLEWETT, S.J.

With a Foreword by
JOHN S. BRUBACHER

FORDHAM UNIVERSITY PRESS · NEW YORK

Nihil Obstat: EDWARD J. MONTANO, S.T.D.
                 Censor librorum

Imprimatur
                 ✠ FRANCIS CARDINAL SPELLMAN
                 Archbishop of New York

                 March 9, 1960

LIBRARY OF CONGRESS CATALOG NUMBER: 60-10737

CONTENTS

v

130787

Foreword

This collection of essays on the thought and influence of John Dewey is a stirring tribute to him. No one will be much surprised that Dewey's philosophical friends and supporters have celebrated the recent centennial of his birth by reading papers and publishing books and essays. But when his philosophical critics and adversaries join in the celebration we can take it as a great compliment to the length of his shadow. It is praise indeed when friend and foe alike can unite to mark the achievements of so controversial a figure.

It is notable that these Catholic essays honor Dewey, not by offering a new critique of his position, but by making an honest endeavor to understand and portray just what his thought and influence have been. For the most part appraisal is only incidental and by inference. This proportion of emphasis has several advantages. For one it lessens the atmosphere of unyielding deadlock in which philosophical debate and exposition so often take place. For another, correspondingly, it makes it seem more possible and likely that long-standing adversaries may find some mutual principles on which their minds are *ad idem*. In a day when democratic and communist nations find themselves at each other's throats it is comforting to feel that some of the philosophical divisions within the West can be approached as dispassionately as they are in this collection of essays. Too often divisions and misunderstandings arise because opponents leap at each other before they have taken the other's measure. Happily there is no danger of that in this book.

Quite the contrary is the case. Some of the contributors to this volume have written so understandingly of Dewey that they almost give the impression of writing sympathetically as well. In fact they do write sympathetically in places. While they drop hints of the incompleteness of Dewey's thought in its entirety they do find numerous specific points at which Catholic and non-Catholic alike can find new insight and draw new inspiration from his writings. In fact some of the authors here place Dewey in such an appealing light at times that the non-Catholic reader may occasionally be confused whether the author is agreeing with Dewey or having unusual success in leaning over backwards in being fair to him. If not confused on that point he may well wonder how anyone who understands Dewey so well can possibly disagree with him in his over-all position. In such instances the average reader may well wish more space had been available for comparison and criticism.

While the authors of this volume have made a sincere and painstaking effort to understand Dewey, there seems to be a general opinion among them that Dewey never made a similar effort himself to understand them or rather their position. One could wish on that account that some of the authors could have contributed chapters to the volume on Dewey in Paul Schilpp's monumental *Library of Living Philosophers*. The genius of the volumes in that Library, it will be remembered, is that renowned philosophers were given an opportunity while yet alive to respond to their critics and interpreters. It certainly would have been interesting in the volume at hand to see how far Dewey would have considered these Catholic scholars to have understood him and in what vein he would have responded to the inadequacies of his position as they see them.

Invaluable as such a volume as Schilpp's is, our times, it seems to me, require concerted effort to reach more of a consensus than his volume does. This is not to say that there is a negligible value in exploiting our differences. Quite the opposite, unless we do exploit them, we shall not discover or invent better theories, to say nothing of a failure to detect the defects in the logic of our present ones. But it could be that we exploit our differences too eagerly and divisively. In periods of relative peace and security such eagerness and individualism can be contained without danger to the common weal. Indeed they may be a welcome antidote to the risk of social complacency. Yet today with democracy and communism as antipodal as they are and with such enormous power charged around these opposite poles of thought, there is imminent danger of a spark leaping between them which will ignite and destroy everything within almost a world-wide radius. Under such circumstances perhaps it would be more appropriate to devote some of our best philosophical energies toward trying to find out the points on which a consensus can be built.

Peace, as the preamble to Unesco states, depends on developing the "intellectual and moral solidarity" of mankind. We cannot afford to let such solidarity be a mere by-product of the philosophical clash of thought. I believe we must consciously strive for it. We must not only strive for greater understanding between East and West but we must try to close ranks in the West as much as possible. Our strength demands it. Most meetings of philosophical associations which I have attended have been devoted to exploiting the differences of its members. I would like to see one dedicated to exploring their agreements. Think of what might come out of a meeting where each one attending would not be eager to press his own point of view or find flaws in another's argument but would concentrate on searching for common understanding and agreement. Instead of immediately taking issue with someone's thesis suppose we were to inquire whether we caught his meaning exactly or whether perhaps with a change of wording we might even mean the same thing. Of course philosophers do this now to a limited extent but suppose it were to be the main spirit of the occasion! If we did I am confident that the areas in which thought coincided would be larger and more numerous than we have any notion at present. The current volume, it strikes me, is an important step in such a direction.

JOHN S. BRUBACHER

THE TRIUMPH OF SUBJECTIVITY: AN INTRODUCTION
TO TRANSCENDENTAL PHENOMENOLOGY

J. QUENTIN LAUER, S.J.

THE BROWNSON SERIES NO. 1, 1958

Introduction

The long life of John Dewey and his central position in American Education in a period that saw the greatest changes since the Renaissance, quite naturally made him the idol of many of his followers and, especially, generated strong opposition among others who saw him as the destroyer of traditional ways of thinking. Changes, indeed, he saw and perhaps caused in the course of his long career; and, in this centenary year of Dewey's birth, the wave of indignation over the sad state of American Education that has swept through certain segments of the American people since Sputnik rose into space, will surely bring about, among other things, some serious re-examinations of his thoughts.

Any valid appraisal and criticism of a man's thought, however, must well up from intellectual charity (sympathy, if you will), and not from either resentment fed by hearsay, or at best, superficial study, nor from partisanship. No true understanding of a man's thought can be had unless we learn by critical and historical study to see how he came to put his questions in the way he did and give the answers he gave to them. "You need to go on and see *how far* a man's theory will really take you, and how much truth can be got out of it, and just where and why it breaks down."

It is in this spirit that the eight contributors to this volume, published in commemoration of the centenary of Dewey's birth, have thought to analyze and appraise certain distinctive features of the thought and influence of the philosopher of science and democracy. There are, as might be anticipated, some passages of even sharp criticism, but the tone of the book as a whole will come as a surprise to those who may have imagined that all Catholics were, necessarily, anti-progressive in all senses of that, by now cloudy, word. While not at all pretending to give a fully rounded picture of the whole of Dewey's philosophy, these studies do center on themes with which the name of Dewey has been inextricably linked: experience, nature, democracy, the meaning

xi

of knowledge, work, education, the meaning of history, and socio-cultural change as seen in China.

The careful reader will detect differences of interpretation among the various contributions, but running through all of them is a unity provided by a humanistically Catholic view of man.

Few words have led to so much confusion in studies on Dewey as "naturalism." In an effort to clarify the meaning of Dewey's naturalism, Professor Collins tracks the changes in his views on nature. The importance for the development of Dewey's views on nature of his revulsion from the theological evolutionism of Herbert Spencer and from the institutionalizations of Christianity with which he was familiar, will come as a surprise to those who airily dismiss concern with the pre-1904 Dewey as antiquarianism.

My essay, centering on the formative years of Dewey's life, is concerned with his conception of democracy as a way of life. I advance the hypothesis that a little-known "mystical" experience of the young Dewey sheds light on the fervent commitment to democracy which he successively justified by arguments from Christianity, neo-Hegelianism, and, later, experimentalism. In relation to Dewey's stress on communication as the lifeblood of democracy, I suggest that his aversion to, and disinterest in, Catholicism as a living force rests in part on his unwillingness to allow that a personal God, distinct from the historical process, became incarnate at a specific point in history and instituted what Dewey chose to call the "method of authority."

Dewey is probably best known to scholar and untutored alike as the proponent of a theory of knowledge-as-doing. Professor Zedler, in an effort to make Dewey's final theory seem less bizarre than it does when viewed from its antecedents, recounts the gradual changes in his interpretation of the fact of knowing.

Sister Joseph Mary Raby, writing on the educational philosophy which Dewey formulated chiefly in his decade at the University of Chicago (1894-1904), finds two quite different meanings for democracy: a form of political government and a way of life. It is the second meaning which is operative in Dewey's philosophy of education, a meaning which includes a distrust of authority, a rejection of all "absolutes," and a belief in the near-infallibility of scientific methods used in no matter what area of life. It is this interpretation of democracy which was to have been institutionalized in "progressive" schools.

Introduction

The place of work in experience and the role of occupations as unifying foci for the variety of studies in primary school curricula was one of the dominant themes in Dewey's writing on education. Father Donohue explores Dewey's interpretation of work and the place of technology in the modern world. He suggests that Dewey's awareness of the changes being wrought on the American scene by urbanization and industrialization qualified him to discuss needed educational changes with more understanding than those of his critics who still thought longingly of Renaissance education as a viable ideal.

Dewey's alertness to present trends and needs colored his attitude toward the writing and study of history, Professor Neill contends. In his understandable repudiation of the exaggerated stress on objectivity, so characteristic of nineteenth-century German historiography, Dewey went almost to the opposite extreme, reducing history to a type of apologetic for what he believed were necessary social reforms.

Professor Pollock's essay attempts to situate Dewey within the larger context of American pragmatism which, in turn, is seen as a response to distinctive challenges of the American scene and as a derivative from the concern for the temporal order which marks certain formulations of the Christian message. Deweyan experience, with its accent on openness and on the novelty of things, is coupled with an attitude toward the natural order which is easily misunderstood.

In the final essay of the collection, Father Berry evaluates Dewey's most important excursion into the cultural affairs of another nation. Invited to China at a critical turn in its modern history, Dewey spent close to two years interpreting Western thought to the Chinese university world and thereby assisting the growth of the new liberal movement among students and intellectuals. Father Berry draws on his knowledge of recent Chinese history to compare the conflicting voices to which the new China turned its ear and offers some reflections on the transitoriness of Dewey's influence.

To say that the heart of Dewey's long philosophical effort was to remake man's image of himself may be an exaggeration. But it is a meaningful exaggeration. Though Dewey resented being looked on as a mere anarchist, a mere destroyer, he never blushed at being considered an iconoclast. And the image he wanted to burn was the image of himself which Christian man had accepted for centuries: a creature of body and spirit, destined for, and hence responsible to, a personal

God, who is distinct from but active in history. While conceding that this view of man had played a useful role in earlier Western history, Dewey argued that it had run its course and for a large number of post-Christians in the United States Dewey was the prophet. If now his influence is on the wane, should this be interpreted to mean that today's youth has suffered a failure of nerve and is looking for that infantile certainty which Dewey so rightly castigated? Before we accept this explanation, it might be well to ask whether Dewey's account of Christianity is the one the rising generation is familiarizing itself with or whether, in accord with Dewey's oft-repeated advice to trust in experience, it is refusing to put on the blinkers of an earlier generation (Dewey's) and is actually searching the evidence for itself. If this is so, then a continuing study of Dewey himself, carried on without bitterness and partisanship, and centered on questions to be resolved or, at least, illumined by an appeal to discussable data rather than to slogans, is a desideratum. It is the hope of all the contributors to this volume that their essays raise questions which are too often avoided or shed light on aspects of Dewey's thinking which need further study.

One of the rewards of an editor is his opportunity publicly to record his gratitude to his co-writers. This is especially true when the editor actually receives a contribution from all who, perhaps in the first flush of enthusiasm, promised one. To the seven other contributors who produced what they promised despite the multiplicity of their tasks and commitments—my warmest thanks. I am particularly grateful to my fellow Jesuits, the Reverend John W. Donohue, S.J. and the Reverend Edwin A. Quain, S.J., Director of the Fordham University Press, and to Miss Emily Schossberger, who assisted him in seeing the manuscript through to publication after my return to Japan in August, 1959. Finally, in the name of all the contributors, I should like to thank Professor John S. Brubacher for his gracious foreword.

JOHN BLEWETT, S.J.

I

The Genesis of
Dewey's Naturalism

JAMES COLLINS

James Collins was born in Holyoke, Massachusetts, and educated at The Catholic University of America. He served as Research Fellow in Philosophy at Harvard University. Since 1945 he has taught at St. Louis University, where he is professor of philosophy. He was President of The American Catholic Philosophical Association in 1953-54. His published books are: The Thomistic Philosophy of the Angels (*1947*), The Existentialists: A Critical Study (*1952*), The Mind of Kierkegaard (*1953*), A History of Modern European Philosophy (*1954*), *and* God in Modern Philosophy (*1959*).

The occurrence in 1959 of John Dewey's centenary does not automatically place us in a favorable position to understand and assess his achievements. He enjoyed such a long period of creative work and the practical movements he supported are still affecting people so profoundly that it is difficult to bring him within the proper perspective for making a just estimate. Yet anyone interested in the philosophical issues he raised can be sure of at least one thing. Dewey's thought is intrinsically worthy of close study, no matter what be the outcome of the educational and social tendencies which claim to draw inspiration more or less faithfully from him. He is a major twentieth-century philosopher and his ideas have a staying quality which will enable them to outlast the tides of intellectual fashion in which they have become involved.

A good way to gain access to Dewey's mind is to focus attention upon some master theme in his philosophy. One topic which animates his work from beginning to end is the question of nature and naturalism. Under one aspect or another, this general problem is close to the center of discussion in every phase of his development. It certainly permeates all the writings of his last thirty years of active work. Indeed, the naturalism of this last period, during which he became a public figure, is so massive and dominant that it seems to resist a careful analytic and genetic study. We tend to give the term "naturalism" a vague and conventional meaning when applied to Dewey, as though the emotion of approval or hostility evoked by its use is self-explanatory and settles the issue. The fact is, however, that his position on nature and naturalism does have a definite structure and a definite history which are open to investigation. The purpose of the present essay is to follow the genesis of his views on this question during the crucial formative years from 1884 to 1909. The conception of nature gradually forged during this quarter-century span became one of the permanent bases of his philosophy and served to determine the sense in which it was a naturalistic philosophy. Dewey's subsequent elaborations of naturalism built upon this foundation by expanding its themes and by dealing aggressively with obstacles to its full acceptance in our society.

Nature as the Irritant against Idealism

Schopenhauer once remarked that no great work is done in philosophy unless the individual thinker is goaded into it by some deeply troubling issue which he cannot soothe over and forget. In Dewey's philosophical development, the role of creative irritant was played by the problem of nature.[1] He was attracted to it almost from the outset and, for a while, thought that he could provide a neat idealistic solution to difficulties arising in this area. After trying to carry out an idealistic interpretation of nature, he found the results too unsatisfactory to avoid making a radical revision of some basic points and thus moving beyond idealism to a distinctive philosophy which could do more justice to the views on nature then coming to the fore. The record of Dewey's preoccupation with this matter is found in the articles published during his years at Michigan and Minnesota (1884-1894). They show that the theme of nature antedated his naturalism itself and that his reflections upon it furnished some of the prime considerations eventually compelling him to make the journey from idealism to naturalism.

What strikes us at once in Dewey's initial publications is their confidence that the idealist can take full account of the current findings in biology and psychology, the sciences of nature making the most rapid and revolutionary advances. Idealism is especially recommended as providing the best philosophical integration for the work being done on reflex action, evolutionary theory, and empirical description of consciousness. Far from excusing the notoriously weak Hegelian philosophy of nature as being an unimportant part of the system, Dewey seeks to improve idealism precisely at this point so that it can become adequate to the scientific findings about natural reality.

He analyzes Wundt's research on reflex action, for instance, in order to show that it brings out pertinent evidence against the Cartesian view of mind without lending any real support to materialism.[2] Reflex action is a basic nervous activity which involves purposive adaptation and hence a teleological category which cannot be reduced simply to physical causation. In studying its significance, we move from the purely physical description to a recognition of mind as being immanent in physical operations. Dewey is already interested in adjustment as a mediating concept both for showing the immanence of purposive mind and for guarding against a simple reduction to physical conditions. The adjusting function is one way in which a goal-seeking mind or spirit realizes its own purposes through the means of the bodily organism.

Thus a test case was made of the explanatory power of idealism to show the presence of telic mind in that area of nature studied by physiological psychology. That is why Dewey's later functional explanation of the reflex arc, without making any use of the theory of purposive spirit, assumed such decisive philosophical importance for him. To be able to dispense with the idealistic account of mind in this significant region in the study of nature suggested to him that idealism is irrelevant to the actual world that holds our interest.

Even in his original idealistic interpretation of reflex action, however, Dewey established two traits about the philosophical study of nature which became part of his permanent doctrine. That the critical thinker should be on his guard against a panoramic or picture-thinking approach to problems raised by experience, was the first point made. Thus he should not look for an easy set of pictures for visualizing the mind-body question, but should seek reflectively after the interpretative principles which can account for the scientifically describable condition of man.

And on the broader scale, Dewey observed that his "object is not to get into the inside of nature and behold with mortal eyes what is going on there, but the less ambitious one of inquiring what principles must be used in order to give meaning to the facts of the case." [3] In the inquiry into nature, we should be skeptical about theories based upon the claim to have intuitive access to the workings of nature and about theories relying upon pictorial explanation. Dewey's constant stress upon treating philosophy mainly as a method rather than a content sprang from his adherence to this rule. He always remained suspicious of "inside stories" about the real structure of nature, even though he did not resist claiming to be on the inside of the only proper method for inquiring into the natural world.

That the facts turned up in the course of Darwin's research radically modify our conception of nature and, in turn, require a rethinking of philosophy, was Dewey's second conclusion. Neither the philosophical Darwinism of Spencer nor the older idealism seemed to him adequate for interpreting the evidences of biological evolution. He criticized Spencer for basing his synthesis upon the picture of age-long accidental changes, since this was a panoramic approach offering no specific account of the presence of intelligence and active adaptation. Spencer either glossed over the problem of intelligence and purpose by the vagueness of his universal formulas or else introduced a covert element of purposiveness into nature as a whole, as the price paid for making a mechanistic account of some particular instances. Even during Dewey's idealistic period, however, he readily admitted that German and British idealism could not meet the challenge of evolution without accepting some incisive modifications. It is important to remark that Dewey's criticism of idealism began as an *internal* reconstruction while he was still its firm adherent. That is why he did not have to cross too wide a gulf or leave behind all his key notions when at last he did move on to naturalism. Furthermore, it is significant that he felt the need to modify idealism in the face of psychological and biological findings about man within the context of nature.

His problem was to accommodate these findings without permitting them to have the decisive word in determining the real status of nature and man. The solution was to redefine the method of experience and the psychological standpoint so that they would fit into the idealistic context.[4] To adopt the psychological method in philosophy means to confine all questions about the reality of things to the manner in which they present themselves in experience. But experience itself refers to the relations which arise within consciousness as a wider whole: the experiential method supposes that consciousness is the only inclusive standard for being and knowing. All philosophically significant exist-ence is relative to consciousness, and even our individual consciousness is relative to the universal consciousness. When we say that conscious-ness is the philosophical absolute in method and reality, however, we are referring neither to an isolated individual consciousness nor to a separated universal one. The decisive word rests with absolute mind or consciousness, taken precisely as a concrete synthesis of the individual and the universal components.

Dewey expected that this reformulation of idealism would enable him to meet the argument of evolutionary realism. The latter position in-cluded every effort to explain consciousness genetically as being in-trinsically dependent upon prior physiological states and ultimately upon a scientifically described evolutionary process, which precedes individ-ual minds and is their causal source. Dewey criticized this explanation with counterarguments which at first seemed incontrovertible to him. The evolutionary approach applies only to your mind and mine, i.e., to the individual aspects of consciousness. But these individual modes, to-gether with all their objective correlates on the side of the evolving or-ganism, are only abstractions made from the concrete totality of ab-solute mind or consciousness in which the full reality of experience resides. Furthermore, our very ability to devise an evolutionary theory about individual consciousness is testimony that the latter can transcend itself and its biological context. It moves beyond its immediate anteced-ents by recognizing its synthesis with universal consciousness, and hence its capacity for studying experience as a totality, within which the course of biological evolution is a particular strand of explanation.

Dewey's final objection against evolutionary realism is in the sphere of methodology. Philosophical issues cannot be settled either by an in-dependent logic or by a philosophy of nature founded upon the em-pirical sciences as its fundamental source of control. From the view-point of Dewey's version of psychological idealism, logic and philosophy of nature must be regarded as abstractions made within the context of the organic totality of individual-and-universal consciousness. Logic treats of the formal structure of thought found within this whole, whereas philosophy of nature deals with its material side or objective content. These approaches are valid abstractions insofar as they respect the controlling reality of spirit or the totality of self-consciousness. But if they subordinate this reality to a supposedly autonomous standard, such as the laws of formal logic or the evolutionary theory of natural selection, then they become vicious abstractions and violate the method and order of philosophy.

This is the high point in the early Dewey's defense of a revised idealism and its claim to deal adequately with the sciences of nature and philosophy of nature. In attempting to make the defense more detailed and pointed, however, he begins to encounter the difficulties which will eventually require him to abandon his psychological idealism. For instance, he agrees with Hegel's empirical critics that no dialectical passage can be made from logic to philosophy of nature.[5] We must start with facts rather than logical categories, and hence we must move from nature to the logical sphere rather than try to follow the reverse path. In granting a relative primacy to the domain of nature, Dewey already comes dangerously close to conceding that we make our unconditioned start with nature as factually experienced and analyzed by the empirical sciences.

Furthermore, in order to distinguish clearly between his own psychological idealism and Hegel's logic of the absolute idea, he must describe nature as the realm of fact and existent relations. Although he does try to save idealism by measuring the factual and concrete traits of nature by the standard of the totality of consciousness, Dewey cannot quiet the suggestion that this reference of natural fact, existence, and relation to another standard is just a further instance of vicious abstraction or of trying to impose a set of logical categories on nature. The question becomes increasingly more pertinent whether experience is correlated primarily with the idealistic postulate of universal consciousness or with natural existents, including our ordinary conscious acts and organic states.

Under pressure from such considerations, Dewey begins to hesitate whether to regard philosophy of nature simply as an abstractive application of a philosophical method grounded in the consciousness-postulate, or as a reflective synthesis of the working procedures of the empirical sciences. He concedes that the former position would weaken the philosophical significance of the actual methods used in the sciences of nature. Yet he also recognizes that the latter alternative would affect much more than the philosophy of nature. It would open the way for specifying the general meaning of experience and philosophical method in terms of a natural reality given fundamentally through the empirical sciences and not through an idealistic conception of the totality of consciousness. An unqualified and fully concrete start would then have to be made with nature as directly experienced by man and with the actual procedures of the sciences of nature.

We can conclude this section on how the problem of nature functioned as an irritant against Dewey's initial adherence to idealism by noting four weaknesses in his reply to evolutionary realism.

1. Dewey's argument on the abstract character of the genetic approach to man simply supposed that the concrete is identical with the idealistic description of consciousness. But this was the point at issue and could not simply be assumed. In practice, Dewey found himself using "concrete fact" in a thoroughly ambiguous way. Sometimes it signified the idealistic notion of "conscious experience in its totality," whereas in other uses it was a descriptive term for the particular elements given in our ordinary acquaintance with, and scientific account of, natural existents and relations. The trouble with the former usage was that, on Dewey's own admission, philosophy "can deal with this absolute self-consciousness only so far as it has partially and interruptedly realised itself in man." [6] Under these unavoidable human conditions, the totality of spirit does not enjoy the status of a founding and specifying fact for the philosophy of nature, but is a dialectical construction measured by some facts of human experience of natural things.

2. One such fact is our ability to work out an evolutionary theory of the minded organism of man. This testifies to our capacity to reflect on evidence and follow out its implications, even in cases which involve our own history. But the analytic and inferential operations required for elaborating a theory about man's genesis do not force us to suppose any merger or synthetic union between individual and universal consciousness, as the idealistic doctrine of absolute spirit argues. Evolutionary theories about man do rest upon the cooperative work of many researchers over the generations, and yet a decisive difference persists between the idealistic notion of consciousness as a whole and the community of scientific researchers. The latter never gets totalized and transcended into some absolute self-consciousness, because the community of investigation remains open-ended and resists hypostasization.

3. As a consequence, Dewey found it impossible to remove the obscurity from the venerable idealistic term "synthesis," even in reference to the relation of individual and universal consciousness. Granted his rejection of an autonomous logic, he could not clarify its meaning merely by means of the dialectical theory of logic. And on the experiential plane, it could be replaced by describing the interdependence between philosophy of nature on the one hand and the complexus of our

ordinary acquaintance with natural events and the scientific ways of
analysis on the other, without making use of the postulate of universal
consciousness at all. Indeed, Dewey was beginning to suspect that this
interdependence which we can experience is only disrupted by trying
to refer all the components in it to the idealist standard of absolute self-
consciousness. Here was also the root of the unremitting hostility he
later displayed toward any form of dualism involving a transcendent
factor. He came to view every type of transcendence after the model of
this idealistic totality which is disruptive of the actual relations holding
between human experience, nature, and scientific inquiry.

4. One special form of dualism which plagued him from the start
was that between time and eternity. He recognized the distinctively temporal character of all natural events and human acts. Now idealism
would require him to treat nature and everyday man as a manifestation
of self-consciousness, to locate their true reality only in their organic
containment within the eternal totality of mind, and thus to conclude
that their "manifestation is an act not occurring in time, but eternally
completed in the nature of the Absolute, and that it occurs only 'partially' and 'interruptedly' *through* (not *in*) time, in a being like man." [7]
On this reckoning, acceptance of the eternal would sap the temporal
order of its intrinsic significance and initiative. Yet the weight of ordinary experience and scientific research favored the view that the natural
world in its temporal aspect is real and valuable in its own mode of
acting.

Thus Dewey felt himself confronted with the choice of either preserving the integrity of nature as a temporal course or reducing it to the
instrumental role of a manifestation of an eternal consciousness. That is
why he soon came to understand the temporal character of nature as
involving the exclusion of any claim for eternity. He generalized the
idealistic account of time and eternity to cover every way of relating
them, and hence he looked upon every defense of the eternal as containing an attack upon the intrinsic worth of nature in its temporal traits.
The polemical note in Dewey's stress on time became a permanent
aspect of his naturalism.

All these problems pointed unavoidably to one negative conclusion
for Dewey. He could not make a fruitful study of nature and man within
an idealistic framework. Whatever idealistic elements might survive in
his later thought, he could not permit them to reassemble into the central thesis that the really real consists in an all-enveloping eternal totality of consciousness or absolute spirit. He must now explore a way of

philosophizing which rests upon the direct polarity between nature and experience and scientific method.

Critique of Ethical and Religious Conceptions of Nature

To appreciate the actual direction which his search for a more adequate philosophy of nature and man took, we must now consider certain difficulties uncovered by Dewey in the area of ethics and religion during the 1884-1894 period. We will choose two prominent topics: his attack on Spencer's way of founding ethics and his treatment of the Christian message. In both instances, we will find that his criticism turns around the meaning of natural reality and that the result is a permanent contribution to his growing naturalism. This difference will also be observed, however, that whereas in the case of Spencer he is treating of a popular philosophy to which he is not personally committed, his reflections on Christianity do concern his own religious position during these formative years. In the case of both idealism and religion, some factors survive in his later philosophy, albeit in a transformed way and as dominated by a new organizing principle concerning nature and man's role in it.

Even during his college days in Vermont, Dewey was interested in the striking contrast between Kant and Spencer on the foundation of ethics.[8] Kant built his ethics around a sharp dualism of the moral agent and the natural world, whereas Spencer relied upon a close unification of them. This raised the question whether nature inhibits the moral life until man finds some autonomous footing apart from it or whether nature furnishes the very impetus and laws for our moral life. Thus in the formulation of the ethical problem familiar to him, Dewey was accustomed to regard one's view of nature as being highly relevant to one's account of the ethical order.

It seemed to him that the Kantian dualism between moral man and determined nature was rapidly becoming untenable in the wake of current scientific findings. Biology, laboratory psychology, and the social sciences were bringing man wholly within the domain of nature as the inclusive subject of scientific investigation. To use Dewey's own metaphor, the arms of scientifically articulated nature were reaching out to engulf man in his entirety. Hence if the ethical order depended upon retaining the Kantian contrast, then it was doomed to be undermined by every advance in the scientific study of man.

At this point, Spencer held out the possibility of renovating moral life precisely by incorporating it within the general process of nature. As he formulated them, the evolutionary laws themselves contain an ethical implication and hence permit an ethical foundation within the context of scientifically described nature, rather than in opposition to it. The Spencerian evolutionary thinker would have the basic assurance that human life is not anarchic but regulated by natural laws which our intelligence can discover. Moreover, he would be able to establish that evolutionary laws specify man's ethical aim to be the development of the cooperative spirit of the social organism rather than the self-centered individual. Again, evolutionary science would bring out the powerful sanction of conscience as embodying the sifted results of social experience. And it would lend the full force of the order of nature to such virtues as honesty and courage, since it would present them as objectively dictated means for attaining the evolutionary goal of the human social organism.

In describing Dewey's attitude toward Spencer, we must distinguish between the general and quite indeterminate proposal to develop ethics within the context of nature and the specific way in which Spencer tried to make a natural justification of ethical judgments. On the more general issue, Dewey modified his position in accordance with his shift from an idealistic ordering of nature itself to absolute spirit to his later centering of ethical values within the natural world. Nevertheless, it is significant that neither in his idealistic phase nor in his full-fledged naturalism did he accept Spencer's precise method for justifying moral values on the basis of the evolutionary laws of nature. His reluctance on this score is important for understanding his view of nature as well as his ethical standpoint. The reasons advanced during his idealistic period for not following Spencer reveal some of his enduring conceptions of nature. They also generate some difficulties which eventually force him to seek for a better philosophical foundation of the theory of nature than idealism can provide.

In the writings now being analyzed, Dewey sets forth three major objections against the Spencerian doctrine that the physical categories underlying the theory of evolution can also determine the moral ideal for man.

1. It is doubtful that any direct induction can be made from the evolutionary traits established by biologists to the moral ideal of social cooperation. If we were to mold our conduct in conformity with Darwin's description of natural selection, for instance, we would have to support an incessant rivalry and unequal sharing in goods rather than the pattern of mutual help and equal opportunity of access to values.

Competition and social divergence would be our graven law. Although evolution stresses the common origin for all human life, it does not follow on physical and biological grounds alone that men therefore must have a community of interest which is moral in kind. It is fallacious to argue that "because there is a physical community of origin there *must* be an ethical community of end." [9] Organisms develop out of the common pool of life precisely by conflict and by reference to a survival goal in which they do not all equally share.

One interesting feature about this argument is that it appeals over the head of Spencer to the working biologist's notion of evolutionary traits. Whatever Spencer may deduce from his own statement of general evolutionary laws, Dewey finds it more informative to study the biological account. We can get a more reliable conclusion about whether or not to found ethics upon the evolutionary account of nature by examining what a Darwin actually regards as the mechanism of natural selection than by following Spencer's elaborate deduction from physical laws. Although this is an effective tactic against Spencer, it raises in Dewey's mind the question of the larger consistency in his own practice. His own appeal to the universal consciousness is just as remote from the biological reports as is Spencer's invoking of the law of the persistence of force. Hence he is faced with the task of attending to his own counsel that one should first develop the theory of nature in close reliance upon actual scientific procedures, and then consider how an ethical doctrine can be elaborated.

2. Dewey also remarks on the ambiguity surrounding Spencer's talk about the goal or end toward which evolution is moving. It can mean either a factual last term and outcome in some future situation or else a present ideal energizing our ongoing action. Even if the universe has an end in the sense of an outcome to a phase of drift, this does not supply man with a moral end for controlling his present decisions. The goal of evolutionary nature is not an ethical one, in the sense that it aims specially at the personal and social fulfillment of man. If we take the cosmic drift as our sole moral basis, we will treat man only as a passing phase and instrument in the universal change. Our moral need is not satisfied by values and ends which are merely set for man as a part of the cosmic scene. Moral ends must be present in man in such a way as to respect his distinctive nature as a self-realizing agent.

Once more, we may notice that Dewey is in possession of an aspect of his view of nature which will survive his passage beyond idealism and will help to characterize his naturalism. Nature is basically characterized by its constant change and factual existence in space and time. The natural process has phases and outcomes, but they cannot be construed as determining the moral goals and scale of values for man. Whatever the patterns we may discern in the cosmic process, it remains morally neutral and cannot provide us with a ready-made basis of values. We cannot just read off the moral goals of man from the making and unmaking which transpire in nature, since their moral relevance comes from their bearing upon man as an agent responsible for his own development. Hence we have to beware of reading our own moralizing interpretations into nature and then appealing to a purely objective cosmic sanction for them. Spencer's justification of ethics makes man into a passive recipient of values and deprives moral ends of their specific reference to the interests and needs of man.

Yet in the course of working out this criticism, Dewey finds it difficult not to apply it forcibly to his own idealism. The idealistic position on individual and universal consciousness permits him to hold that moral values are present in man, but not that they also have their source from human activities and interests. From the idealistic standpoint, man is a self-realizing agent only in the sense of manifesting his truer self or the universal consciousness present in him. Whereas Spencer reads his own moral proclivities into natural process, idealism reads into it the aims of absolute spirit. In both cases nature is asked to provide more of a guide and sanction for moral ideals than it is fitted to yield, and man in the concrete is given less responsibility for shaping his values than he is able and eager to take. The solution toward which this situation points is to achieve some direct bond between man and nature, so that moral values can arise from this relationship rather than from an extrinsic legislation.

3. Finally, Dewey questions whether there are indeed any ends in nature, when it is considered by itself alone.

> Nature has no end, no aim, no purpose. There is change only, not advanced toward a goal. . . . We utterly deny that the physical world, as physical, has any end; that nature, as natural, can give birth to an ideal.[10]

Teleology finds no place in physical explanation, and hence no analysis of physical categories and the evolutionary laws founded on them can furnish a moral ideal or end for human conduct. Once we are in possession of a moral ideal, then the scientific study of nature is very helpful for discovering the conditions retarding and aiding its realization.

But we should not confuse the seed of moral life with the soil where it is planted and grows.

This last text brings out one major tension in Dewey's early program of accommodating nature and its scientific explanation to the idealistic presuppositions. What he denies is that there are ends and ideals in nature taken precisely "as physical," "as natural." But the argumentation he uses to support this denial is still based on the idealistic notion that a knowledge of ends depends on our conceiving the universe as a whole. Clearly enough, such knowledge is not supplied by the natural sciences and can come only from the theory of absolute spirit. To treat nature as natural means, then, to regard it apart from reference to the absolute consciousness which sets the general purpose and meaning for natural process. Yet Dewey is starting to realize that it is possible to forego all claims to understand the total cosmic purpose and still to have some knowledge of ends, considered in a particular and plural way. This can be done if we take into account the interests and aims of men as we find them, not as they are explained within idealism. Particular ends and ideals are established by men in their dealings with nature and with each other. If we restrict ourselves to this humanly derived significance for moral ends, then we can recognize their presence in the natural world without having to read them into natural process from a deductive premise taken either in Spencer's evolutionary formula or in the idealistic absolute.

Nature has no inherently inscribed values and ends. Dewey adheres to this as a reliable statement and includes it in his later naturalism. But the fact that ends do arise in our human experience leads him to revise his original idealistic interpretation of the statement that nature, as natural, cannot give rise to an ideal or an end. Nature does give birth to the kind of being which envisions ideals and establishes ends for action. What makes moral purposes meaningful is not the relating of nature to a universal consciousness, but the relating of it to men in their concrete existence and planning activities.

But before exploring how values, ends, and norms arise from the direct relation and intercourse of nature and man in society, Dewey must face the further objection that the Christian conception of things requires us to relate man only indirectly to nature and to orient his intellectual and moral interests basically away from it. This is the reason why Dewey cannot avoid treating of a Christian conception of nature. His handling of this theme is not a superfluous work but an essential strand in his gradually developing conception of nature. His growth toward naturalism is bound up with his achieving a critical, but by no means entirely negative, position toward what he takes to be the Christian view of the man-and-nature relationship.

The prevalent idea in Dewey's religious conferences at Michigan is that we must distinguish between the essential Christian idea and the hardened conventions of institutional Christianity.[11] The former is not only distinct from the latter, but is now engaged in the historical act of disengaging itself from the institutional forms. This contrast is the forerunner of Dewey's later distinction between the religious attitude and particular religions. For our purpose, however, the significant point is that the antithesis originated in his search for a direct highway between man and nature. He felt that institutional Christianity had erected a barrier between them, forbidden any direct relations, and routed all their traffic to the absolute as their only legitimate point of meeting.

Here is the philosophical source of Dewey's antipathy toward the Christian tradition, an antipathy which is so puzzling to those who are familiar with the humanistic resources of Christian thought. He customarily interprets the distinctions between the spiritual and the worldly, the eternal and the temporal, the hereafter and the here-and-now, as dualisms in a pejorative sense. They express a separative movement on the part of institutional Christianity to withdraw man as much as possible from natural concerns, to insulate him from any fresh experience and challenge of natural events, and to concede meaning to the latter only as imperfect images of a spiritual purpose. On this basis, Dewey concludes that every affirmation of the transcendent and the supernatural entails a separatism and a depreciation of earthly life. He hardens his equation between the transcendent and the antinatural into a permanent pattern of thought, ruling out beforehand any possibility of revision in the light of examining various ways in which the above distinctions are intended. The pressure behind his polemical stiffness concerning the dualisms of institutional Christianity is his concern to open up and maintain a direct route for man's activities in the natural world.

Yet it is noteworthy that Dewey does not regard the Christian idea itself as antinatural. Instead, he argues that this idea was never properly realized by the dualistic forms of traditional Christianity and that it is now actively seeking for a more adequate means of expression. The Christian idea never was a specialized religious truth but was a first approach to the naturalistic meaning of human experience. The core truth was propounded as the realization of the meaning of experience, as the working truth which all experience bases itself upon and carries within itself. This truth was that man is an expression or an organ of the Reality of the universe. That, as such organ, he participates in truth, and through the completeness of his access to ultimate truth, is free, there being no essential barriers to his action either in his relation to the world or in his relations to his fellow-men.[12]

The last phrase in this text expresses what Dewey deems to be the really salvageable element in the Christian idea. For even in this vague form, it allies the Christian principle with the general naturalistic effort to remove the barriers preventing a direct intercourse between individual man, the natural world, and human society. If we want to identify the concrete ways in which the Christian idea is now acting to overcome these obstacles for fulfilling the meaning of experience, Dewey bids us to consider "the development of science, the conquest of nature through the application of this science in invention and industry, and its application to the activities of men in determining their relations to one another and the resulting forms of social organization." [13] These are the contemporary bearers of the Christian idea, its ways of realization in the modern world.

In offering this interpretation, Dewey explicitly acknowledges that he is engaged in a task of reconstruction.[14] Thus one of his earliest developments of the basic theme that the work of philosophy consists in critical reconstruction occurs in connection with the religious conception of man and nature. The essential Christian idea must be reconstructed in order to eliminate any reference of man to an order of being and value that transcends nature. Religious energies have to be radically reorientated toward the experiential whole of nature and man, lest they be drained off from the primary work of the understanding and control of nature and the improvement of human social relations. In seeking to find an acceptable core in the Christian outlook rather than remove it entirely, Dewey remains closer to Hegel and Comte than to Nietzsche and the scientific materialists. Yet in the course of naturalizing the Christian idea, he also discovers himself to be reconstructing his own earlier psychological idealism. The primary meaning for the totality of experience is not found in the polarity of individual and universal consciousness but rather in the polarity between human actions and the natural world. Reconstruction of the Christian message about experience and man's place in the universe is thus one of the major paths in Dewey's journey from idealism to naturalism.

The vagueness still clinging to even the reconstructed religious outlook can be removed by specifying the more adequate instruments for
actualizing it under today's conditions. We can identify these working
forms in accordance with the axiom that if the Christian idea is at all
revelatory, then it must reveal truths and continue to do so in our own
historical age. Dewey remarks that the most effective and constant
sources of increment of knowledge and practical control today are the
scientific method and its applications in technology and democratic
process. They constitute the real incarnation of the Christian idea for
contemporary man. "Revelation means effective discovery, the actual
ascertaining or guaranteeing to man of the truth of his life and the reality of the Universe." [15] Measured by this criterion, the religious spirit
must now place its entire hope in the scientific method's exploration of
the ways of natural process, as well as in the democratic means for
enriching the human community. The only valid standing henceforth
for the religious attitude is as an encouraging symbol of the ongoing relations which science and democracy are striving to achieve between men
in society and the natural order.

Dewey patiently undertakes even the particular work of making an
exegesis of Biblical passages and common Christian notions about the
kingdom of God and the truth which liberates man. His purpose is to
show that they can be translated, without remainder, into the context
of man and nature as the only kingdom within human reach. The truth
which makes man free is the recognition that we can realize our
potentialities only within the environment of natural needs and opportunities. The repetition of the word "only" at this point is intended to
underline the significant fact that Dewey's teaching on the sole cognitive
competence of the scientific method is the other side of the coin which
reformulates the Christian idea. He cannot be sure that the reconstruction of the latter is definitive until he assigns all the reliable sources
of knowledge and disciplined power to scientific method and democratic
procedures.

> It is because science represents a method of truth to which, so far as
> we can discover, no limits whatsoever can be put, that it is neces-
> sary for the church to reconstruct its doctrines of revelation and
> inspiration, and for the individual to reconstruct, within his own reli-
> gious life, his conception of what spiritual truth is and the nature of
> its authority over him. Science has made real to us, and is bound
> to make still more real, the actual incarnation of truth in human ex-
> perience and the need for giving heed to it. . . . [In conformity with
> the Christian outlook] it is assumed, however unconsciously, that all

truth which is worth while, all truth which promises to be of practical avail in the direction of man's life, may be gotten at by scientific method.[16]

Thus Dewey is transferring from institutional Christianity to his own reconstructed idea of Christian truth and hence to the naturalistic position the absolute confidence in a revealing source of truth and practical control. Only, this source is now to be understood not as the transcendent God and not as the idealistic absolute spirit but as the effective presence of scientific method and its organization of environment and society. Paradoxically enough, then, Dewey helps to consolidate his methodological and metaphysical claims about the scientific method and the natural field of experienceable reality by means of his reconstruction of the Christian idea. It lends a certain absoluteness to his naturalism and a sense of exclusive dedication to the good for man which might otherwise not characterize it.

Deweyan naturalism does not treat science and democracy purely as descriptive principles of method. They are more properly regarded as normative counterprinciples against inserting any third domain of reality or method of investigation between the complex, dynamic whole composed of inquiring man and nature as a visible process of interchange with man. These principles function as assurances both against diverting human plans and moral ideals away from the symbiosis of man and nature and in favor of devoting our energies and hopes completely and solely to the study, control, and enjoyment of this relationship.

Evolution Seals the Circle

Our purpose in the remainder of this study is to examine the essays which Dewey composed between 1897 and 1909 and published in 1910 under the title of *The Influence of Darwin on Philosophy*. Together with his book on experimental logic, these essays were the main philosophical fruit of his Chicago professorship and his first years at Columbia University. They were concerned with one serious residual problem from his previous critique of idealistic and religious conceptions of nature. The outcome of that critique could plausibly be interpreted as being nothing more than the substitution of the new dualism of man and nature for the older ones under fire. Such a dualism might open the way once more for ordering our experience toward a principle of unity located in the transcendent God or the absolute consciousness of idealism. Dewey found it necessary to seal in the mutual relations of man and nature in such a manner as to prevent any real reference of inquiry and desire beyond the man-and-nature complexus. He found a way of doing this by making his own reconstruction of Darwin's import for philosophy, and thus by challenging Spencer's claim to provide *the* philosophical system of evolutionism. With this reinterpretation, Dewey came into firm possession of the chief components in his conception of nature. His naturalism was well established in its main lines by 1909, and thereafter it was only necessary to work out in fuller detail its various aspects and extend them into the particular facets of human experience.

The substitutional method used in naturalistic reconstruction. One striking result of Dewey's study of Darwin is his resolve to model his theory of philosophical reconstruction after the evolutionary reconstruction of biology. The pattern of progress which holds good in biology must also be the pattern of progress in philosophy. This means that unserviceable doctrines are to be replaced by experimentally more adequate ones just as inexorably and definitively in philosophy as in the physical and biological sciences. It would be just as senseless to worry about antiquated philosophical problems as about the concepts of pre-evolutionary biology. Hence the philosopher must reconstruct his discipline by a deliberate use of the two-phase method of elimination and substitution.

The method of philosophical reconstruction, as carried on in the naturalistic spirit, has an eliminative aspect which simply removes as meaningless in an evolutionary age certain of the long-standing disputes. The example used by Dewey shows that he wants to be even more rigorous in philosophy than Darwin had dared to be. Darwin confessed in an autobiographical statement that his mind wavered between attributing the order of the universe ultimately to chance or to a designing intelligence. Dewey comments that there are two ways of taking this hesitation. Either the question is a genuine issue which is too difficult for our minds to encompass or else it is a meaningless difficulty from which we must try to extricate ourselves entirely. Now philosophy is learning not to claim for itself any distinctive method or data, but to work out the general implications of the method and data furnished by the sciences, especially biology. Hence in our age of evolutionary science "philosophy forswears inquiry after absolute origins and finalities in order to explore specific values and the specific conditions that generate them." [17] This forswearing implies that the whole question about the ultimate principle of order in nature is a meaningless one. We are bound to reject both sides of the Darwinian alternative and to hold that the issue itself must be dropped from philosophy. To reconstruct the philosophy of nature means to unburden our minds of the very problems which do not hold out the prospect of being settled within an immanent and particularized evolutionary mode of inquiry.

From this standpoint, Dewey's naturalism is nothing more than that set of questions about nature and human experience thereof which survives the process of elimination according to these scientific canons. In later years, he registered strong disapproval of the way that logical positivism used a physicalistic standard to outlaw many problems as meaningless. But his own naturalism owed its genesis to a similar elimination of what he judged to be meaningless according to the pattern of biological inquiry and evolutionary interests.

An effective reconstruction must be substitutional as well as eliminative. In outlawing questions about ultimate origins and goals, it must replace them positively by a concern for specific lines of growth and particular ends of activity. There is a psychological and even a therapeutic aspect to Dewey's description of the substitutional method. To philosophize in the naturalistic manner means to undergo a process of healing and growth, to mend the wounds occurred in eliminating past concepts and then to spurt ahead in developing the new ones which fit an evolutionary view of nature. As far as traditional points of dispute are concerned, "we do not solve them: we get over them. Old questions are solved by disappearing, evaporating, while new questions corresponding to the changed attitude of endeavor and preference take their place." [18] Darwin's *Origin of Species* is the greatest dissolvent of philosophical issues in the precise sense that it redirects our main interests and renders the previous scene in philosophy simply archaic and unproblematic for us.

Dewey's thinking on the question of philosophical diversity and progress is wholly dominated by the biological metaphor and by a consequent psychologizing of the task for the naturalistic critic. He conceives of philosophical progress as transpiring through a linear series, in which one position totally supplants another, after the fashion of scientific theories. The philosophical issues and ideas of the past become vestigial and useless, so that they atrophy and eventually disappear when the course of scientific research directs our interests elsewhere. The traditional habits of mind may persist temporarily, and then the naturalistic critic must trace out their particular origins, their past responsiveness to the situation, and their present condition as outmoded illusions. He must treat the states of mind which persist in reopening the old problems in the same way that the psychologist deals with reports about the converging Zöllner lines.

Dewey relies on a convictional shift generated by new scientific interests, as well as on a psychologizing of recalcitrant positions, to deal with the diversity among philosophers and the recurrence of philosophical issues. But this is scarcely sufficient to take account of the actual ways in which philosophers proceed. They explore issues not by any linear displacement but by a societal continuance of the basic modes of interpretation. Their concern is directed to the questions which persist under many kinds of cultural, scientific, and psychological conditions. These questions do not disappear when one philosopher chooses to appeal to a generalization of evolutionary thought as a solvent. Moreover, the metaphor of a vestigial survival of outmoded problems and theories leads Dewey to rely indulgently upon the same panoramic mode of thinking which he had previously criticized with vigor in Spencer's case.

Naturalistic pathos against the transcendental. Dewey was aware that his substitutional method, considered only as a theoretical recommendation, could not secure the total disengagement of minds from the doctrinal positions and attitudes of the past. As he phrased it, evolutionary thought and the naturalism stemming from it are not merely an additional law but a complete about-face.[19] They involve a withdrawal of respect for ultimate explanations, fixed structures, and universal purposes, so that men can concentrate upon nature in its particular phases, its fluent qualities, and its capacity for limited aims and satisfactions. And to bring about this reversal, a practical act is required in addition to a theoretical critique. Hence Dewey found it necessary to surround his version of the inquiry into nature and human experience with a new affective atmosphere, which would encourage a permanent practical adherence to it. Naturalistic reconstruction would thus have to reach into our emotions and concrete valuations as well as our theoretical principles.

As an instrument for arousing a new naturalistic pathos, Dewey began using the term "transcendental" with a strongly polemical ring in his writings after about 1894. As he had employed it in his idealistic period, it had signified only the method of relating objects and a knowledge of objects to their context and ultimate foundation in the doctrine of absolute mind or consciousness. But now he began to use it to mean that, in this process of tracing out the basic presuppositions of objectivity, there is also involved an active denigrating of empirical objects and states of mind. They lose their intrinsic significance and worth in the degree that they are given an underpinning in universal consciousness. Indeed, the transcendental type of thinker enjoys derogating them for the greater glory of God or the greater expansion of the absolute. In painting this somewhat horrendous portrait of the transcendental mind, Dewey was not so far removed from Nietzsche's call for loyalty to the earth by abandoning belief in an absolute which is distinct from man and nature.

To the reply that the transcendental standpoint does eventually establish the importance of finite things and the natural sciences, Dewey makes a quick and scornful retort. The transcendental vindication comes in the form of a wholesale engulfing. In the order of knowledge, it amounts to a praise of truth-at-large and of the universal presence of conscious mind. But it fails to supply us with any definite recommendations for resolving the particular problems of life or for improving the scientific methods which do face these problems at their own level. And in the moral order, the transcendentally oriented mind is prone to give blanket approval to all existing conditions as being justified expressions of the absolute. The only practical advice we get is not to worry about anything, since the absolute consciousness has eternally healed and rectified all situations.[20] But nothing is forthcoming as to how we can go about manifesting this happy state in terms of our empirical situation.

The case for naturalism receives practical and emotional support from this pathos against the transcendental outlook. That outlook encourages a vague and sterile mentality, which remains unable to analyze our actual problems or improve our daily lot. Instead of beguiling ourselves with wholesale talk about the absolute mode of reality, Dewey advises us to concentrate upon the specific instruments of inquiry and policy for bettering our control over nature and our social living. The pathos against a world-fleeing transcendentalism is thus converted into a positive ethos of scientific study and cultivation of naturally available values. We are prepared to withdraw all interest from a search after the absolute, if for no other reason than that such a search may entail a dangerous diverting of human skills away from the responsibilities of our world. It is precisely at this point where naturalism as a philosophical doctrine moves beyond ordinary respect for nature and human society. It contends that this respect cannot be wholehearted and effec-

tive until we treat the question of the absolute as theoretically meaningless and practically disastrous for man.

One notable feature of this theory of the transcendental must be
criticized. Dewey expands its range customarily to include not only the
idealistic notion of absolute mind, from which he was reacting, but also
every theistic affirmation of a transcendent God. He does not justify in
detail this extended usage, but blurs together the idealistic absolute and
the God of personal theism. It then becomes impossible for us to respect
the proper distinctions and to make a precise test of the soundness of
Dewey's argument in any particular case of a philosophy which he may
regard as transcendental. This procedure defeats the ends of inquiry,
since it prevents any controlled analysis of the position in question or
any pointed comparison of its view of natural reality with the naturalistic view. Although Dewey is satirical about a wholesale defense of
absolute truth and goodness, he himself makes a wholesale use of his
theory of the transcendental to include many sorts of non-naturalistic
positions. The unsettled philosophical question concerns whether the
undesirable consequences for scientific work and practical control follow
with necessity from every theory to which he attaches the label of
transcendental. No answer can be given while we allow the question to
remain in Dewey's formulation, which is not so much a precise articu-
lation of the connections as a blanket assertion that they must exist in
every case where the real is not identified with nature and the human
activities it sustains.

The example of Darwin. It was not until after he had worked out his
capacious meaning for the transcendental that Dewey was in a good
position to complete his naturalistic interpretation of Darwin and thus
effect a passage from biological evolution to evolutionism as a philosophical doctrine. There is a revealing contrast between Freud and Dewey
in respect to their way of including Darwin in the modern intellectual
movement. Freud takes what we may call a stigmatic approach to
modern science. He regards the Copernican revolution, Darwinian evolution, and his own exploration of the unconscious as so many successive
wounds inflicted upon Western man's pride of place, origin, and rational control. For his part, Dewey prefers to give a liberational meaning
to the growth of modern science.[21] He views the movement from
classical physics to evolutionary biology to his own experimental logic
as so many moments in the healing of Western man from transcendental
preoccupations and the freeing of him for a greater appreciation of his
active role in nature. They are successive stages in a gradual extension

of scientific method from the physical world to the sphere of life and finally to man's intellectual and moral activities. With each step, the opportunities for understanding, control, and satisfaction increase.

There is an internal relation between the three moments in the expansion of the scientific way, however, such that, until Darwin made his contribution, it was not yet possible for a fully developed philosophical naturalism to appear. Hence it was vital for Dewey's purposes to make a reconstructive appraisal of Darwin's work, in order to present it as the penultimate discovery paving the road for his own philosophical position. Only after Darwin had overcome the reluctance to submit living things to the general procedures in science did it become feasible to bring human reality thoroughly within the range of these same procedures. And only after the psychological and social sciences had made a good start in naturalizing man as an object of scientific investigation was the situation ripe for making Dewey's own philosophical attack on the transcendental attitude and his generalization about nature and man. In bringing man within the scope of his evolutionary explanation, Darwin was also providing philosophy with sufficient evidence for sealing the circle of natural being and limiting our cognitive and valuational interests to human operations within the natural domain.

Taken in this reconstructive way, then, the figure of Darwin is used as part of the argument favoring the acceptance of naturalism. Dewey burdens the Darwinian treatment of the species problem and the genesis of mind with definite philosophical consequences of a naturalistic sort. On these two scores, he seeks to invest his own position with scientific and historical inevitability and to show that other philosophies belong to a pre-evolutionary outlook, which can no longer seriously hold our assent.

Since Darwin's greatest advance was made in revising the biological notion of species, Dewey presented the whole metaphysics of theism and transcendental idealism as being essentially dependent upon the now outmoded Greek view of biological species. His argument was that only the acceptance of species as a fixed form which progressively realizes its own preordained end lends strength to the metaphysical assertion of the superior reality of a fixed order of essences and ends, which can be known only through a special rational insight.

These inferences were extended to nature: (*a*) She does nothing in vain; but all for an ulterior purpose. (*b*) Within natural sensible events there is therefore contained a spiritual causal force, which as spiritual escapes perception, but is apprehended by an enlightened reason. (c) The manifestation of this principle brings about a sub-ordination of matter and sense to its own realization, and this ultimate fulfilment is the goal of nature and of man.[22]

But this whole fabric for interpreting nature, Dewey contends, is only an extrapolation on a grand scale of a biological theory of species which Darwin has swept away. His evolutionary research shows that species have a definite temporal origin, that their structure is subject to constant modification, that chance variation rather than purposive planning accounts for their successful adaptations, and that they are wholly subject to a history and death within nature and apart from any further reference beyond it.

The consequences of evolutionary research for one's philosophical conception of nature can be spelled out in terms of the three inferences mentioned above. First, there is not a sufficient basis in the events we can study for concluding that nature itself is purposive. The random variations are too pervasive for us to think that the entire natural process is planned by an intelligent agent working out its own ends. Ends do play a part in human affairs, but then we can see that in their origin and import they are purely natural, immanent, and plural. Next, the so-called laws of evolution are not transcripts of some hidden spiritual force but are convenient summaries of trends made for the convenience of our reading and controlling of natural events.[23] We can learn to remain satisfied with a study of natural being just as it displays itself to our perception, scientific analysis, and practical planning. And finally, the worth of our analytic and planning activities comes from their direct relevance to nature and human affairs, not from their serving any further purpose or realizing any transcendent plan. Nature and man find their continuing fulfilment in the experience and values which arise from their interrelated activities, without any subordination to a God or an absolute center of consciousness.

The work of Darwin and subsequent evolutionists in making a genetic study of man and especially the human mind is also used by Dewey to strengthen the case for philosophical naturalism. The inclusion of man within the evolutionary process helps Dewey to resolve two prominent issues. One of these is the idealistic argument he himself had previously used to the effect that the evolutionary origin of individual minds is reconcilable with the subordination of nature as a whole to absolute mind. The striking feature about all the evolutionary sciences of man is that they uncover strong positive reasons for involving the human mind in the evolutionary sweep, and yet find no good reasons for adding that nature and man are real only as realizing the purpose of cosmic mind. All the weight of the evidence points toward an evolutionary account of human reality, but it leaves quite unsupported any transcendental reference of man and nature to an eternal purposive consciousness.

Another major question affected decisively by an evolutionary explanation of man is the kind of relation holding between nature and man. Dewey is specially concerned about this implication, since it enables him at last to avoid the charge of dualism without obliterating what is distinctive about man. Nature and man are not coeval, independent entities. Man comes to be through an evolutionary growth of nature, and it is within the totality of nature that he develops his intelligence and pursues his goals. Once we agree to take the human mind only as we experience it in its natural being, then we must admit it to be an evolutionary outcome, an active principle arising within nature and finding there its whole sphere of inquiry and values. There is something distinctive about our intelligence, not by reason of its being an expression of some absolute mind but by reason of the properly human activities in which it consists. Distinctive modes of being develop within natural process, but to recognize them is not to open a door for the kind of dualism which will reinstate some transcendental principle.

In his highly concentrated 1909 dialogue on nature and its good, Dewey completes the revision of his previous opinion that nature cannot give rise to moral ideals and values. He remains opposed to the excessively moralizing view of nature advanced by idealism and by Spencer, but he is now able to offer a naturalistic account of intelligence and value. Nature cannot be said to care for values until it produces an intelligence which can select and fight for what it prefers.

> Not, then, when Nature produces health or efficiency or complexity does Nature exhibit regard for value, but only when it produces a living organism that has settled preferences and endeavors. The mere happening of complexity, health, adjustment, is all that Nature effects, as rightly called accident as purpose. But when Nature produces an intelligence—ah, then, indeed Nature has achieved something. Not, however, because this intelligence impartially pictures the nature which has produced it, but because in human consciousness Nature becomes genuinely partial. Because in consciousness an end is preferred, is selected for maintenance, and because intelligence pictures not a world just as it is *in toto,* but images forth the conditions and obstacles of the continued maintenance of the selected good.[24]

This text tells heavily against Spencer's notion that the laws of nature directly intend a moral aim and dictate to our passive intelligence what its values and goals must be. Nature is mindless and purposeless until it brings the minded organism of man into being. But then we can define human intelligence adequately as the function of holding particular ends in view and working selectively with the naturally available means for realizing these chosen ends or goods. There is no need to invoke either a moralizing nature or a universal consciousness to explain mind and value.

From this point onward in Dewey's own philosophy, he feels that naturalism is securely based against both the transcendental types of philosophy and reductive materialism. His attention is devoted henceforth to working out the detailed applications of his naturalistic position, especially the new theory of experience and value which it implies. His investigations after 1909 are consciously carried on within the already established outlines of a philosophy which maintains that humanly meaningful reality is found solely in the dynamic relations between inquiring and valuing man and the rest of nature.

Nature and Naturalism

One question remains outstanding as a result of this study of the genesis of Dewey's naturalism. Are his findings about nature indistinguishably one with his philosophical naturalism? That they do not strictly coincide is clear enough from a comparison between a few of the components in his conception of nature and some of his philosophical arguments.

We have already considered how Dewey's early reflections on nature served as an irritant provoking some new ideas. On the main points of provocation, however, Dewey's movement away from idealism need not have been directed toward naturalism. A realistic approach to nature is also on guard against the illusions of panoramic thinking and the claims to get into the inside of nature. Theistic realism is more concerned with getting at adequate principles of explanation for the experienced facts than with seeking an intuitive vision of the whole of nature. And it regards the experienced facts as having an intelligibility of their own which cannot be disrupted by being referred to the concept of total consciousness. The temporal, spatial, and changing character of the natural world expresses its own reality, and that reality cannot be revoked or rendered illusory by being related to anything else. Recognition that the natural world is a spatial and temporal process, having meaning and worth precisely in these modes of being, is not confined to naturalism. Liberating itself decisively from the idealism-naturalism alternative, a realistic view of the personal creative God encourages us to respect and enrich the natural ways of existing, knowing, and valuing.

Dewey's critique of some prevailing ethical and religious conceptions of nature contains some sound features, which are not reserved exclusively for a naturalistic philosophy. A realistic theism also holds that man does not simply read off his moral values from the book of nature, as though he were passively related to the natural world. Valuating and determining our moral goals are distinctively human acts: they do not occur in isolation from the rest of nature but they do require human intelligence and interest in order to come into being. Nevertheless, there need be no incompatibility between using our intelligence and funded experience in determining the aims of action and also searching after God as our ultimate good. The defense of particular ends of human action is not bound up with a rejection of God, although it does require a stubborn insistence on man's own responsibility in making his selections and realizing them.

Dewey moves away from a descriptive examination of the traits of natural being and toward a philosophical naturalism in his treatment of Christianity and the transcendental. Yet just here his inquiry becomes unsatisfactory because of its very restricted historical basis of induction for studying the ideals and institutions of Christianity. His stylized objection that institutional Christianity prevents the direct communication of man and nature does not survive the test of comparison with actual Christian views of the natural world. In the Christian tradition as everywhere else, there is a pluralism of attitudes toward nature. The function of the discriminating mind is not to lump them together but to examine each one separately on the question of the relation between Christian values and natural ones. This is a safer and fairer procedure than Dewey's methodic dualism between the institutions and the idea of Christianity, since it avoids the arbitrariness of his descriptions.

As for his theory about the transcendental, it is better as a weapon of persuasion than as a tool of analysis. By coalescing many sorts of idealism and of theism under the heading of a transcendental doctrine, Dewey does not overcome them so much as he prevents the patient study of how various forms of idealism and theism consider the domain of nature. It cannot be said of them all that they denigrate the natural objects of experience or that they ask us to choose between particular scientific procedures and the truth about the ultimate principle of natural reality. For advancing the inquiry into nature in our own day, it seems advisable to refrain from posing the question of God and nature in terms of a transcendental metaphysics versus anti-transcendentalism, as being too vague for rigorous treatment.

Finally, the appeal to Darwin's example has to be evaluated critically as an instance of the substitutional-reconstructive method as it transforms the historical materials. One thing which stands out clearly from a comparative study of how the different philosophies have interpreted Darwinian evolution is the variety of inferences drawn from it.[25] There is a definite gap between biological theories of evolution and philosophical forms of evolutionism. The work of Darwin and his scientific successors does not have a one-way univocal meaning for philosophy and does not lead automatically to a naturalistic view of evolving nature. Dewey's conviction that it does is the consequence of his own prior philosophical commitment, as the following text shows.

> The conception of evolution is no more and no less the discovery of a general law of life than it is the generalization of all scientific method. . . . Philosophy must go to school to the sciences; must have *no* data save such as it receives at their hands; and be hospitable to *no* method of inquiry and reflection not akin to those in daily use among the sciences.[26]

The theory of biological evolution does not itself provide the generalization of all scientific method, for this is a philosophical interpretation which Dewey makes in the course of reconstructing the significance of evolutionary thought. Similarly, the two negative exclusions which he emphasizes flow from his fundamental naturalism; they are not inevitably entailed by our going to school to the sciences. We can be faithful to a direct experiential acquaintance with nature and to a careful study of what evolutionary science and other disciplines say about the natural world, without having to stipulate that there are no data and no methods other than those furnished by the sciences. If it is precisely a question of the degree of kinship between scientific methods and those used in philosophy, then the likeness is determined more by the range of our questioning and the findings responsive to it than by Dewey's prior negative norms. The latter are not imposed as conditions for doing good scientific work and need not be prescribed for philosophies of nature which attend to the scientific account of things.

A specific instance in which Dewey tries to draw more out of the scientific achievement than it can yield is provided by his treatment of the

species problem. What he calls the Hegelian bacillus in his blood is dominant in his effort to make every metaphysical doctrine on the essential
structure, finality, and order of things dependent upon the Greek view
of biological species. The importance of this notion is undeniable,
especially in Aristotle's philosophy. But it is too narrow a pivot whereby
to summarize and overcome all these metaphysical positions. They
involve some nonbiological meanings for species, and they rest on some
direct inspection of the ways of nature which is not uncritically determined by the biological metaphor. The results of evolutionary research
certainly require some deep modifications in philosophies which remain
responsive to scientific findings and theories, but the process of modify-
ing and enlarging one's philosophy is not the same as submitting to a
naturalistic substitution.

Dewey's thought is admirably sensitive to many aspects of natural
existence. He keeps us alive to the process and novelty of natural events,
to the tireless creativity of nature, to the integrity of its spatial and
temporal traits, and to the unity which man establishes with the rest of
natural reality through his inquiring and valuing activities. The meaning-
fulness of nature within the perspective of human experience and
scientific methods is his insistent theme and his great contribution to
philosophy.[27] We can honor our debt to him in these respects without
embracing his philosophical naturalism. The gap remains between
Dewey's defense of the human significance of nature and the naturalistic
principle that we should confine our inquiries, values, and ends to the
man-and-nature totality.

NOTES

1. Referring to previous philosophical meanings for "nature," Dewey remarks
   that "few terms used in philosophy have a wider or a looser use, or involve
   greater ambiguity." Article by John Dewey on "Nature," in *Dictionary of
   Philosophy and Psychology,* edited by J. M. Baldwin (New York: Macmillan,
   1902) II 139.
2. "Soul and Body," *Bibliotheca Sacra* 43 (1886), especially 244-48. His later
   functionalist interpretation is given in "The Reflex Arc Concept in Psychology," *Psychological Review* 3 (1896) 357-70.
3. "Soul and Body," 240.
4. "The Psychological Standpoint," *Mind* 11 (1886) 1-19; "Psychology as Philosophic Method," *Mind* 11 (1886) 153-73. The former article contains a
   criticism of Spencer's evolutionary realism. For the role of these articles in
   Dewey's general development, see M. G. White, *The Origin of Dewey's Instrumentalism* (New York: Columbia, 1943) 34-48.

5. "Psychology as Philosophic Method," 170-73.

6. *Ibid*. 164.

7. *Loc. cit.*

8. The "Biography of John Dewey," edited by J. M. Dewey, included in *The Philosophy of John Dewey*, edited by P. A. Schilpp (second ed., New York: Tudor, 1951) 3-45, is still invaluable for intellectual influences on Dewey. On the Vermont days, consult the two articles by L. S. Feuer: "H. A. P. Torrey and John Dewey: Teacher and Pupil," *American Quarterly* 10 (1958) 34-54; "John Dewey's Reading at College," *Journal of the History of Ideas* 19 (1958) 415-21. See also, G. Dykhuizen, "John Dewey: The Vermont Years," *Journal of the History of Ideas,* 20 (1959) 515-44.

9. "Ethics and Physical Science," *The Andover Review* 7 (1887) 582. Similar in approach is his 1904 essay, "Herbert Spencer," reprinted in *Characters and Events* (New York: Holt, 1929) I 45-62. On the relation between Dewey's ethical naturalism and other American criticism of Spencer's ethics, cf. W. F. Quillian, Jr., "Evolution and Moral Theory in America," in *Evolutionary Thought in America,* edited by S. Persons (New Haven: Yale, 1950) 398-419.

10. "Ethics and Physical Science," 579, 580. What made George Santayana's *The Life of Reason* so important for the genesis of American naturalism was its presentation of a naturalistic sense in which nature does indeed give birth to an ideal. Dewey himself insists that it is only through giving rise to man that nature does perform this function.

11. "Christianity and Democracy," in *Religious Thought at the University of Michigan* (Ann Arbor: Inland Press, 1893) 60-69. A preliminary description of the published Michigan materials is given by W. Savage, "The Evolution of John Dewey's Philosophy of Experimentalism as Developed at the University of Michigan," (unpublished University of Michigan doctoral dissertation; Ann Arbor: University Microfilms, 1950).

12. "Green's Theory of the Moral Motive," *The Philosophical Review* 1 (1892) 610. Dewey is here repeating the view expressed in "Christianity and Democracy," 64-5.

13. "Green's Theory of the Moral Motive," 610. Dewey's 1908 essay, "Religion and Our Schools," reprinted in *Characters and Events,* makes this naturalistic religious suggestion about the increase of scientific knowledge of nature: "Possibly if we measured it from the standpoint of the natural piety it is fostering, the sense of the permanent and inevitable implication of nature and man in a common career and destiny, it would appear as the growth of religion." *Characters and Events* II 515-16. This is a good definition of the Deweyan naturalistic meaning for the religious attitude. On the religious availability of humanistic naturalism, see G. R. Geiger, *John Dewey in Perspective* (New York: Oxford University Press, 1958) 219-24.

14. "Reconstruction," *The Monthly Bulletin* of The Students' Christian Association of the University of Michigan, 17 (1893-94) 149-56.

15. "Christianity and Democracy," 64.

16. "Reconstruction," 154.

17. *The Influence of Darwin on Philosophy and Other Essays* (New York: Holt, 1910) 13; henceforth this book is referred to as *Influence of Darwin.* Dewey

adds: "Once admit that the sole verifiable or fruitful object of knowledge is the particular set of changes that generate the object of study together with the consequences that then flow from it, and no intelligible question can be asked about what, by assumption, lies outside." *Ibid.* 14. For theism, however, God is not outside of the natural process but distinct from it in such a way that it embodies a causal reference to God. Hence Dewey must suppress this causal reference from his description of the conditions, objects, and consequences involved in natural process. See below, note 23.

18. *Influence of Darwin,* 19. J. H. Randall, Jr., "Dewey's Interpretation of the History of Philosophy," in the Schilpp volume, *The Philosophy of John Dewey,* 77-102, distinguishes sympathetically between destruction and critical reconstruction of historical materials. But he also observes that Dewey is interested more in power than in justice as a motive in using history of philosophy, and that his tolerance of previous views stops short of any doctrine defending a transcendent reality beyond nature. G. Boas, "Instrumentalism and the History of Philosophy," in *John Dewey: Philosopher of Science and Freedom,* edited by S. Hook (New York: Dial, 1950), maintains that anyone faithful to temporalism must accept the obsolescence of doctrines on a transcendent reality, and adds: "I see no way of an Instrumentalist's answering the question of why obsolete ideas survive except anthropologically." (p. 85). Faithfulness to the temporal character of nature is different from fidelity to temporalism, however, since the former does not stipulate that the temporal and eternal ways of being must be incompatible. Hence there is more to the persistence of the problem of God than is provided by an anthropological explanation: it is a question raised for human intelligence precisely by the temporality of our experience of natural things and human societies.

19. *Influence of Darwin,* 259.

20. *Ibid,* 24-25.

21. *Ibid.* 8-9. In a letter to William James (March 27, 1903), Dewey states that his own instrumental analysis of active process in nature and scientific inquiry results in the subordination of both idea and fact, both idealism and pragmatism, to a naturalism stressing the ongoing active process of nature and inquiry. The letter is found in R. B. Perry, *The Thought and Character of William James* (Boston: Little Brown, 1935) II 522-23; see 528. His philosophy is thus viewed as fulfilling and moving beyond the previous trends in modern science and philosophy.

22. *Influence of Darwin,* 10.

23. Dewey finally rejects the view that causation involves a productive efficient agency and necessarily determining force. Thus he hopes to remove the philosophical inference to either a powerful God or an absolute self-consciousness, as well as the appeal of Spencer to natural causal tendencies as the basis of ethics. See John Dewey: "The Superstition of Necessity," *The Monist* 3 (1892-93), 362-79; "The Ego as Cause," *The Philosophical Review* 3 (1894) 337-41. In the latter article, Dewey uses the reduction of causality to uniform conditions in order to close off the inference to the ego as a separate causal agent.

24. *Influence of Darwin*, 44.
25. Cf. James Collins, "Darwin's Impact on Philosophy," *Thought* 34 (1959) 185-248.
26. *Influence of Darwin*, 262, 269.
27. M. R. Cohen, *Studies in Philosophy and Science* (New York: Holt, 1949), 140, objects that Dewey's naturalism is too anthropocentric and that "it offers no vistas of nature beyond the human scene." But Dewey does maintain that the traits of nature found within our experience and required for scientific inquiry are also characteristic of the rest of nature. The pertinent criticism is that the integrity of these traits and their philosophical importance do not depend necessarily upon any closure of inquiry within the man-and-nature circuit. On Dewey's effort to identify this closure with the experimental way in philosophy, consult C. W. Hendel, "The New Empiricism and the Philosophical Tradition," in *John Dewey and the Experimental Spirit in Philosophy*, edited by C. W. Hendel (New York: Liberal Arts Press, 1959). 1-31.

II

Democracy as Religion:
Unity in Human Relations

JOHN BLEWETT, S.J.

Father John Blewett, S.J. is a professor of education at Sophia University, Tokyo. After his ordination in 1953, he studied for a year in Germany and did graduate work at Stanford University and at St. Louis University, obtaining his doctorate in 1959 from the latter institution. He has contributed to various Catholic periodicals, principally to Social Order.

The lives of many great men have been shaped by a vision of social reality which seems to transform their understanding of the things that count and to twist their sense of the socially relevant to factors which many contemporaries overlook. Ignatius of Loyola, while convalescing after a painful operation, reads the accounts of saintly heroes of earlier centuries along with a meditative biography of Christ, and finds his former ideal of knightly service to a human king shifting to a Christocentric view of the universe where service to the on-living Christ focuses all his activities. The young Jawaharlal Nehru, wealthy, Cambridge-educated, suddenly sees before him the wretchedness of the masses of voiceless peasants and feels a stab of pain at the realization of his own ignorance of suffering and his sheltered aloofness from the woes of his people.[1] Like the illuminating flash in which a Dostoevsky sees the plot of a great novel unfold before him, these "visions," whatever their psychological origin, issue in action and, often enough, in social reformation. Sometimes the action follows on the heels of the vision, though decades may pass before the full import of the vision is revealed. Loyola starts almost immediately to take stock, to lay plans, to fashion himself (and allow himself to be fashioned) for whatever service lies ahead, but it is only two decades later, in 1540, when he founds the Society of Jesus, that the meaning of his vision becomes clear.

In the life of John Dewey there seems to have occurred such a decisive experience. According to his own report, it took place sometime between 1879 and 1881 while he was teaching in a small Pennsylvania town with the unimaginative name of Oil City. Troubled by his attitude toward prayer, wondering whether he really meant business in calling upon God, he suddenly experienced a sense of release, a feeling of peace. His account of it to a friend some sixty years later is more worth reading in full since it is not widely known. As his confidant recalled Dewey's report:

> It was not a very dramatic mystic experience. There was no vision, not even a definable emotion—just a supremely blissful feeling that his worries were over. Mystic experiences in general, Dewey explains, are purely emotional and cannot be conveyed in words. But when he tries to convey his in words, it comes out like this:—
> 'What the hell are you worrying about, anyway? Everything that's here is here, and you can just lie back on it.'
> 'I've never had any doubts since then,' he adds, 'nor any beliefs. To me faith means not worrying.'
> Although his religion has so little affirmative content,—and has nothing to do, he is sure, with his philosophy,—Dewey likens it to the poetic pantheism of Wordsworth, whom he was reading at that time, and to Walt Whitman's sense of oneness with the universe. To forestall your own remark, he reminds you that it is very likely a sublimation of sex, and points out that this doesn't make it any less normal or important.[2]

It would be absurd to interpret this experience as a blueprint for the intellectual mansion which Dewey spent a lifetime in building, but it is not unwarranted to see it as announcing the theme on which he played countless variations during the incredibly productive seven decades from 1882 when he entered Johns Hopkins and published his first article to his death in 1952. In this paper I will explore Dewey's work during his first decade of university teaching, at the University of Michigan from 1884 to 1894 (with one year's leave of absence at the University of Minnesota), to trace the way in which this "feeling" of faith, understood as *freedom from worry and sense of oneness with nature,* colored his interpretation of democracy. I will argue that, contrary to

Dewey's appraisal, this "feeling of faith" has influenced his philosophy quite noticeably by serving as one of those prelogical or unconscious psychological dynamisms which subtly guide, without often explicitly determining, the individual in his selection of the elements he judges to be relevant for his map of the world. My account, though largely expository, will include some remarks on alternatives to Dewey's understanding of democracy, which he either failed to consider or rejected as outmoded. Those who may be inclined to write off a study of Dewey's early thought as merely antiquarian may find some comfort in the fact that many of the theses of *Democracy and Education* (1916), *Human Nature and Conduct* (1922), and *Freedom and Culture* (1939) were adumbrated, if not developed, before 1894.

Democracy as Celestial Ethic

If in his twilight years Dewey had followed the example of Augustine of Hippo and published a series of retractations before his death, he would certainly have included among his errors many of his early essays on ethical questions. He would have smiled wryly as he drew the red pencil through some central theses of an early tirade against Herbert Spencer: the validity of a "spiritual" philosophy identical in its main features with Christianity and the futility of relying on natural means to develop the other-regarding selflessness which is the soil of virtue.[3] He would have labeled as prescientific his early view that loving attention to Christ and prayerful meditation on the things of God develops most effectively the religious sentiments which distinguish the true believer from the neurotic religionist ceaselessly probing into the murky depths of his feelings and inner experience.[4] Among the chaff of the early essays, however, Dewey would have found some grain, notably an article of 1888 on "The Ethics of Democracy." A sprightly contribution to a series of papers from the pens of faculty members, Dewey's essay opened with the teasing declaration, "Apparent contradictions always demand attention."[5] The "contradiction" which centered Dewey's attention was the fact that, though theoretical treatises outlining the deficiencies of democracy were appearing in increasing number, mankind seemed to be tending toward an acceptance of democracy as a way of life. Dewey selected Sir Henry Maine's study, *Popular Government,* as an example and used its allegedly disdainful downgrading of democracy as an anvil to pound out his own spirited account of the "American theory" that democracy is more an ethos or social climate

than a form of government; that each individual is "society concentrated," not a mere ballot-caster or indistinguishable unit in a mass of
mediocrity; that the democratic citizen as sovereign is on the socio-
political plane the free individual who *vis-à-vis* God is his own priest.[6]

Dewey reproached Maine with blindness to the movement of history.
The aristocratic polity, which he was championing as more stable and
more conducive to the development of the good man, was heading
toward bankruptcy, for men were awakening to the fact that even the
wise and the good, when entrusted with power, lose their wisdom and
goodness. Even an ideal aristocracy, such as that sketched in Plato's
Republic, fails to measure up, Dewey argued, for though it may coincide
with democracy in conceiving its purpose to be the establishment of
conditions favorable to the growth of the virtuous man, it assumes that
most men are incapable of working out their destiny. It rests on a
"blasphemy against personality," which is presumed to be concentrated
in the leaders; it sanctions and undergirds hero-worship, "which means
man despised"; it denies human equality as a state in which "every man
has a chance and knows that he has . . . the chance to become a
person." If democracy is a way of life, then inevitably the day must
come when men in their life of work will no longer tolerate inhumane
working conditions. In an aristocracy or an Aristotelian city-state the
life of work may be scorned as degrading while accepted as inevitable
as the class divisions upon which it depends, but in a democracy, Dewey
insisted, industrial relations must partake of the democratic spirit by
being subordinated to the demands of society.[7] In 1888 this view was
little less than revolutionary.

Although the lines of Dewey's argument in this essay are sometimes
blurred by rhetorical overgrowths and although "democracy" tends to
be so etherealized as to have no relation to such contemporary or
near-contemporary realities as the neglect by white men of the "personality" of the Indians, the smugness of a "Rum, Romanism, and rebellion" mentality, and the activities of carpet-baggers and Tammany Hall,
the essay is invaluable for highlighting Dewey's belief in *democracy
as a way of life.* Scornfully he rejected the notion that democracy is
merely a form of government. As true would it be to describe a home
as a brick-and-mortar building or a church as a room with pews and
pulpit. As a form of "moral and spiritual association" democracy
describes the friendly willingness of neighbor to help neighbor, the
readiness to believe in the power of discussion to settle the questions

and vexations that rise from the association of man with man, and the implicit trust which a man at peace with himself and his near associates will accord to the newcomer, the stranger.

As a way of life, democracy represents the apogee of man's efforts to sow righteousness and harvest peace and good will, for it is the "ultimate, ethical ideal of humanity." [8] It is, indeed, a state of affairs "in which the distinction between the spiritual and the secular has ceased, and as in Greek theory, as in the Christian theory of the Kingdom of God, the church and the state, the divine and the human organization of society are one." [9] If we stop for a moment to analyze that last statement, we may wonder if Dewey did not inadvertently slip in a quotation from a curial theologian of the papal states of the thirteenth century. Had he lived three centuries earlier in one of the city-states of the Mathers and the Winthrops, he would not have been too far afield in his description of that polity as bodying forth the oneness of "the divine and the human organization of society." But in 1888 such an assertion was arrant nonsense—unless the "divine" element in society were man himself, considered as linked in misty oneness with ambient nature. What Dewey described in this passage, I would suggest, was not the United States of 1888 but the feeling of faith of his Oil City experience, conceptualized in the near-Hegelianism which the philosophical side of his nature was currently wooing.

Though one hesitates to use the word "ultimate" in the same sentence with Dewey's name, I would venture to suggest that the ultimate commitment that guided Dewey through his long life was to democracy as a way of life. Flowering from a particular vision of human history, in which concord and harmony are the central virtues and the factionmakers, the champions of "divisiveness," the chief public enemies, this belief in democracy guided Dewey in his efforts to dethrone any system or power—psychological, philosophical, theological, or political—which he judged to be incompatible with it. As a very young man, Dewey believed that a Hegelianized Christianity proclaimed the same sweet reasonableness and so represented the loftiest peak which the spirit of man had yet ascended. This view, however, changed midway during the decade at Ann Arbor so that between 1891 and 1894 Dewey became a Saul of Tarsus in reverse. If a dedicated person is a religious person—a possible use of a notoriously nebulous word—then American history has known few such religious men as John Dewey. His attacks against whatever he chose to label a dualism are the obverse of his persistent, untiring quest of unity, and nowhere did he pursue unity so hotly as on the plane of human relations. Democracy was dualism dethroned.

Early Schooling in Democracy

If we look for the origins of Dewey's commitment to democracy, we should not exaggerate the importance of his "mystic experience." Neither should we be misled by his oft-quoted comment on the "inward laceration" [10] which he suffered from the "dualisms" which he inherited from his surroundings. This memory of early distress might lead us to suspect that from his Vermont home he carried away little more than a sense of spiritual anguish to be resented the more it gnawed. Dewey himself, in an autobiographical excursus in an essay on a famous Vermonter of the early nineteenth century, Dr. James Marsh, voiced his gratitude for having been born "at a time and a place where the earlier ideal of liberty and the self-governing community of citizens" had not yet been contested by the fundamentally "European ideal" of the citizen subservient to the state.[11] The Vermonter, Dewey continued, probably stood without equal in believing that governments, like houses, could and should be remodelled in accord with the growth and changing needs of the citizenry. Patriotism, then, could not mean for a Vermonter a placid acquiescence in outmoded forms of government. It was, rather, an attachment to "the claims of a common human society as superior to those of any particular political form." Dewey's tribute to the political wisdom of the people among whom he grew up may, perhaps, be dismissed by the skeptic as revelatory of the feelings of a septuagenarian more than of the reality of community life in the Burlington of his boyhood. But does not Dewey point to the control by the town citizenry of its government which so stirred the admiration of De Tocqueville? The community "may almost be said to govern itself, so feeble and so restricted is the share left to the administration, so little do the authorities forget their popular origin and the power from which they emanate," that perceptive visitor had commented some twenty years before Dewey's birth.[12] The belief that the best judge of a man's interest is the man concerned, which underlies Dewey's lifelong stress on participation as an essential quality of the democratic way of life, was rooted in the traditions and manners of the people from whom he sprang.

The friendly association with teachers and fellow-students, which Dewey enjoyed in his graduate education at Johns Hopkins from 1882 to 1884, must have deepened his belief in the power of cooperation to achieve what the independent action of an individual could only begin. (It was a friend from those days, James McKeen Cattell, who in 1904 came to Dewey's rescue by smoothing his way to a professorship at Columbia after his resignation from Chicago.) When in 1884 Dewey came to teach at the University of Michigan, he was not treated as a junior clerk in a large office by the older professors. Instead, he was greeted as an equal. "Acceptance as an adult responsible member of the faculty," his daughter noted, along with the educational success of the state-supported, coeducational university, started the chain of ideas which later formed her father's theory of education.[13] Dewey's marriage in 1886 to Alice Chipman, a woman who had been reared to follow her own lights and who was sharply critical of what she considered to be social injustices, linked him with a person who was convinced "that a religious attitude was indigenous in natural experience and that theology and ecclesiastic institutions had benumbed rather than promoted it."

De Tocqueville's comments on the genius for self-government of the New England townsfolk imply that they were healthily watchful over the authorities elected to carry out their directives. Dewey's remarks in his essay of 1888 on "The Ethics of Democracy" on the inevitable tendency of even "good" aristocrats to divert the stream to their own fields reflects this wariness of his people. But something more than watchfulness and wariness are needed to make democracy tick. Something more even than a right to a voice in decisions affecting oneself is needed, for this need not imply a ready acceptance by one's equals nor —as the *nouveaux riches* of any generation can testify—is participation in decision-making inconsonant with being kept in one's place. Before a man will ungrudgingly and graciously welcome his fellow to conjoint living, to democracy as a way of life, he must be persuaded that he is not inviting a dunce to scatter what he has so patiently harvested. He must have grounds for respecting him. Dives must find in Lazarus an equal before he will consider him as a friend.

In the history of Western man the call to a belief in human equality and to a consequent respect for one's fellow (to oversimplify considerably) has been sounded by two trumpets: the Stoic and the Christian. The fact that even the slave has feelings and can think, that wisdom is not necessarily the playmate of the rich, that the same primal fire burns in the heart of hero and harlot—these were the themes of the Stoic catechism on equality, themes that, transposed into a different key, were revived in the seventeenth and eighteenth centuries by political philosopher and social reformer alike. Birth into a wealthy and cultured home is, in the Stoic catechism, not so much a claim to importance as a reminder that the truly liberated man is the cosmopolitan, the man whose home is the world, whose brother and sister are the wise of no matter what country or clime. Seneca feels the narrowness of Nero's palace. With Epicurus he can feel at home. The *philosophe* salutes as a brother savant the Confucian scholar whose belief in man's reasonableness he learns of through the laudatory accounts of Jesuit missionaries. Though what an American naturalist would call a "supernatural" element was not totally absent from the Stoic belief in human equality, it was not central to it. The Logos or Reason in which all men shared would not accost the person at death with the startling declaration that his feeding and clothing the poor, his visiting the imprisoned and instructing the ignorant were service of Itself in its temporal disguise. The Logos had not thundered forth a creative "Let there be light" into primaeval darkness.

In the Christian explanation of equality, on the contrary, the centrality of the belief in man's origin from and return to God cannot be blinked. To peon and pope alike the message is the same: each must give account at death of his own actions, particularly of his giving or withholding of love to those in need. Each man is accountable to a personal God, and in this sense (if in no other) men are equal.

There is some evidence that in his first years at the University of Michigan Dewey found in his interpretation of Christianity a propulsive force for his belief in human brotherhood and equality. For a little-known compilation of texts from the writings of the Scotch novelist and itinerant preacher, George MacDonald, Dewey selected several passages smacking of the Christian belief in the equality of all men. Echoes of the parable of the Good Samaritan are heard in a passage linking faith and good works in a way that might have troubled an ante-lapsarian Calvinist but pleased the social gospelers: "the way to worship God, while the daylight lasts, is to work; the service of God, the only 'divine service' is the helping of our fellows; I want to show that this is the simplest, blessedest thing in the human world." [14] In response to the question, "Who is my neighbor?" Dewey cited MacDonald as saying: "not the man only whom my compassion would lift from some slough; but the man who makes my clothes; the man who prints my books; the man who drives me in his cab." [15] And on a later page he included MacDonald's comment on meanness, whether of action, of thought, or of judgment as the "one thing a Christian soul recoils from." [16] Meanness, like aristocracy, means man despised. Dewey did not find very early in his career that the worship of God through works for mankind is incompatible with the sombre belief that some men set their hearts on a rejection of that very God. In an address to a group of Christian students at Ann Arbor in late 1884, his first year of university teaching, Dewey insisted that refusal of belief in God cannot be lamely ascribed to intellectual negligence. It is definitely a moral lapse, a sin. Conceding that the sober witness of the Bible to the reality of God and His claims on man strikes the unregenerate as hard doctrine, the young professor argued that the truth of this Biblical teaching comes home to one only when "the commands it lays upon the will have been executed." [17]

It took a hardy soul to speak so vigorously about sin in the heyday of optimism and belief in man's unlimited perfectibility. Powerful voices were booming that such chatter stemmed from nursery terrors and anthropomorphic projections. In the *Andover Review* and the *Bibliotheca Sacra,* theological journals to which Dewey offered some of his early essays, the thundering of the new heathen, the materialistic scientists, found frequent echoes. The times were desperate. The Indians were howling in attack, and the defenders of the citadels of godliness had recourse to any blunderbuss they could lay hands on. Dewey did not slink back from the fray. In an article of 1887 on "Ethics and Physical Science" he upbraided the proponents of a "scientific ethics" for virtually dispossessing man of his ethical heritage in their eagerness to subordinate him to the far-off end of a better world. That Christian ethics had little to recommend it to the Spencerians, the scientists in question, is plain from the clear description of it which Dewey attributed to them.

> It [theological or Christian ethics] rests upon the arbitrary decrees of the will of God, and this will is an unverifiable assumption, or at best is purely supernatural and hence out of relation to the true ends of humanity. The aim which theological ethics proposes is of equal flimsiness with the foundation, or, according to some of the more ardent, is even immoral, consisting in devotion to one's personal salvation in a future realm and is therefore, either utterly disparate with man's daily activities here, or in conflict with them. And the sanction is, if we may trust these writers, worthless, even if not morally degrading, being the escape from some arbitrary penalty, or the winning of some equally arbitrary reward.[18]

Curiously enough, Dewey did not object in his rebuttal of the scientists to this description of theological ethics, quite possibly because he accepted it as a summary of what passed for Christianity in some churches of his acquaintance. Instead, he charged the enemy's position by tallying what may be called the "undemocratic" assumptions implicit in their "scientific" ethics.

Against the universal agreement of all ethicians that all men should be equal stock-holders in the ethical community, Dewey argued, the evolutionists stand in protest, for they canonize "conflict" with all the brute nastiness it entails for the weak and helpless, as the means to an eventual state of human bliss. Secondly, their claims that the end of the universe is worked out through man as instrument can only mean that man is subordinated to that end where, in truth, he is called to work out his own destiny.[10] Finally, the evolutionists strip the life of all men save those of the final generation of real meaning, for they place the goal of human history at the end of time. That goal is a world to be enjoyed only by the last to leap from the womb of time, "something which the past ages have been obliged to do without," not a center equidistant from all points on the human circumference, giving meaning to the struggles of the Cro-Magnon as well as to his more sophisticated descendants.[20] The fact that this center, "an ideal unity of purpose and meaning," is the neo-Hegelian universal consciousness or spirit which formed the theme of the *Prolegomena to Ethics* of Thomas Hill Green, one of Dewey's acknowledged masters, should not blind us to the egalitarian function it served. Like the Stoic Logos, it was shared in by little "spirits" like man and this served to ennoble even the sot. Though Dewey may have had reservations about identifying it with the Jahweh of the Bible, though he would, even in this liberal Christian phase of his career, have scorned to speak of it as Creator, he used it skillfully against an evolutionary ethics which might have seemed to support the conclusion that the "fit" worthy of "survival" in the modern age lived on Park Avenue and were well known on Wall Street.

Dewey's interest in ethical questions during his early years at Ann Arbor was matched by his close attention to the latest developments in the "new psychology." Here, too, he found support for his strong belief in democracy as a way of life. He reported in 1884 to the largely clerical readership of the *Andover Review* some of the wonders of the laboratory-centered research of Wundt and Helmholtz. Unlike the scholastic schematism of the British empiricists, the "new psychology" dipped into the ocean of experience and was "content to get its logic from this experience, and not do violence to the sanctity and integrity of the latter by forcing it to conform to certain preconceived abstract ideas." Experience is no longer dictated to and told what "it *must* be in order to square with a scholastic logic," for the new psychologists are convinced that their discipline, which has been nurtured by their recent questioning of experience, will not betray them.[21] Along with this fearless openness to, and reverential probing of, the ordinary experiences of Everyman, the new psychologists are outstanding for their reliance on a new shareable method, that of experimentation, instead of on the older technique of introspection with all its subjective vagaries.

In this enthusiastic essay of 1884 Dewey did not draw out the implications of laboratory psychology for his belief in democracy, but they would bloom with the passing of the years. If the ideas at the back of our mind predispose us to attend to certain kinds of data and ignore others, then Dewey's fascination with "that rich and colored experience, never the same in two nations, in two individuals, in two moments of the same life," [22] inclined him from early adulthood to look for the discrepant, the not-quite-the-same, the unique. In a sense he was commenting on his own stance when in 1900 he contrasted his hardly-yet-born instrumental logic with "prescientific" modes of thought in the following terms:

> The discovery of difficulties, the substitution of doubt for quiescent acceptance, are more important than the sanctioning of belief through proof. Hence the importance of noting apparent exceptions, negative instances, extreme cases, anomalies. The interest is in the discrepant because that stimulates inquiry.[23]

Such an attitude presumes that all things are of value and that your evening paper should not so draw you that you fail to notice your wife's new hat. "When interest is occupied in finding out what anything and everything is," Dewey continued his discussion of types of logic, "any fact is just as good as its fellow. The observable world is a *democracy*. The difference which makes a fact what it is is not an exclusive distinction, but a matter of position and quantity, an affair of locality—and aggregation, traits which place *all facts upon the same level*." [24]

Students of Chinese thought have called attention to the manner in which the basic principle of harmony in human living was understood by Chinese sages to be a reflection on the human plane of the equilibrium of opposing forces in the world of nature.[25] The readiness with which an Ignatius of Loyola (to use an example from a different milieu) could exhort his religious subordinates to obedience to their superiors by reminding them of the "fact" that one heavenly body is swayed by another higher in the heavens indicates that in "prescientific" eras men had not been blind to the interplay between the phenomenon of order in nature and in human society. Dewey availed himself of this "prescientific" device to find, not hierarchical order, but democratic harmony in the world of scientific facts. Since the observable world is a "democracy," then it follows quite neatly that "laws are not edicts of a sovereign binding a world of subjects otherwise lawless; they are the agreements, the compacts of facts themselves, or, in the familiar language of Mill, the common attributes, the resemblances."[26] Nature is a community of interlinked units with no "higher" and "lower," no heavenly matter intrinsically superior to the slippery, never-quite-being-fulfilled *Stoff* of the sub-lunary world. Nature is not a Pandora's box housing malevolent forces. It is, at least potentially, a cornucopia showering good things on man, a maternal force ready to be attuned to the needs of her children and banishing worry thereby. Oneness with the onrushing fruitfulness of nature through the medium of scientific method is a perpetuation of that "supremely blissful feeling" which Dewey had enjoyed in the quiet "mystic experience" of his Oil City days.[27]

Open Communication, Lifeblood of Democracy

If Nature is a linkage of equal units, a sharing of samenesses-with-a-difference, then Nature become vocal in man should body forth this fact through the inter-communication of unit with unit. Democratic man should not be miserly. Least of all should the vanguard of brotherly pilgrims, the scientists, fail to share the riches they uncover in their probing of Nature. Like the scouts sent to explore the Promised Land, they should return to their people with the fruits of their discoveries and communicate to them their vision of the riches lying ahead. This conviction of Dewey was honed to a new sharpness in the early 1890's by the reports he received from a friend, Franklin Ford. In his work as a journalist in New York, Dewey recounted in a letter to William James, Ford had been refused permission by his employers to investigate the "social bearings of intelligence and its distribution." Undeterred, he had carried out his study and was not edified to learn that the reluctance of editors to publish certain findings was only one aspect of a larger problem, the obstacles and blockages in the channels of communication. Private groups, lobbies, vested interests—were these not the "aristocrats" of bygone days, still intent on their age-old effort to shackle the commoner and suborn truth to their pocketbooks? Against such villains must the crusade be carried on by spokesmen for the common good or the "whole" whose intellectual chastity could not be violated by the Beau Brummells of industry, finance, or the Church. In his letter to James, Dewey seems to be swimming with the immensity of the project ahead. He believes "that a tremendous movement is impending, when the intellectual forces which have been gathering since the Renascence and Reformation, shall demand complete free movement, and, by getting their physical leverage in the telegraph and printing press, shall, through free inquiry in a centralized way, demand the authority of all other so-called authorities." [28] In urging the importance of Ford's work to James, Dewey sketched the type of person he judged would be set in motion by it in his description of James as one who "has the intellectual interest developed, the thirst for inquiry with no special interest or precept or church or philosophy to 'save.' "

Morton White is quite correct in finding in this letter one of the first intimations of Dewey's break with objective idealism,[29] but a fact of equal, or even greater, importance for his later career, adumbrated in this letter, has not received the attention it deserves—namely, his implied rejection of a final commitment to any institution or system of thought as prejudicial to the common good and his fervor in dedicating himself to the establishment of open communication as the new "seat of intellectual authority." [30] Quite plainly in this letter Dewey identified "free inquiry in a centralized way"—a happy description of what he usually called scientific method—with the new authority in human affairs. To appreciate the direction Dewey hoped this new authority would take during his lifetime we can do no better than to turn to a reflection written some forty years later by one of Dewey's intimates and co-author with him of two textbooks on Ethics, James Hayden Tufts.

> My generation has seen the passing of systems of thought which had reigned since Augustine. The conception of the world as a kingdom ruled by God, subject to his laws and their penalties, which had been undisturbed by the Protestant Reformation, has dissolved. We watch the process, but as yet are scarcely awake to its possible outcome. The sanctions of our inherited morality have gone. Principles and standards which had stood for nearly two thousand years are questioned. The process goes on among us in methods which are perhaps no less radical [than the Communist experiment in Russia] because they are not violent.[31]

Dewey enlisted in the early 1890's in the move to purge the world of representatives of the "old order," because he had been enraptured by a vision of the universe as an orchestra directed exclusively by man in accord with the latest findings of scientific inquiry.

Chief among the voices from the past was Christianity with its message that the old order had long since passed away when in the fulness of time the Word became flesh and enstated a divine-human "dualism" in the heart of history. The most visible form of Christianity, the Catholic Church, claimed to be the authoritative perpetuation of that Communication of long centuries ago and had scandalized don and dunce alike in Dewey's boyhood by announcing at the Vatican Council of 1870 that the bishop of Rome, the Roman Pontiff, was the final judge in time on the meaning of Christ's message and had been so from the beginning of Christianity. Against the contention that all issues are open to doubt and debate it insisted that some few were not, though it encouraged dispassionate study and meditative consideration of the reasons for this insistence. In the early 1890's Dewey levelled his artillery against this refusal from the old order to disintegrate into the fertilizer for the new democratic world. In a little known lecture of March, 1892 he spelled out his reasons for the opposition to institutional Christianity which would mark so many of his later works.

Cult and doctrine, Dewey began, have been shown by research to be only the weeds in the garden of the religious spirit, whose flowers spring from the social and intellectual life of the human community. Christianity especially should not demand the acceptance of particular points of dogma, for Jesus taught little more than that "God is truth; that as truth He is love and reveals himself fully to man, keeping back nothing of Himself; that man is so one with the truth thus revealed that it is not so much revealed *to* him as *in* him; he is its incarnation." Living on the Olympian heights of Truth-incarnate-in-himself, man can exult in his freedom, for he is "free negatively, free from sin, free positively, free to live his own life, free to express himself, free to play without let or limitation upon the instrument given him—the environment of natural wants and forces." Athwart the path of the emancipated man, however, stand the unreconstructed churches with their claim to a "certain prerogative in laying down what is this truth, a certain exclusiveness in the administration of religious conduct." In its monopolistic desire to decide the meaning of Christian teaching, "the visible church" had been overplaying its hand for centuries by trying to repress scientific inquiry but only in the end to see itself spurned by the new priests of revelation, the scientists who "went out into the vineyard of nature and by obedience to the truth revealed the deeper truth of unity of law, the presence of one continuous living force, the conspiring and vital unity of all the world." Other religions may speak of mysteries beyond man's ken, but Christianity is synonymous with revelation, and "revelation means effective discovery, the actual ascertaining or guaranteeing to man of the truth of his life and the reality of the Universe." [32]

In equating revelation with discovery and the source of revelation with man in his social relations Dewey linked up Christianity (now so emasculated as to be barely recognizable) and democracy. Did not Christ teach that the Kingdom of God is within or among us? Well then, should not this teaching result in a religion which takes it seriously? Dewey's vision of democracy-as-religion is so remarkable that extended quotation alone can give us the "feel" of it.

> The significance of democracy as revelation is that it enables us to get truths in a natural, everyday and practical sense which otherwise could be grasped only in a somewhat unnatural or sentimental sense. . . . If God is, as Christ taught, at the root of life, incarnate in man, then democracy has a spiritual meaning. . . . Democracy is freedom. If truth is at the bottom of things, freedom means giving this truth a chance to show itself, a chance to well up from the depths. . . . The truth is not fully freed when it gets into some individual's consciousness, for him to delectate himself with. It is freed only when it moves in and through this favored individual to his fellows. . . . The supposition that the ties which bind men together, that the forces which unify society, can be other than the very laws of God, can be other than the outworkings of God in life, is a part of that practical unbelief in the presence of God in the world which I have already mentioned . . . It is no accident that the growing organization of democracy coincides with the rise of science . . . Democracy thus appears as the means by which the revelation of truth is carried on. It is in democracy, the community of ideas and interest through community of action, that the incarnation of God in man . . . becomes a living, present thing, having its ordinary and natural sense.[33]

If Dewey's audience felt somewhat bewildered at the end of this address, they might well have been excused, for the marriage of God and man at the altar of democracy, the transformation of that two-in-one-ethos into the theandric democrat of the world on the point of coming, and the discovery of the divine presence in the flaming bush of common action were not the common themes of chapel talks.

If they hankered for concrete evidence of the disloyalty of the "visible church" to the revelations of scientists, they could have found an interesting source in the autobiography of Charles Darwin, which was rolling from the presses in 1892. There they might have read of the encounter of Huxley and the Anglican Bishop Wilberforce of Oxford thirty-two years before when the latter enlivened his denunciation of Darwin's views as contrary to Biblical revelation by asking Huxley to enlighten him whether it was from his grandfather's or his grandmother's side that he traced his ape ancestry. Did they feel that this was an unfair thrust, they must have been delighted with Huxley's biting reply: "I should feel it no shame to have risen from such an origin. But I should feel it a shame to have sprung from one who prostituted the gifts of culture and of eloquence to the service of prejudice and of falsehood." [34]

Dewey's writing in 1892 and 1893 rang changes on the themes that tumbled forth in his address on "Christianity and Democracy," and spelled out in some detail the implications for human living of religion as communion-with-nature-and-man-in-freedom-from-fear. He reassures a student audience that the burden of the teaching of John the Evangelist and Saul of Tarsus is that man *is* saved and that, consequently, a pursuit of personal salvation is pointless. He suggests that the religious prophet to whom people will next turn is the one who will interpret the religious meaning of the flow of life of democratic man, transposing into a key attuned to modern ears the message which Jesus had interpreted for the people of his age—that man is at peace with God. He bids "the church," which has played out its part in the drama of man's revelation to himself of his earlier unsuspected divinity, "to universalize itself and thus pass out of existence," presumably by renouncing its claim to speak with authority on ethical and religious questions.[35] In a study on Renan, Dewey tries to account for the backsliding of the savant who in 1848 had been serenely confident of the imminent canonization of Science in the temple of Humanity but who, in 1890, expressed his fears that mankind, stripped of its idealistic and supernatural illusions, faces bleakness in the stretches ahead. Admitting that scientists had failed during the preceding half-century to bring "the human spirit and the human interpretation" to their findings, Dewey suggests that Renan had underestimated the vitality of old beliefs and the cunning of vested interests in preventing science from establishing itself in the field of ethical inquiry. Then, in conclusion, he lifts the veil on the import of the struggle to bind scientific method to moral inquiry:

> I cannot but think that the Renan of '48 was wiser than he of '90 in the recognition of the fact that man's interests are finally and prevailingly practical; that if science cannot succeed in satisfying these interests it is hardly more than an episode in the history of humanity; that the ultimate meaning and control will always be with

the power that claims this practical region for its own—if not with science, then with the power of the church from which Renan was an early apostate.[36]

Dewey's discovery that man's practical concerns, no matter how splendidly cloaked with "rational" explanations, ultimately define the meaning of life, was one of the turning-points in his life. The arena of struggle, it follows, lay not in the misty realm of dogma but on the plains of men's interests. And Dewey did not underestimate the foe— that Shadow from the past that the sun of every age seemed to startle to life. It was not to be described as "mother" or "the sheepfold" or as "the city on a mountain." It was that sinister Power whose long history provided her with all the weapons of control known to man— with the miracle, mystery, and authority of the Grand Inquisitor. In an essay of late 1891 Dewey had sketched, apropos a larger topic, the way the "scholastics" had looked on intellectual inquiry. (And was scholasticism not the extension of the Shadow into the realm of thought?) In perfect consistency with their religious beliefs the scholastics "did not conceive that thought was free, that intelligence had rights, nor that there was any possible science independent of data authoritatively laid down." Thought, in this context, resembled a barrel to be filled with whatever "tradition," "revelation" or "external authority" might pump into it. Consequently, it is quite understandable that the scholastics never dared "to examine the material, to test its truth; to suppose that intelligence could cut loose from this body of authority and go straight to nature, to history itself to find the truth." [37] Free and independent science was a child of a later age. Dewey had no great quarrel with the scholastic method as a tool for medieval man. Indeed, he could applaud "the principle of authority" of the early and medieval Church for subduing the barbarians to a life sufficiently disciplined to enable them to appropriate the treasures of the Graeco-Roman world.[38] But a continuation of the scholastic method and of the Church which (as it appeared to him) vigilantly crammed its maw with carefully selected, predigested food—this was a scandal not to be brooked. The Church, in effect, was the prize example of the vested interests which Franklin Ford had caught out in the despicable game of kinking the lines of communication on which democratic man so depends.

But man does not quench his thirst for truth merely by drinking from the fountain of facts which daily living gushes forth. He must sieve them through the vision of reality which animates his living and guides his activities. Though no dark authority from ages past should be allowed to declare a vision for modern man, some control over society's network of communications must be exercised. In an account of a newspaper which in 1891 and 1892 he was struggling to launch, Dewey described the vision, the principle of selection, which would guide his editorial policy. "Thought News" the paper was to be named, and, although some wag had wagered that "Ten to one, 'Thought News' will contain news already covered by the newspapers and twenty to one that its thought will be exclusively that of its editors," Dewey was in earnest about the matter. In his explanation of editorial policy Dewey recalled Huxley's gibe that philosophy is a matter of "lunar politics" and conceded that many students would probably applaud the accuracy of the thrust unless they could be shown that philosophical studies, no matter how abstract, are related to some central fact. What is that fact?

> That fact is the social organism. When philosophic ideas are not inculcated by themselves but used as tools to point out the meaning of phases of social life they begin to have some life and value. . . . When it can be seen, for example, that Walt Whitman's poetry, the great development of short stories at present, the centralizing tendency in railroads and the introduction of business methods into charity organizations are all parts of one organic social movement, then the philosophic ideas about organism begin to look like something definite. The facts themselves get more meaning, too, when viewed with relation to one principle than when treated separately as a jumble.[39]

The social organism, the social whole, the common good, the people, nature-and-man-in-oneness—call it what you will. It is that great sea of experience which in the murkiness of the past welled up from the brute world of screeches and chatterings, became articulate in the first stammerings of primaeval man, and was now rising higher and higher as men were linking themselves into a new unity through newspaper, telephone and telegraph. That roar of many voices must be orchestrated into unity. A new prophet was needed. If democracy was god, could not Dewey be that prophet?

Coming only a month after Dewey's declaration that the prophet of the modern age must voice the aspirations of democratic man and less than a year after his disclosure to James of the finding of Franklin Ford, this statement on the centrality of the "social organism," couched though it is in Hegelian terms which later he would use in a different sense is, I submit, an excellent description of Dewey's vision of life. In what scientifically verifiable way Walt Whitman's poetry was organically linked to centralization of railroad interest Dewey could not really have said. But he could proclaim a misty union between the two with the same assurance with which, some sixty years later, he asserted to a puzzled inquirer that a "situation," the unit of ethical inquiry, "stands for something inclusive of a large number of diverse elements existing across wide areas of space and long periods of time, but which, nevertheless, have their own unity." [40] To proclaim is the work of the prophet. The message to which Dewey bore witness is basically what he felt at Oil City: that man and nature are interlinked and that worry is a needless futility. In terms of activity, it is that man can discover the "very laws of God" in "the forces which unify society" and should rejoice to communicate his findings to his fellows.[41]

The New Humanity

In the Christian vision of the world mankind was renewed by being offered the opportunity to participate in the life-giving death of Christ through incorporation into the Church, a society open to each and all, irrespective of race, socio-economic condition, or political opinion. Protestant and Catholic were in rough agreement that, no matter how this fact might be explained, one facet of it could not be minimized: the initiative of God in the creation of the world and in the redemptive work of Christ. "What hast thou that thou hast not received, and if thou hast received, why dost thou glory as though thou hadst not received?" St. Paul had questioned the Christian community at Corinth, and his affirmation that man's power to enter the community of Christ, the Church, is a gift of God had helped to anchor deeply in the Christian conscience the conviction that especially in the order of salvation man is dependent upon God. There is an "ongoing process" in the universe—the initiation of mankind into the family of God. It is a process wherein (according to Catholic teaching) the very elements of nature are bent to the service of man, for the water of Baptism, the wheat and wine of the Eucharist, the reasoned consent of man and wife, and the whispered words of priestly absolution are transformed through the power of Christ into life-giving and life-restoring sacraments. The universe strains toward fulfillment, and in a sense that fulfillment, that consummatory experience, is daily attained when God lays hold of wheat and wine to change them into His Body and Blood. The universe reaches fulfillment too in every virtuous act of man, for in that act man consecrates himself and that segment of space-time wherein he is situated to his own good, which is the glory of God. But this movement of the universe through the hands of man is initiated by God and directed toward Him, Alpha and Omega.

The process of redemption begins anew with each individual and can never be left behind as a particular phase of world history. The individual man must *work out* his salvation in a universe which is precarious in that he can misuse it, misdirect it, sin.

It is doubtful whether Dewey ever took time to study Catholic teaching. His writings are so charged with outworn cliches about Catholicism that one is driven to admiration that the champion of "scientific method" could have been so gun-shy of reputable sources of Catholic teaching. A man who in 1900 could maintain that Christianity, because of its stress on personal salvation, minimized the social aspects of conduct and "regarded the social life, from the family to the state, as having primary relation to man's appetites, in themselves evil"; who in 1908 could maintain that Catholic moral philosophy in the Middle Ages was "prevailed upon to damn the body on principle"; and who in 1922 could lightly refer to the "Jesuit maxim" of the "end justifying the means," was not interested in ferreting out what Catholics actually believe.[42] Dewey was no more interested in the facts in this matter than was the judge, who denied Bertrand Russell the right to teach, interested in determining precisely what Russell did uphold on matters of sexual morality.[43] One reason for this strange blindness is, I would suggest, that quite early in his career Dewey denied God a ticket of admission to the democratic world then allegedly forming and wrote off institutional Christianity as irremediably perverse.

But how could the strange fact be explained that the teaching of Jesus which Dewey had been able to decipher had been so badly misunderstood by previous generations? Dewey offered a cloudily ingenious explanation of this seeming anomaly in late 1892, not many months after his address on "Christianity and Democracy," and only two months before his appraisal of Renan. A Hegelian rhapsody on the movement of history, the explanation began with a clearly naturalistic account of the origin of Christianity: "If we regard it [the Christian 'idea'] as having historical relations and not something intruded into the world from outside, without continuity with previous experience . . . [it] must have been the generalization of previous life." The Word did not become flesh. The "idea," struggling for recognition in the arena of history, finally comes to consciousness among a despised Semitic people and from them gradually spills over into the cultures of the Mediterranean world. The fact that all who were "in Christ Jesus were no longer under the law" was a heady wine, for the first sip of it "only quickened men's consciousness of their slaveries . . . only made men feel more deeply the limitations of their activity and hence their 'finitude.'" [44] Instead of recognizing the human origin of this abrogation of law for the redeemed, the generations before modern man interpreted it as something "wholly supernatural" and, Dewey implies, grovelled in the idolatry of a new servitude—the worship of a God distinct from historical process. The dialectic is that of Hegel, but the passion is that of the prophet of democracy when he writes: "Until such time, then, as the new principle [the complete freedom of redeemed man] should succeed in getting itself organized into forms more adequate to itself (the development of science, the conquest of nature through the application of this science in invention and industry, and its application to the activities of men in determining their relations to one another and the resulting forms of social organization) this principle must have seemed remote from, negative to, all possible normal life."

The palimpsest of history on which centuries of Christian thinkers had scrawled, could now yield up the dim outlines traced by nature itself—thanks to the new light, the theory of evolution, which post-Darwinian man was able to bring to his reading. According to this theory the "unity of process," which natural scientists had uncovered in nature, "has ceased to be either a supernatural datum or a merely philosophic speculation. It has assumed the proportions of fact." [45] One wonders if this "fact" had not been felt by Dewey in his Oil City experience and was now coming to verbal formulation with the help of an evolutionistic vocabulary.

This "fact," Dewey went on to say, is democracy in the realm of social relations, it is the whole toward which aristocratic and feudal institutions had been pointing. "When that which is perfect is come," Dewey quoted St. Paul's panegyric of love, "that which is in part shall be done away." Man is healed—or, better still, man has reached the sun-drenched plateau from which for the first time in history he can smell the noisome rot strewn in the valleys of the past. Never again must he descend to that misty waste brooded over, oppressed by, the weight of the Absolute.

The new, democratic man must be freed, too, from the incubus of a "metaphysical self." Dewey used this term initially to designate Green's concept of the impingement of the Absolute on the sense and affective parts of man by which knowledge and moral striving are generated. He enlarged its scope to refer to whatever might be included in the term, soul, and also, it seems, any element of personal stability which might lead an individual in making a moral decision to disregard or minimize relevant data from the present. "The more one is convinced," he wrote in late 1893, "that the pressing need of the day, in order to make headway against hedonistic ethics on the one side and theological ethics on the other, is an ethics rooted and grounded in the self, the greater is the demand that the self be conceived as a working, practical self, carrying within the rhythm of its own process both 'realized' and 'ideal' self." [46] This working, practical self befits the democratic man, for it is not tied down to precedent or forms. Like the frontiersman, it is open to the new, ready to innovate, concerned to hold all commitments in the tentative mood, for who knows what lies beyond the next hill? Though, in the passage just cited, Dewey's target was Green's unavailing efforts to unify the here-and-now man with the Absolute, his larger target was the man who refuses to mesh his "private" self with the demands of the social organism. Moral evil is no longer a willing deviation from what one takes to be obligatory. It is reinterpreted as a type of rigidity.

> When we condemn an act as bad, because selfish, we always mean, I think, exactly this: the person in question acted from interest in his past or fixed self, instead of holding the self open for instruction; —instead, that is, of finding the self in the activity called for by the situation. I do not see that it is a bit better to *get* goodness *for* the self than it is to get pleasure for the self. . . . *Fiat justitia, ruat coelum* will serve, if it means: Let the needed thing be done, though the heavens of my past, or fixed, or presupposed self fall. The man who interprets the saying to mean: Let me keep my precious self moral, though the heavens of public action fall, is as despicable personally as he is dangerous socially.[47]

Man's belief in a soul or "fixed" element in his composition is as prejudicial to social reform as was earlier man's belief in God, conceived as creative source of the universe, hurtful to his efforts to reach complete freedom. Believers in a soul are—though Dewey does not draw the comparison—ranged with the British empiricists in psychology and the scholastics in philosophy, men afraid to allow here-and-now experience to unfold its loveliness before them. They insist on shackling the present to their rigid forms, their precepts derived from authority.

In one of his last appearances at Ann Arbor, Dewey continued his apostolate of evangelizing the churches to fall in step with the spirit of the age. The ideals Christianity had introduced into the world—the inalienable worth of the individual, the need to establish the Kingdom of God, revealed truth as the guide of life—have been worked into the social fabric of the modern world, he asserted, and for this reason "it is idle to go on repeating the old ideals and cherishing the old aims." The higher unity in the name of which Christianity is called to reconstruct its doctrines of revelation and inspiration is that of the new religion of scientific truth-making. This is so "because science represents a method of truth to which, so far as we can discover, no limits whatsoever can be put." [48] Precisely because respectable people—parents and clergymen, among others, it goes without saying—too often refuse to allow the realm of morals to be studied by scientific method and insist on bullying the most weak and defenseless of the race, little children, into following orders, instead of understanding them, a "chaos in moral training" has resulted. Evidence for this lamentable state of affairs Dewey found in the results of a questionnaire about one-hundred of his students at Ann Arbor answered concerning the type of motivation their parents had appealed to in their moral education. Although all ethical teachers are in agreement that conduct springing from fear of punishment and hope of reward is not moral, Dewey asserted in one of those vast, quite incorrect generalizations which scar many of his writings, nevertheless the students testified that appeals to fear and to religious considerations had been most frequently used in their homes. Dewey's desire was to disabuse parents of their fears of giving reasons to their children for the actions they expected them to carry out; and on this account he deplored parental failure to act in accord with the conviction of almost every contemporary moral teacher that "the reasons and duties of the moral life either lie within itself or at least may be studied by themselves without direct reference to supernatural considerations." [49]

If you tell your child that she must go to bed at eight o'clock or suffer from drowsiness the next day, you are giving her reasons which she can test in her own experience. But if you warn her that failure to do so will offend Jesus or displease her guardian angel or spot her soul, you are threatening her with the help of data that she cannot possibly check. That way lie neurosis and human warp, needless fears and the consequent infantile longing for certainties which drive men from one dogmatism to another rather than to the only layer of ghosts, scientific method. The Dewey who wanted to put order into the chaos in moral education by exorcising the "supernatural," drank from the same cup as Lucretius, that fierce lover of distressed devotees of the gods. There was in him much of the compassion of Gautama Buddha who wanted to spend himself in shattering the illusions of sense-bound men.

But, unlike Lucretius and Buddha, Dewey lived after Christ. Opposed

to—or better, clarificatory of—his "mystic experience" of Oil City with
its call to freedom from worry and to a sense of oneness with Nature,
stands the revolutionary challenge of Christ to accept His yoke and bear
His burden and thereby find rest and peace in the very march through
Nature to its creative Source. That Dewey was correct in asserting
man's kinship with Nature, the prelogical or "unminded" partner in his
pilgrimage, is beyond dispute. That his emphasis on the sense of
liberation and release experienced by the man who works for and with
his fellows is not misplaced, comes as no shock to one who believes
in the primacy of charity. That a feeling of kinship for Nature or a
belief in democratic good works is incompatible with a reasoned belief
in God and the centrality of Christ in human history is not at all clear.
Nor is it immediately evident. It is a question and, like every question,
calls for study and reflection. It is not answered by being dismissed,
but, like Banquo's ghost, rises most unexpectedly to demand a hearing,
a public hearing. If a hearing is denied it, may it not be queried whether
blockages of communication are a prerogative of supporters of the
"method of authority?"

NOTES

1. For a brief, accurate account of Loyola's experience see James Brodrick,
   The Origin of the Jesuits (London: Longmans, Green, 1940) 10-12. Nehru
   describes his awakening to the plight of the peasants in *Toward Freedom*
   (New York: John Day Co., 1941) 54-60.
2. Max Eastman, "John Dewey," *The Atlantic Monthly* 168 (Dec. 1941) 673.
3. "Ethics and Physical Science," *Andover Review* 7 (June 1887) 577, 582.
4. "The Place of Religious Emotion," *The Monthly Bulletin* of the Students'
   Christian Association of the University of Michigan, 8 (Oct. 1886) 23-25.
5. *The Ethics of Democracy,* ("University of Michigan Philosophical Papers,"
   Second Series, No. 1. Ann Arbor: Andrews and Company, 1888) 1.
6. *Ibid.* 14.
7. *Ibid.* 25-6.
8. *Ibid.* 18.
9. *Ibid.* 28.
10. "From Absolutism to Experimentalism," *Contemporary American Philosophy,*
    ed. George P. Adams and William P. Montague (New York: Macmillan,
    1930) II 19.
11. "James Marsh and American Philosophy," *The Journal of the History of
    Ideas* 2 (1941) 147. This essay was written in 1930 on the occasion of a
    commemorative exercise in honor of Marsh.
12. Alexis de Tocqueville, *Democracy in America,* ed. Philips Bradley (New
    York: Vintage Books, 1954) I 60.

13. Jane Dewey, "Biography of John Dewey," *The Philosophy of John Dewey,* ed. Paul A. Schilpp (2d ed.; New York: Tudor Publishing Co., 1951) 21.

14. J. Dewey (ed.), *Selections from the Writings of George MacDonald or Helps for Weary Souls* (New York: T. R. Knox and Co., 1885) 9. A reprint of this compilation was issued by the Chicago firm of F. L. Dusenberry in 1889. MacDonald's son, Greville, recounts that his father received few receptions so stirring as that at Ann Arbor during his lengthy lecture-tour in the States in 1872-73. All the Protestant churches, except one, closed down on the Sunday of his father's preaching so that the congregations could hear him. It may well be that the memory of MacDonald was still green at Ann Arbor when Dewey arrived there and that the *Helps for Weary Souls* was a response to local interest, if not demand. For further details see Greville MacDonald, *George MacDonald and His Wife* (London: Allen and Unwin, 1924) 455-56.

15. *Helps for Weary Souls,* 5-6.

16. *Ibid.* 23.

17. "The Obligation to Knowledge of God," *The Monthly Bulletin* of the Students' Christian Association of the University of Michigan, 6 (Nov. 1884) 24.

18. "Ethics and Physical Science," *Andover Review* 8 (June 1887) 575-76.

19. *Ibid.* 580-81, 585.

20. *Ibid.* 589. For another interpretation of this essay see Neil G. McCluskey, S.J., *Public Schools and Moral Education* (Columbia University Press, 1958) 203-204. In stressing one aspect of Dewey's argument, I am not unaware that a more thorough examination of it would highlight the philosophical inadequacy of Dewey's formulation of key issues.

21. "The New Psychology," *Andover Review* 2 (Sept. 1884) 288.

22. *Ibid.* 278.

23. "Some Stages of Logical Thought," *Philosophical Review* 9 (Sept. 1900) 484.

24. *Ibid.* 485 (italics supplied).

25. Cf. Arthur Wright, "Struggle vs. Harmony," *World Politics* 6 (Oct. 1953) 33.

26. "Some Stages of Logical Thought," *Philosophical Review* 9 (Sept. 1900) 485-86.

27. See above, page 34.

28. The letter, written on June 3, 1891, may be found in Ralph B. Perry, *The Thought and Character of William James* (Boston: Little, Brown, 1935) II 517-19.

29. Morton White, *The Origin of Dewey's Instrumentalism* (New York: Columbia University Press, 1943) 102.

30. This term is a chapter-heading from Dewey's *The Quest for Certainty,* published in 1929.

31. James Hayden Tufts, "What I Believe," *Contemporary American Philosophy,* ed. Charles Adams and William P. Montague (New York: Macmillan, 1930) II 333.

32. "Christianity and Democracy," *Religious Thought at the University of Michigan* (Ann Arbor: The Inland Press, 1893) 60-61, 62, 63, 64.

33. *Ibid.* 66-8.

34. *The Autobiography of Charles Darwin and Selected Letters,* ed. by Francis Darwin (New York: 1958 Dover Publications reprint of *Charles Darwin, His Life Told in an Autobiographical Chapter and in a Selected Series of His Published Letters,* published in 1892 by D. Appleton and Co.) 252.

35. These assertions appear in "The Relation of Philosophy to Theology," *The Monthly Bulletin* of the Students' Christian Association of the University of Michigan, 14 (Jan. 1893) 67-8.

36. "Renan's Loss of Faith in Science," *Open Court* 7 (Jan. 1893) 3515.

37. "The Present Position of Logical Theory," *Monist* 2 (Oct. 1891) 4, 5.

38. See as an example "The Significance of the Problem of Knowledge," University of Chicago Contributions to Philosophy, I, 3 (Chicago: University of Chicago Press, 1896) 9-12.

39. For my account of Dewey's newspaper venture I am relying on Willinda Savage's doctoral dissertation, "The Evolution of John Dewey's Philosophy of Experimentalism as Developed at the University of Michigan" (University of Michigan, 1950) 145-47.

40. John Dewey and Arthur F. Bentley, *Knowing and the Known* (Boston: Beacon Press, 1949) 315.

41. See above, page 34 and page 37, for the context of these remarks.

42. The three quotations in this sentence are from: a) "Moral Philosophy," *The Universal Cyclopedia,* ed., Charles K. Adams (New York: Appleton, 1900) VI 242; b) "Intelligence and Morals," an essay of 1908 reprinted in *The Influence of Darwin on Philosophy and Other Essays* (New York: Holt, 1910) 54; c) *Human Nature and Conduct* (1929 Modern Library edition of the 1922 original) 240.

43. Dewey's defense of Russell's right to a fair trial and to teach is contained in "Social Realities versus Police Court Fictions," his contribution to *The Bertrand Russell Case* (New York: Viking, 1941).

44. "Green's Theory of the Moral Motive," *Philosophical Review* 1 (Nov. 1892) 610. This was the first of two articles which Dewey wrote at this time on the inadequacy of Green's moral philosophy. The section on Christianity or the "Christian idea" was included to illustrate a general principle which Dewey used to explain why Green only partially overcame the "dualisms" of earlier thinkers.

45. *Ibid.* 611.

46. "Self-Realization as the Moral Ideal," *Philosophical Review* 2 (Nov. 1893) 663. This was the second of two articles on Green's philosophical inadequacies.

47. *Ibid.* 661.

48. "Reconstruction," *The Monthly Bulletin* of the Student's Christian Association of the University of Michigan, 15 (June, 1894) 151, 154.

49. Dewey, "The Chaos in Moral Training," *Popular Science Monthly* 45 (August 1894) 440, 441.

III

Dewey's Theory of Knowledge

BEATRICE H. ZEDLER

> *A member of the Department of Philosophy of Marquette University, Professor Beatrice Zedler obtained her doctorate from Fordham University in 1947. She has contributed articles, primarily on medieval Arabian philosophers, to* New Scholasticism, Modern Schoolman, *and* Proceedings of the American Catholic Philosophical Association. *Her essay, "John Dewey in Context," appeared in* Some Philosophers on Education (*1956*).

To one who complained, in the presence of students, that Dewey was sometimes hard to understand, John Dewey once said: "Let some of these young men explain me: it could make a career for some of them." [1]

If he had been referring to his theory of knowledge, his remark would have been most appropriate. One could indeed make a career of examining fully Dewey's views on this subject through his long and active life. But without undertaking so exhaustive a study, we might try to record some of the stages in the development of this theory as they appear in some of his principal writings. This genetic approach may give us a better understanding of his mature philosophical position on the nature of knowing.

From 1884 to 1903

An early article, written the year that Dewey completed his graduate studies, contains a clue both to his later position on knowledge and to the motivation of his own philosophical commitments. Dewey opposes the view that would consider knowing as "a colorless intellectual thing" or knowledge "in its origin as a faculty apart, separate from our will and our desires." "But the fact is," he says, "that there is no knowledge of anything except as our interests are alive to the matter, and our will actively directed toward the end desired. We know only what we most *want* to know." [2]

In this stress on the union of knowing and willing, with the willing directing the knowing, he suggests the reason for his own early attachment to Hegel. Hegel's thought, he tells us in an autobiographical essay, "supplied a demand for unification that was doubtless an intense emotional craving, and yet was a hunger that only an intellectualized subject-matter could satisfy." It helped him to overcome the painful sense of divisions and separations that were, he says, borne in upon him "as a consequence of a heritage of New England culture, divisions by way of isolation of self from the world, of soul from body, of nature from God." He adds that "Hegel's synthesis of subject and object, matter and spirit, the divine and the human was . . . no mere intellectual formula; it operated as an immense release, a liberation." [3] Dewey had made the acquaintance of German philosophy during a year of private study. During his graduate work at Johns Hopkins, this initial attraction was deepened because of the current interest in German thought and especially because of the influence of one of his teachers, George Sylvester Morris. [4]

Professor Morris had an intense dislike for the dualism of British philosophy which isolated two factors in knowledge: the knowing subject and the object to be known. To this "mechanical relation" of subject and object he opposed the Hegelian "organic relation" in which the "empirical consciousness" of the particular man and the objects of knowledge are embraced by a larger living whole, the "universal consciousness." [5] Some of Dewey's most enduring antagonisms and preferences are traceable to this influence, notably his attacks on British empiricism and on dualism in any form, and his profound interest in "organic relations," an interest which for some years he was to express in Hegelian terms.

In an 1884 article, in which Dewey gives an Hegelian critique of Kant, he says that since subject and object of knowledge are both manifestations of Reason, the relation between them is not external or mechanical but organic. In the context of Hegel's refusal to distinguish sharply between subjective and objective existences, we can no longer refer to "things and thoughts as two distinct spheres." [6] "There is but one world, the world of knowledge," Dewey says a few years later, "not two, an inner and an outer, a world of observation and a world of conception; and this one world is everywhere logical." [7]

The Hegelian basis for Dewey's rejection of a dualism of knowing subject and known object is more explicitly stated in his article, "The Psychological Standpoint." [8] Here, after some incisive criticism of the British empiricists, he suggests that between subject and object there is a bond existing in an eternal consciousness. Noting that his discussion is repeatedly pointing to Absolute Idealism, he adds: "Were it admitted that subject, mind, and object, matter, are both but *elements within,* and both exist only *for,* consciousness—we should be in the sphere of an eternal absolute consciousness, whose partial realisation both the individual 'subject' and the 'external world' are." [9] The relation between the individual consciousness and the universal consciousness he expresses in this way: "The individual consciousness is but the process of realisation of the universal consciousness through itself. Looked at as process, as realising, it is individual consciousness; looked at as produced or realised, as conscious of the process, that is of itself, it is universal consciousness." [10]

In his first book, *Psychology,* an explicit application to knowledge is made. Knowledge involves both an individual element and a universal element. As to the *knower,* it is individual; as to the *known,* it is universal:

> "Knowledge may be defined as the process by which some universal element—that is, element which is in possible relation to all intelligences—is given individual form, or existence in a consciousness. Knowledge is not an individual possession. . . . To obtain knowledge, the individual must get rid of the features which are peculiar to him, and conform to the conditions of universal intelligence. The realization of this process, however, must occur in an *individual.*
> ". . . the essence of the truth already exists, and all the self can do is to make it its own. It can give it individual *form* by reproducing this universal existence in consciousness or self." [11]

This view of knowledge as a reproduction of some universal content "in the form of individual, unsharable consciousness" [12] seems scarcely recognizable as the position of the John Dewey we know today, yet clues to the later Dewey are found even in the Hegelian Dewey. In this same work, Dewey suggests that it is the relatedness of things that is the very basis of the possibility of knowing:

". . . if things had nothing in common, if each was absolutely distinct from every other, no thinking would be possible. . . . Thinking is possible because there exists in things thought an ideal, universal element. The discovery of this element constitutes thinking; when discovered, it is always expressed in the form of a relation." [13]

"*Actual Knowledge is Concerned with a World of Related Objects.* . . . the world of objects is not a series of unconnected, unrelated objects. Each is joined to every other in space and in time. We never experience any breach of continuity. We pass naturally, by some connecting link, from one to another. We live, in short, in an ordered, harmonious world, or cosmos; not in a chaos. All objects and events are considered as members of one system; they constitute a *uni-verse,* one world, in which order, connection, is the universal rule." [14]

The Hegelian stress on the relatedness of all things in the universe was to find an added justification, Dewey thought, in the discoveries of modern science; Dewey himself thus prepares the way for his transition from idealism to naturalism. In an interesting text, he comments as follows on the influence of science on Leibniz's idea of the world as organic:

"I do not think . . . that it can truly be said that he [Leibniz] was led to the idea simply from the state of physiological investigation at that time. Rather, he had already learned to think of the world as organic through and through, and found in the results of biology confirmations, apt illustrations of a truth of which he was already thoroughly convinced." [15]

Morton White suggests that this comment describes Dewey's own philosophical development. His concept of the world as organic arose from his idealism and was later to be confirmed and modified by his contact with Darwinism.[16] In the essay that has been called "the last great defense of Hegel to be found in Dewey's logical writings," [17] Dewey did in fact suggest that the objective idealism of Hegel could best be understood in the light of modern science; that because Hegel was born too soon, before modern science had fully conceived the world as "an organism of significant relations and bearings," Hegel's philosophy was given a subjective interpretation. Dewey stresses not only that "Hegel . . . anticipated somewhat the actual outcome of the scientific movement," but that he represented "the quintessence of the scientific spirit." [18]

The transition from Hegel to Darwin in Dewey's theory of knowledge was therefore not as abrupt as it might at first seem. As Morton White puts it, Dewey

". . . need only convert the universal consciousness into nature, the individual into the organism, and the object of knowledge into environment. The result, translated into naturalistic terms, is that the organism and its environment are both parts of nature. It follows that whatever holds true of nature in general, holds true of human organisms in particular, and that the activity or capacity known as 'knowledge' appears in man in accordance with the principles of organic evolution." [19]

Among other leading clues to Dewey's later theory of knowledge in the earlier writings are these: his uniting of cognitive and appetitive factors; his hint of ideas as plans of action; his distinction of sensation from knowledge; his stress on the active role of the self in knowing. Let us consider each in turn.

Returning, in his *Psychology,* to a consideration of knowledge as a reproduction of some universal content in the form of individual consciousness, Dewey makes more explicit what he means by the universal element and the individual element in consciousness: ". . . the universal element is knowledge, the individual is feeling, while the relation which connects them into one concrete content is will." [20] He adds:

"Feeling, knowledge, and will are not to be regarded as three *kinds* of consciousness; nor are they three separable parts of the same consciousness. They are the three aspects which every consciousness presents, according to the light in which it is considered. . . ." [21]

Consciousness as cognitive, or knowledge, "is the state of being aware of something"; it tells us about something; it gives information. Consciousness as emotional, that is, feeling, expresses the value or interest that this information has for the self, that is, it implies that an idea is not just a colorless fact "but also a way in which the self is affected." [22] To one who would regard the perception of a tree or the learning of a proposition in geometry as purely cognitive, Dewey would say:

". . . feeling is necessary, for unless the mind were affected in some way by the object or the truth, unless it had some interest in them, it would never direct itself to them, would not pay attention to them, and they would not come within its sphere of knowledge at all." [23]
"Knowledge is an affair not only of objective relations, but of value for me." [24]

Consciousness as volitional, or will, engages the mind in action so that it will realize or bring about a certain intention, purpose, or end.[25]

Will manifests itself in two ways: as "in-coming will" or as "out-going will." *In-coming will* takes some portion of the universe and brings it into relation to self, into individual form: e.g. the knowledge of a tree or the recognition of the truth of geometry.[26] *Out-going will* takes some content which is individual and gives it existence in the universe:

> "The first stage is a desire, a plan, or a purpose; and these exist only in my or your consciousness, they are feelings. But the activity of self takes hold of these, and projects them into external existence, and makes them a part of the world of objects and events. If the desire be to eat, that is something which belongs wholly to the individual; the act of eating is potentially present to all intelligences. . . . If the plan be to build a house, the plan formed is individual; the plan executed, the house built, is universal. This act of will resulting in rendering an individual content universal may be called *outgoing* will, but its essence is the same as that of in-coming will. It connects the two elements which, taken in their separateness, we call feeling and knowledge." [27]

Dewey holds not merely that "knowledge is not possible without feeling and will," [28] but that "the process of knowledge is a process of volition," and that "in studying knowledge, we simply neglect the process in behalf of the *product*." [29]

Dewey has previously suggested that this *product* is an individual existence in our consciousness of some universal content. He has implied that this "individual existence of some universal content" is frequently a reproduction within us of an already existing universal content: e.g., the perception of a tree, the conception of government, the news of the death of a friend; in these instances the will, *in-coming will,* would have brought the objective reality to the individual self. But he has also implied, in his discussion of *out-going will,* that the "individual existence of some universal content" might be an individual desire, purpose, plan which achieves its relation to the "universal content" insofar as the will realizes it, transforms it into objective reality; for example, the idea of a house which one is planning to build becomes an individual existence *of a universal content* (i.e., common to all intelligences) when the will executes the plan and gives the house objective reality.[30] In this second meaning of knowledge as product, there is a foreshadowing of the view of ideas as plans of action.

Some of Dewey's comments on knowledge as *process* give further clues to his later position. Sensations, he says, are neither knowledge nor knowing. Distinguishing between "having" and "knowing," he says: "Knowing does not consist in having feelings of heat, of contact, of color, and of sound." [31] Sensations are data and stimuli for the mental processes.[32]

"Sensations, *per se,* never enter into knowledge. Knowledge is constituted by interpretation of sensations, that is, by their idealization. The sensations furnish the data, but these data must be neglected, selected, and manipulated by the self before they become knowledge." [33]

The discussion in *Psychology* of the various stages in the process of knowledge stresses the active role of self:

". . . perception or knowledge of particular things is not a passive operation of impression, but involves the active integration of various experiences. It is a process of reaching out after the fullest and richest experience possible. In illustration, consider the process of scientific observation. The mind does not wait for sensations to be forced upon it, but goes out in search of them, supplying by experiment all possible conditions in order to get new sensations and to modify the old by them. Secondly, such processes as imagination and thinking are not mechanically working *upon* percepts, but are their transformation and enrichment in accordance with the same law of a demand for the unified maximum of meaning. Thinking transforms perception by bringing out elements latent in it, thereby completing it." [34]

Dewey firmly rejects the theory that individual objects are impressed upon the mind as wholes without any constructive activity of the mind, and that this process gives us knowledge of reality.[35]

By 1893 there are anticipations of the later vocabulary, as when Dewey says that "the mind can attend to anything only as that thing enters into some action, only as it is to be put to use," [36] or when he says that a chief use of philosophy is to change ideas "from assumptions which control us into tools of inquiry and action." [37] And by 1900 he is speaking of thought as "a doubt-inquiry function." [38]

The direction of Dewey's development that we have been observing in his theory of knowledge is neatly expressed in the title of his autobiographical essay, "From Absolutism to Experimentalism." [39] The influence of Professor Morris; the interest in the organic relations of Hegel; the stress on knowing as an activity distinct from having, united with feeling and willing, and implying, in the function of the out-going will, that ideas are plans of action—all these were the background for the "Experimentalism" towards which he was tending. The transition was gradual, but as Morton White notes, by 1903 with the publication of *Studies in Logical Theory,* Dewey was an ex-idealist.[40] In this work he gives some sharp criticism of Absolute Idealism,[41] and expresses views which are to be emphasized and elaborated during the next three and a half decades.

From 1903 to 1938

A work-by-work analysis of the writings from 1903 to 1938, the year the *Logic* was published, would be forbiddingly long and needlessly repetitious, but we might try to consider, in the works of that period, some of the most frequently recurring themes that are pertinent to Dewey's theory of knowledge.

We have already seen that Dewey had learned from Hegel to think of the world as organic and that he had seen some confirmation of this view in modern biology. In his mature period the Hegelian doctrine was to be superseded by the teaching of Darwin. Stressing the epoch-marking character of Darwin's work, Dewey remarked that "the greatest dissolvent in contemporary thought of old questions, the greatest precipitant of new methods, new intentions, new problems, is the one effected by the scientific revolution that found its climax in the 'Origin of Species.' " [42] This work, he notes, introduced a mode of thinking that was bound to transform the theory of knowledge. The aspects of this theory which seemed to him especially revolutionary were the stress on change in reality and the consequent denial of the fixed, the final, and absolutely permanent; the assumption of a continuity of all things in the world of nature as against a dualism of any kind; and the implications of the principle of natural selection, which Dewey describes as the principle that "all organic adaptations are due simply to constant variation and the elimination of those variations which are harmful in the struggle for existence that is brought about by excessive reproduction." [43]

By this principle of natural selection, man has evolved from the variations of less complex beings, and as a being of nature is necessarily in an environment which may contain factors that are favorable, neutral, or hostile to his life-activities. Like any other organism, he must adjust to his environment in order to survive. Such an adjustment does not mean a passive acceptance of the environment; it means rather a changing of the factors of the environment in the interest of life, e.g., neutralizing hostile occurrences or transforming neutral events into cooperative factors. The higher the type of life, the more adjustment takes this active form.[44] Dewey illustrates this by a contrast between the savage and civilized man. The savage takes things "as they are," making use of caves, roots, water, where he finds them. The civilized man will build reservoirs, dig channels, irrigate what had been a desert; he will improve native plants by selection and cross-fertilization and invent machinery to till the soil and harvest the crops. Of any organism it can be said that it "does not stand about, Micawberlike, waiting for something to turn up"; it acts upon its surroundings.[45] The organism is engaged in a transaction with the environment. The environment acts on the organism, and the organism in turn acts on the environment to bring about those changes that are favorable to its needs. This basically is what Dewey means by experience: the environment-stimulating-the-individual-to-modify-the-environment.[46]

Man is *in* experience and continuous with nature.[47] No aspect of man's being is outside of, or exempt from, the evolutionary process. What is called "mind" is a function emerging from matter. When we consider life in operation, "body presents itself as the mechanism, the instrumentality of behavior, and mind as its function, its fruit and consummation." [48] The bodily phase of action may be studied in two ways. It may be considered in connection with the processes it shares with inanimate things and then it is viewed as a variegated complex of physico-chemical interactions. But bodily action is not wholly assimilated to inorganic action; one must also consider that "chemico-physical processess go on in ways and by interactions which have reference to the needs of the organism as a whole and thus take on psychical quality, and in human beings . . . are in such connection with the social environment as confers upon them intellectual quality." [49] Mind would seem to be, then, basically a more complex case of the chemico-physical processes at work lower down on the evolutionary scale. It is something acquired, built up through interaction with environment.[50] " 'Mind' is an added property assumed by a feeling creature when it reaches that organized interaction with other living creatures which is language, communication." [51] Life in society thus helps to educe mind in man.

But Dewey is reluctant to use the word, "mind." Historically it has for him the connotation of a thing that is at once separate from body and outside and aloof from the world of nature. It recalls the persistent but outmoded dualism that Dewey is impelled to fight against in the name of modern science and of twentieth-century philosophy. He suggests that if for a whole generation men were forbidden to use mind and matter as nouns and were obliged to use adjectives and adverbs instead (e.g., "mental" and "mentally," "material" and "physically"), we should find many of our problems much simplified.[52] At least we would avoid thinking of the mental and physical as distinct substances and might learn to think of them rather as functions and qualities of action. If we must use the term "mind," we should take our clue from such a non-technical use as this: "The mother minds her baby." Here "mind is care in the sense of solicitude, anxiety, as well as of active looking after things that need to be tended." This is equivalent to saying that we should regard "mind" primarily as a verb, "to mind," denoting an activity that is at once intellectual (since it involves "noting" something), affectional (as caring and liking), and "volitional, practical, acting in a purposive way." So understood, mind will denote not an independent, isolated entity, but "all the ways in which we deal consciously and expressly with the situations in which we find ourselves." We will not so easily forget, then, that mind "is formed out of commerce with the world and is set toward that world." [53]

The evolutionary context that enables us to discern the nature of man and man's "mind" points also to the nature of man's thinking. "The significance of the evolutionary method in biology and social history," Dewey says, "is that every distinct organ, structure, or formation, every grouping of cells or elements, is to be treated as an instrument of adjustment or adaptation to a particular environing situation." [54] When there is a maladjustment between the organism and its environment, its faculties become tools or instruments working to restore harmony. This is true also of the higher organism, man. As long as his needs and desires are fulfilled, he does not have to think. But when his desires are thwarted, when he has troubles to cope with, or difficulties to overcome, he calls upon thought to regain for him a harmony with his environment.[55] Man thinks because he has to think. "In the absence of that organic guidance given by their structure to other animals, man had to find out what he was about," says Dewey.[56] He notes that

> "The child has to learn to do almost everything: to see, to hear, to reach, to handle, to balance the body, to creep, to walk. . . . A little chick just out of the shell will after a few trials peck at and grasp grains of food with its beak as well as at any later time. . . . An infant does not even begin to reach definitely for things that the eye sees till he is several months old, and even then several weeks' practice is required before he learns the adjustment so as neither to overreach nor to underreach." [57]

The baby's "primary problem is mastery of his body as a tool of securing comfortable and effective adjustments to his surroundings, physical and social." The operations of conscious selection and arrangement by which he solves this problem constitute thinking. The problems and troubles which stimulate thinking may vary, but Dewey wishes to stress that "thinking is a kind of activity which we perform at specific need, just as at other need, we engage in other sorts of activity, as converse with a friend; draw a plan for a house; take a walk; eat a dinner; purchase a suit of clothes." [58] Thinking always begins with a *forked-road situation,* a situation which interrupts the smooth gliding of our activity by presenting a difficulty, a dilemma, which proposes alternatives.[59]

Although Dewey introduces his discussion of the nature and occasion of thinking from the standpoint of naive experience, he intends his remarks to apply to concrete scientific research as well; he finds no gulf, no difference in kind between the methods of the plain man and those of science.[60] Mankind's scientific thinking, like mankind's ordinary everyday thinking, has developed out of the basic problems of life:

"Anatomy and physiology grew out of the practical needs of keeping healthy and active; geometry and mechanics out of demands for measuring land, for building, and for making labor-saving machines; astronomy has been closely connected with navigation, keeping record of the passage of time; botany grew out of the requirements of medicine and of agronomy; chemistry has been associated with dyeing, metallurgy, and other industrial pursuits. In turn, modern industry is almost wholly a matter of applied science. . . ." [61]

For both the man in the street and the man in the laboratory, thinking is done to answer a definite need.

In a formal analysis of the subject-matter of thought, Dewey distinguishes (1) the *antecedents* or conditions that evoke thought; (2) the *data* or immediate material presented to thought; (3) the *proper objective* of thought. He explains these points as follows:

"Of these three distinctions the first, that of antecedent and stimulus, clearly refers to the situation that is immediately prior to the thought-function as such. The second, that of datum or immediately given matter, refers to a distinction which is made within the thought-process as a part of and for the sake of its own *modus operandi.* . . . The third, that of content or object, refers to the progress actually made in any thought-function; material which is organized by inquiry so far as inquiry has fulfilled its purpose." [62]

By the antecedents of thought Dewey means a "whole disturbed situation" that calls forth and directs thinking, a "situation in which the various factors are actively incompatible with each other." The situation is objective, but has a subjective phase in the experience of the confused and conflicting tendencies.[63] The antecedents of thought are therefore the forked-road situation, the conflict which we have already seen Dewey stress as the starting-point of thought.

In the conflict certain factors are selected as matters relevant to the solving of the problem. These are the *data,* the given, the presented, the "facts," the secure and unquestioned in the contention of incompatibles.[64] They are the capital that thought can count on, matters of sensation that are the raw material of thought.[65] But they are not just "given"; they are "taken." "*As* data they are *selected* from the total original subject-matter that gives the impetus to knowing." [66] They are not merely found, but deliberately sought out as clues, as in the clinical tests the physician performs on the patient to discover the sick man's symptoms.[67] But whether the data be facts discovered by laboratory techniques, whether they be sense qualities of ordinary experience, or whether they be what some thinkers called objects, e.g., stars, rocks, trees, they are not complete and finished, but "material to serve," evidence, signs, clues of something still to be reached.[68] These evidences, though factual and sure, do not, however, guarantee that the data are the data of *this* particular problem.[69] Whether the exclusions and selections have been rightly made in relation to this problem can be decided only experimentally. For these data will give rise to a *meaning,* an inferred existence, an idea which is not sure but needs to be made sure by being tested to see whether it succeeds in solving the problem. If it does, then the selection of data was rightly made and the idea itself is verified. Apart from acting upon the idea, no amount or kind of intellectualistic procedure can throw any light upon its validity." [70]

This relates closely to Dewey's third distinction in his discussion of thought: its proper objective. Since the purpose of thought is to meet the specific need or solve the problem that evoked the thinking, the objective is achieved when the idea is verified. For the idea or meaning, "having been selected and made up with reference to performing a certain office in the evolution of a unified experience, can be tested in no other way than by discovering whether it does what it was intended to do and what it purports to do." [71]

Within this view on the nature of man's thinking is implicitly contained a theory of what knowledge is and of what knowledge is not. Let us see how Dewey makes this explicit.

If we ask where in the analysis of thought, knowledge is located, we would have to look for it in the process by which the idea is verified. For "knowledge is an affair of *making* sure," [72] it is a "mode of doing." [73] Or if we regard knowledge as the outcome of thinking or inquiry,[74] it must not be separated from the process by which it is achieved. Though Dewey concedes that there is a sense in which knowledge, as distinct from thinking or inquiring, does not come into existence until "thinking has terminated in the experimental act which fulfils the specifications set forth in thinking," he adds that "the object thus determined is an object of *knowledge* only because of the thinking which has preceded it and to which it sets a happy term." Knowledge is knowledge only in virtue of the inquiry that has led up to it.[75]

Unlike the "analytic realist" who holds that although experimentation may be essential in *getting* knowledge, it has nothing to do with knowledge itself, Dewey maintains that the operation of experimentation is necessary to knowledge. The contrast in these two positions is illustrated by Dewey's story of the man who under peculiarly precarious circumstances has been rescued from drowning. A bystander remarks that now he is a saved man. But another man, Dewey's symbol of the analytic realist, replies: "Yes, but he was a saved man all the time, and the process of rescuing, while it gives evidence of that fact, does not constitute it." Dewey objects to the implication that the happy conclusion is separated from the active process by which that conclusion was reached. Reality would thus be separated from the process by which it is achieved. He stresses that the object of knowledge is "something which the processes of inquiry and testing, that constitute thinking, themselves produce." [76]

But if knowledge is not to be wholly identified with its resultant object, neither should it be regarded as an awareness of antecedent realities or sense data. Knowledge is not an affair "of grasping antecedently given realities" [77] or of Aristotelian first principles either.[78] It is not "a revelation of antecedent existences or Being." [79] Its object is "not reality at large, a metaphysical heaven to be mimeographed at many removes upon a badly constructed mental carbon paper which yields at best only fragmentary, blurred, and erroneous copies." [80] Even if knowledge *were* a copy of reality, a "kodak fixation," it would be fruitless, for "knowledge which is merely a reduplication in ideas of what exists already in the world may afford us the satisfaction of a photograph, but that is all." [81]

If the reduplication should be not of an antecedent reality at large but of what Dewey has called "data," this too would be pointless. Sense data are not knowledge; though "had," they are not known. If we already have "the given," the facts, "why should we take up the wholly supernumerary task of forming more or less imperfect ideas of those facts. . . ?" Dewey shows the futility of regarding knowledge as a copy of data in his example of the man lost in the woods. The man's actual visible environment, trees, rocks, etc., are there, and it would seem superfluous to form an idea of them. What he needs is an "interpretation of the locally present environment in reference to its absent portion," i.e. a mental map, an idea that is a plan of action and that when tested through action will guide him home.[82] Dewey advises us to "interpret the aim and test of knowing by what happens in the actual procedures of scientific inquiry." [83]

To define knowledge as a possession or awareness of data or of antecedent reality is to revive the outmoded dualism of a knowing subject and an object.[84] Those who do this create mysteries by assuming the existence of a soul or spirit, non-natural, extra-natural, or supernatural, that is set over against the body and the world. Such a knowing subject, like a disembodied spirit, would then be *outside* the course of natural existence, passively mirroring it like a spectator,[85] or trying to get outside itself to "lay its ghostly hands upon the things of an external world." [86] This assumption of a dualism between knowing subject and object thus *creates* a problem of knowledge as we might create a problem of digestion if we insisted that the stomach and food material inhabited different worlds; we would then wonder about the possibility and extent of any transaction between stomach and food and we would very likely divide the world into two great camps, "foodists" and "eaterists," forgetting that to be an eater is to be an eater of food.[87] But just as stomach and food occupy the same natural world, so also the knowing subject and what it knows inhabit the same natural world, and Dewey sees nothing more mysterious in the problem of knowledge than in the problem of digestion.

To keep the proper perspective we must remember the non-cognitive and Darwinian context in which man and his knowing occur. What is primary for Dewey is "the interaction of organism and environment, resulting in some adaptation which secures utilization of the latter." [88] Knowledge is secondary and derivative; it is not primary, separate, or self-sufficing; it is a natural occurrence, "involved in the process by which life is sustained and evolved." [89] It has as its proper object "that relationship of organism and environment in which functioning is most amply and effectively attained." [90]

Dewey adds some important clarifications to his doctrine of knowledge. He wishes to show just what is meant in his context by stressing that knowledge is practical. The Darwinian context from which his doctrine emerges might seem to suggest that knowledge is grossly utilitarian both in its origins and in its consequences. But while some acts of knowing may originate in the need to satisfy hunger and thirst or to survive materially in the struggle for existence, other acts of knowing may originate in "intellectual troubles"; for example, "discrepancies within some current scheme of propositions and terms" might occasion reflection.[91] As to its consequences, they may or may not be practical, in the sense of "some quite definite utilities of a material or bread-and-butter type." Dewey intends only to refer all thinking, all reflective considerations to *consequences* for final meaning and test, but adds: "Nothing is said about the nature of the consequences; they may be aesthetic, or moral, or political, or religious in quality—anything you please." The stress on action or practice in his theory does, he acknowledges, play a fundamental role, but it concerns not the nature of consequences, but the nature of knowing. That is:

> "A knowing as an act is instrumental to the resultant controlled and more significant situation; this does not imply anything about the intrinsic or the instrumental character of the consequent situation. That is whatever it may be in a given case." [92]

He is stressing that the knowing itself is "literally something which we do." He has abandoned the old traditional separation of knowing and doing and installed doing as the heart of knowing.[93] Knowledge makes a difference in and to things.[94] It is a change in reality by means of active control of nature or the course of events.[95]

Dewey would reinstate knowledge as an art. He recalls the happier days when "art" and "science" were virtually equivalent terms,[96] when the "divorce of knowledge and action, theory and practice had not been decreed." [97] But the Greek social and economic life separated men into two distinct classes. In Aristotle's day slaves and artisans were employed in furnishing the means of subsistence, while others, higher on the social scale, were free to seek knowledge for the sake of knowing.[98] In contrast with such contemplative knowing, the so-called knowing of the artisan is considered base, for it brings about changes in things, in wood and in stone. It cannot be disinterested because it has reference to results to be attained, food, clothing, and shelter. Its direction to an end beyond itself testifies to its imperfection "for want, desire, affection of every sort, indicate lack. Where there is need and desire—as in the case of all practical knowledge and activity—there is incompleteness and insufficiency." [99]

But the old separation of knowing and doing, with the disparagement of the latter, is crumbling. Modern tendencies put art and creation first.

In modern science "knowing has been assimilated to the procedure of the useful arts;—involving, that is to say, doing that manipulates and arranges natural energies." [100] Scientific thought is now seen to be a specialized form of art.[101]

For "art denotes a process of doing or making." It involves the modeling of clay, chipping of marble, casting of bronze, laying on of pigments, construction of buildings, singing of songs, playing of instruments, enacting roles on the stage. The *work* of art, which is active, is therefore not the same as the *product* of art—the temple, painting, statue, poem, but the work takes place when a human being cooperates with the product.[102] Dewey notes, too, that art explicitly recognizes what it has taken so long to discover in science, the factor of need and interest: "the control exercised by emotion in reshaping natural conditions, and the place of the imagination, under the influence of desire, in re-creating the world into a more orderly place." [103]

For Dewey, knowing is a doing or making: "an act which confers upon non-cognitive material traits which *did* not belong to it. It marks a change by which physical events exhibiting properties of mechanical energy, connected by relations of push and pull, hitting, rebounding, splitting and consolidating, realize characters, meanings and relations of meanings *hitherto* not possessed by them." Knowing is therefore an art, and knowledge, its product, is a work of art.[104] The dividing wall between science and art, knowing and doing, should therefore dissolve. If any distinction of primary and secondary is to be maintained, then art would be primary. For art is the distinguishing trait of man, and science or knowledge is the handmaiden of art.[105]

1938 and After

Dewey recognized that the implications of regarding science as an auxiliary to art needed to be worked out. In his *Essays in Experimental Logic*, 1916, he noted that "scientific procedure as a practical undertaking, has not as yet reflected itself into any coherent and generally accepted theory of thinking, into any accepted doctrine of logic." [106] In his *Logic: The Theory of Inquiry*, published in 1938, he presents a doctrine of logic in which he develops ideas found in his earlier works. We shall note here some of the points from the *Logic* that are most relevant to his theory of knowledge. Here, even more expressly than in the earlier works, there is an identification of reflective thought with an inquiry that has been initiated by doubt.[107] Here, too, Dewey shows how "biological functions and structures prepare the way for deliberate inquiry and how they foreshadow its pattern." He adds to this consideration of the "biological matrix of inquiry," a discussion of "the cultural matrix of inquiry.[108]

The doubt which initiates inquiry is not something merely "subjective." Although "there is no such thing as disinterested intellectual concern with either physical or social matters," yet—except in pathological cases—the reason why *we* are doubtful is because the situation is inherently doubtful. Such a disturbed, unsettled, or "indeterminate situation" constitutes the *antecedent condition* of inquiry. This becomes a *problematic situation* in the process of being subjected to inquiry.[109] But since every indeterminate situation that can be converted into a problem, has some definite constituents, we must first search out and observe the constituents that are settled. They are equivalent to what Dewey called in his earlier work, the *data,* though he here prefers to call them "the facts of the case." They will suggest a possible solution to the indeterminate situation, that is, an idea, a meaning, hypothesis. "Observation of facts and suggested meanings or ideas arise and develop in correspondence with each other." [110] Whether the facts are really the facts of this case will be tested just as the ideas or hypotheses must be tested. "Both are finally checked by their capacity to work together to introduce a resolved unified situation." [111] The *object* of inquiry will be its outcome: "that set of connected distinctions or characteristics which emerges as a definite constituent of a resolved situation and is confirmed in the continuity of inquiry." [112] Inquiry itself Dewey defines as follows: "The controlled or directed transformation of an indeterminate situation into one that is so determinate in its constituent distinctions and relations as to convert the elements of the original situation into a unified whole." [113]

Here, as in earlier works, Dewey insists that knowledge is not a possessing or a viewing of antecedent realities, of facts or meanings, or of objects apart from inquiry. There is no immediate knowledge: no direct grasping of any a priori first principles that are not subject to re-examination.[114] The apprehension of such objects as a typewriter, book, radiator, etc., is not knowledge, nor are sense-perceptions or sense data knowledge, but such data and objects might function as facts of the case in an inquiry.[115] They are materials given *to be known* when inquiry occurs; the non-cognitive "given" should not be confused with the known.[116] Nor should knowledge be identified with a viewing of the object that results from inquiry as though that object were separate from the inquiry. This would be a case of ignoring the concrete conditions and operations by means of which the fulfillment has been brought about,[117] and forgetting that the object is a known object only after it has been instituted *as known* through the operations of inquiry.[118] A selective extraction of one phase of the actual pattern of inquiry, whether it be an emphasis on antecedent reality, data, or object, is, Dewey thinks, so one-sided as to yield a fallacious theory of knowledge.[119]

What, then, is knowledge? It is the outcome of competent and controlled inquiry, but this does not mean it is a fixed, external end to which inquiry is subordinated. For knowledge cannot be defined apart from its connection with inquiry. It is the "settlement" of a particular situation by a particular inquiry.[120] Dewey says that "knowledge is related to inquiry as its warrantably assertible product." [121] Knowledge is "warranted assertibility." [122]

Now the inquiry in terms of which knowledge is defined makes changes.[123] It "effects *existential* transformation and reconstruction of the material with which it deals; the result of the transformation, when it is grounded, being conversion of an indeterminate problematic situation into a determinate resolved one." All controlled inquiry therefore contains a *practical* factor: an activity of doing and making. Since the operations of doing and making institute the grounded determination or warranted assertion that is knowledge,[124] knowledge would seem to be, as Dewey already said elsewhere, a product of art or a work of art.[125]

A later work, *Knowing and the Known,* by John Dewey and Arthur F. Bentley, tries to clarify some vocabulary; it seeks a "few firm names" for use in connection with the theory of knowledge. It refrains, however, from defining knowledge, which it describes as "No. 1 on a list of 'vague words.' " [126] The naturalistic postulate of Dewey's theory of knowledge is restated here, that is that knowings and knowns are natural events, and that "knowing is to be regarded as the same kind of event *with respect to its being known* . . . as an eclipse, a fossil, an earthquake. . . ." [127]

In a chapter written by Dewey alone, two interesting points might be noted. One, already familiar from his early writings, is his union of the intellectual, emotional, and practical, and his criticism of any philosophy that tears them asunder, erecting each into an entity.[128] The other, a rather unfamiliar remark in Dewey's context, is the point that science, although a practical human activity that necessarily involves doing and making, is concerned with the advancement of knowing.[129] Its aim is thus distinguished from that of common sense knowing which is for the sake of carrying on the necessary affairs of everyday life. But the reference to the advancement of knowing as the aim of science is perhaps consistent with his earlier emphasis that the instrumentalist stress on action, practice, and the practical, concerns the nature of knowing, not the nature of the consequences; the consequences may or may not be practical.[130] And in the later work, Dewey does conclude that "science is itself a form of doing. . . ."[131]

Comment

We have followed Dewey "from Absolutism to Experimentalism" in his theory of knowledge. He has said of himself that he yielded to "diverse and even incompatible influences; struggling to assimilate something from each and yet striving to carry it forward in a way that is logically consistent with what has been learned from its predecessors."[132] His progress from Hegel to Darwin would seem to illustrate his meaning, for "Dewey took what is living in Hegel, and rejected what is dead, and reconstructed what he took in terms of his biological functionalism."[133] Dewey has rejected the view of knowledge as a reproduction within the individual consciousness of some already existing universal content. He has developed the view of knowledge as an individual desire, purpose, or plan which is transformed into an objective reality through the activity of the out-going will. He has concluded that since inquiry is an activity of doing and making and since knowledge is the "warrantably assertible product" of inquiry, knowledge is therefore a work of art.

Dewey has tried to show how thinking actually proceeds in its attempt to reach its most effective working.[134] He believes he has taken knowledge just as it is and has described it as one would describe any other natural function or event. And his account does in fact describe what sometimes occurs. When our smooth ongoing activity is interrupted by a difficulty, trouble, or "forked-road situation," we are stimulated to think about how the problem can be solved. We do try to locate the problem precisely, to take account of the data or facts of the case, and to consider whether the meanings or "ideas" that the data suggest do or do not answer the problem. But the account of the *process* by which knowledge is sometimes acquired Dewey takes as an account of what knowledge *is*. And the process by which the truth of an "idea" becomes known he identifies with a doing or making: a transitive action that confers upon non-cognitive material traits that it did not previously have. The antecedent situation and the data therefore cannot be said to be known, except insofar as they happen to be the outcome of some doing or making.

It is clear, then, that he is ruling out all speculative knowledge, for knowledge is called speculative "in relation to the things known which are not operable by the knower, like man's knowledge of natural or divine things." [135] But for Dewey anything "not operable by the knower" and not acted on in inquiry cannot be said to be known. Antecedent "brute existences" may be "had," but they are not known; this kind of "having," however, is here left unexplained. For Dewey has a deep-seated antipathy to anything suggesting a "spectator view of knowledge." To look at a thing and know what it is, even as a prelude to practical knowing, would imply a dualism of mind and its object. It would mean that man is in part exempt from the needs and the strivings of other forms of life with which he is continuous; this Dewey cannot admit.

For Dewey, all knowledge is practical knowledge: knowing how to make or how to do something. It is therefore concerned with the operable. Though Dewey would not phrase his position by saying that man has a practical intellect that can be perfected by the virtue of art, yet he does regard art as the distinguishing trait of man. It is a process of doing (e.g., manipulating and arranging natural energies) or making (e.g., constructing a building). Impelled by desire or need, man's art creates or re-creates something. Art, in Dewey's context, has been called "the most inclusive metaphysical category." [136] Certainly for Dewey knowing belongs within this category. It, too, arises from desire or need and is basically a transitive activity of doing or making. And its outcome, knowledge, he explicitly calls a work of art.[137]

Dewey has objected to having his theory of knowledge compared with other theories, "undertakings of a wholly different nature," which would then be used as a ready-made standard by which to test the validity of his position. Such a comparison would, indeed, seem futile unless one would undertake a critique of the whole naturalistic context within which the theory appears. Dewey makes no secret of the naturalistic basis of his theory.[138] In his efforts to attack the artificial dualism of mind and body, of knower and object, engendered by modern philosophy, he has gone to the opposite extreme. He has made mind a function of matter, the object a product of the knower's transitive action, and knowing a purely natural event no more mysterious than the process of digestion. With any truly metaphysical analysis of knowing ruled out by the assumptions of his context, the account of knowledge is limited to the description of a pattern of inquiry, which is itself patterned upon art.

Here, man even in his knowing is *homo faber,* for his knowing is a making. But, with one commentator, we might ask whether Dewey has not conceived the relation of making and knowing too narrowly.[139] For there might be a Making that is not man's making, and where such Making occurs, there could also be man's knowing.

NOTES

1. Irwin Edman tells this story in *John Dewey: His Contribution to the American Tradition* (Indianapolis, New York: Bobbs-Merrill, 1955) 24.
2. "The Obligation to the Knowledge of God," *The Monthly Bulletin* (University of Michigan) 6 (Nov. 1884) 24.
3. "From Absolutism to Experimentalism," in George P. Adams & Wm. Pepperell Montague, *Contemporary American Philosophy* (New York: Macmillan, 1930) II 19.
4. *Ibid.* 14-15, 18.
5. Morton White, *The Origin of Dewey's Instrumentalism* (New York: Columbia University, 1943) 10-33. These pages contain a good account of the philosophy of Professor Morris in its relation to the philosophy of Dewey. The entire book is very helpful for a study of Dewey's early thought.
6. "Kant and Philosophic Method," *Journal of Speculative Philosophy* 18 (April 1884) 169-71. In a book review of F. H. Johnson's *What Is Reality* in *The Inlander* (University of Michigan) 2 (Mar. 1892) 283, Dewey also criticizes "the assumption of the old dualism between the thought world and the thing world," and says that "Hegel's logic is neither subjective nor objective analysis, but analysis of the life which underlies and overlies all division into objective and subjective."
7. "Is Logic a Dualistic Science?" *Open Court* III (Jan. 16, 1890) 2043. On this same page Dewey also remarks: ". . . knowledge, experience, the material of the known world are one and the same all the way; it is one and the same world which offers itself in perception and in scientific treatment; and the method of dealing with it is one and the same—logical."
8. "The Psychological Standpoint," *Mind* 11 (Jan. 1886) 1-19.
9. *Ibid.* 12-13.
10. *Ibid.* 19. Cf. also "Psychology as Philosophic Method," *Mind* 11 (April 1886) 155-57.
11. *Psychology* (New York & London: Harper, 1898) 5-6. The pages cited from this reprint of the 1891 third revised edition do not differ in their content from the first 1887 edition. White, *op. cit.* 51, comments that the phrase, "universal intelligence" is a reference to what Dewey elsewhere calls "universal consciousness."
12. *Psychology,* 6.
13. *Ibid.* 204. On p. 222 Dewey says: "Reasoning . . . is dependent upon the

presence of a relation, that is, of a universal factor." Cf. also J. A. McClellan & John Dewey, *Applied Psychology* (Boston: Educational Publishing Co., 1889) 88, 90.

14. *Psychology,* 82. Cf. also 145, 199, 233.
15. *Leibniz's New Essays Concerning the Human Understanding: A Critical Exposition* (Chicago: S. C. Griggs, 1888) 34. In "The New Psychology," *Andover Review* 2 (Sep. 1884) 285, Dewey also notes that traces of the concept of organism were found long before the rise of biology as a science, but that the influence of biology on this concept was very great.
16. White, *op. cit.* 61.
17. *Ibid.* 94.
18. "The Present Position of Logical Theory," *The Monist* 2 (July 1892) 10, 14-16.
19. White, *op. cit.* 46.
20. *Psychology,* 21. It should be noted that in saying that knowledge is "universal," Dewey means that its subject-matter "is common to all intelligences."
21. *Ibid.* 17.
22. *Ibid.* 15-16.
23. *Ibid.* 18; cf. also his comments on attention, 134, 138.
24. *Ibid.* 297.
25. *Ibid.* 17.
26. *Ibid.* 22. Dewey explains this first manifestation of will as follows: "Here material which exists as common material for all consciousness is brought into relation with the unique, unsharable consciousness of one. The activity of will starts from the interests of the self, goes out in the form of attention to the object, and translates it into the medium of *my* or *your* consciousness —into terms of self, or feeling. If we consider this activity in the value which it has as manifesting to us something of the nature of the universe, it is knowledge; if we consider it in the value which it has in the development of the self, it is feeling; if we consider it as an activity including both the universal element which is its content, and the individual from which it starts and to which it returns, it is will."
27. *Ibid.* 23. Dewey adds: "Feeling is the subjective side of consciousness, knowledge its objective side. Will is the relation between the subjective and the objective." In a later passage, p. 347, he stresses again: "Will always unites *me* with some *reality,* either transforming an element of the me into objective reality, or bringing that objective reality into the sphere of my immediate feeling. It thus connects the content of knowledge with the form of feeling."
28. *Ibid.* 18.
29. *Ibid.* 368.
30. *Ibid.* 15-16, 23.
31. *Ibid.* 81.
32. *Ibid.* 44-45, 160.
33. *Ibid.* 138.
34. *Ibid.* 158.
35. *Ibid.* 157. In "How Concepts Arise from Percepts," *Public School Journal* 11 (Nov. 1891) 128-30, Dewey develops more positively a "constructivist"

view of knowledge. Cf. 129: "The only way to know the triangle is to make it—to go through the act of putting together the lines in the way called for. . . . To know a thing completely is to know it in its mode of genesis . . . in its relations and bearings." As Morton White points out, *op. cit.* 69, constructivism is not yet pragmatism. The concept is still spoken of here as a mode of mental action; Dewey still implies that the action or construction is in some way going on only in the geometrician's head.

36. "Anthropology and Law," *The Inlander* 3 (April 1893) 308.
37. "Why Study Philosophy?" *The Inlander* 4 (Dec. 1893) 108. He also says here that philosophy "constructs, or at least reconstructs intellectual tools for present use."
38. "Some Stages of Logical Thought," an article first published in 1900 and reprinted in *Essays in Experimental Logic* (New York: Dover, n.d.) 216.
39. In Adams & Montague, *Contemporary American Philosophy* II 13-27.
40. White, *op. cit.* 148.
41. Dewey's contribution to *Studies in Logical Theory* is reprinted as Chapters II-V of *Essays in Experimental Logic* (New York: Dover, n.d.). In these chapters much of the discussion is directed against the idealism of Lotze. Cf. 131-32 for Dewey's criticism of Absolute Idealism.
42. "The Influence of Darwinism on Philosophy" (1909), in *The Influence of Darwin on Philosophy* (New York: Peter Smith, 1951) 19.
43. *Ibid.* 11, 1-2, and passim, and *Essays in Experimental Logic,* 87.
44. "The Need for a Recovery of Philosophy," from *Creative Intelligence* (1917); in W. G. Muelder & L. Sears (editors), *The Development of American Philosophy* (Boston: Houghton Mifflin, 1940) 377-78.
45. *Reconstruction in Philosophy* (Boston: Beacon, 1957 reprint of 1920 text and 1948 Introduction) 85, 86.
46. In "The Need for a Recovery of Philosophy," in Muelder & Sears, *op. cit.* 376, experience is defined "as an affair of the intercourse of a living being with its physical and social environment."
47. *Democracy and Education* (New York: Macmillan, 1923) 145.
48. "Body and Mind," in *Philosophy and Civilization* (New York: Minton, Balch, 1931) 302-3.
49. *Ibid.* 306-7. Though stressing a continuity of mind with matter and denying that mind is purely immaterial, Dewey does not regard his view of man as materialistic. Materialism, he says, isolates "the means and conditions," i.e. the bodily functions, from what they actually do, whereas he stresses purposes, ends, and outcomes of such functions. He is not maintaining that human action is identical with that of lower animals, since in man "Organic processes are seen to be the constituent means of a behavior which is endued with purpose and meaning, animate with affection, and informed by recollection and foresight."
50. *Human Nature and Conduct* (New York: Holt, 1922) 138, 176-77.
51. *Experience and Nature* (1929) (New York: Dover, 1958 reprint) 258.
52. *Ibid.* 75.
53. *Art As Experience* (New York: Minton, Balch, 1934) 263-64.
54. *Essays in Experimental Logic* (1916) (New York: Dover reprint, n.d.) 93. This work will hereafter be referred to as *EEL.*

55. *Reconstruction in Philosophy,* 138-39.
56. *The Quest for Certainty* (New York: Minton, Balch, 1929) 3.
57. *How We Think* (Boston: Heath, 1910) 157-58.
58. *EEL,* 77.
59. *How We Think,* 10-11.
60. *EEL,* 85-86.
61. *How We Think,* 167-68.
62. *EEL,* 104-5.
63. *Ibid.* 122-25.
64. *Ibid.* 136-37.
65. *Ibid.* 145-46.
66. *The Quest for Certainty,* 178.
67. *Ibid.* 174.
68. *Ibid.* 99; *EEL,* 146-47.
69. *EEL,* 345-46.
70. *Ibid.* 137-40, 240-41, 242.
71. *Ibid.* 171.
72. *Experience and Nature,* 154.
73. *The Quest for Certainty,* 102, 231.
74. *The Influence of Darwin on Philosophy* (1910) (New York: Peter Smith, 1951 reprint) 184.
75. *EEL,* 15-16.
76. *Ibid.* 32, 143, 145, 334.
77. *Experience and Nature,* 154.
78. *EEL,* 203-4. Though conceding that Aristotle and his followers were sincerely concerned with the question of attaining grounds of assurance, Dewey thinks they assumed first principles and primary intuitions "in order to get the pegs of certainty to which to tie the bundles of otherwise contingent propositions."
79. *The Quest for Certainty,* 44, 103.
80. *Philosophy and Civilization,* 48, 40.
81. *The Quest for Certainty,* 137.
82. *EEL,* 256-57, 351, 232, 238-40.
83. *The Quest for Certainty,* 103.
84. *Experience and Nature,* 278.
85. "The Need for a Recovery of Philosophy," in Mueder & Sears, *op. cit.* 379-80.
86. *The Influence of Darwin,* 81.
87. "The Need for a Recovery of Philosophy," in Mueder & Sears, *op. cit.* 380; *EEL,* 269-71, 275.
88. *Reconstruction in Philosophy,* 87.
89. *Ibid.* 87; *Influence of Darwin,* 106.
90. *Philosophy and Civilization,* 48. In this location of knowledge, Dewey thinks that he resolves the long-standing conflict of the empiricists and the rationalists. Cf. *Influence of Darwin,* 271-304; *Reconstruction in Philosophy,* Ch. II & IV; *Quest for Certainty,* Ch. VII.
91. *EEL,* 59-60.
92. *Ibid.* 330, 331-32.

93. *The Quest of Certainty*, 36.
94. *Philosophy and Civilization*, 38; *The Quest for Certainty*, 204.
95. *Philosophy and Civilization*, 40, 54.
96. *The Quest for Certainty*, 74.
97. *Philosophy and Civilization*, 315.
98. *Democracy and Education*, 296-305.
99. *Reconstruction in Philosophy*, 110.
100. *Experience and Nature*, 357; *The Quest for Certainty*, 79.
101. *Philosophy and Civilization*, 104.
102. *Art As Experience*, 47, 214.
103. *Philosophy and Civilization*, 120.
104. *Experience and Nature*, 381-82.
105. *Ibid.* 358; *Art As Experience*, 26.
106. *EEL*, 216.
107. *Logic: The Theory of Inquiry* (New York: Holt, 1938) iii, 7.
108. *Ibid.* Chapter II, 23; Chapter III.
109. *Ibid.* 115, 105-6, 107.
110. *Ibid.* 108-9.
111. *Ibid.* 111, 114.
112. *Ibid.* 119, 520.
113. *Ibid.* 104-5. It is a fundamental thesis of Dewey's book to show how logical forms originate in operations of inquiry.
114. *Ibid.* 139-41; on Aristotelian first principles, cf. 10-12, 142, 343-47.
115. *Ibid.* 139, 143-44.
116. *Ibid.* 522.
117. *Ibid.* 177.
118. *Ibid.* 521.
119. *Ibid.* 514, 521.
120. *Ibid.* 7-8, 21. Dewey adds that there is no guarantee that the settled conclusion will always remain settled; every settlement introduces conditions of a new unsettling. Cf. 35, 345.
121. *Ibid.* 118.
122. *Ibid.* 9.
123. *Ibid.* 34. Cf. also 246, 287, 463.
124. *Ibid.* 159, 160, 180.
125. *Experience and Nature*, 381-82.
126. *Knowing and the Known* (Boston: Beacon Press, 1949) xi, 48, 287.
127. *Ibid.* 87.
128. *Ibid.* 276-77.
129. *Ibid.* 281-82. Dewey here introduces a sharper distinction between science and common sense than is found in his earlier works.
130. *EEL*, 330-32.
131. *Knowing and the Known*, 284. In this same chapter, it is interesting to note that there is a softening of the emphasis on knowledge as power, on science as a means of obtaining mastery over nature. Though Dewey admits that such mastery may be an important consequence of science, he is concerned about the human uses to which this mastery is put. Cf. 283-84.—In the Appendix to the volume Dewey states that what is new in his treatment of knowl-

edge is "in regarding the *problem* as belonging in the context of the conduct of inquiry and not in either the traditional ontological or the traditional epistemological context." Cf. 317. For a good review of *Knowing and the Known,* cf. that by James Collins, in *Modern Schoolman* 27 (May 1950) 322-26.

132. "From Absolutism to Experimentalism," in Adams & Montague, *op. cit.* 22.

133. John H. Randall, Jr., "Dewey, 1859-1952," *Journal of Philosophy* 50 (Jan. 1, 1953) 9.

134. *The Influence of Darwin,* 77, 96-7.

135. St. Thomas, *Sum. Theol.* I. q. 14, a. 16.

136. Randall, *loc. cit.*

137. For a discussion of the contrast between the position of John Dewey and St. Thomas Aquinas on practical and speculative knowledge, cf. Norbert J. Fleckenstein, *A Critique of John Dewey's Theory of the Nature and the Knowledge of Reality in the Light of the Principles of Thomism* (Washington, D.C.: Catholic University of America Press, 1954) 153-56; also Ferrer Smith, "A Thomistic Appraisal of the Philosophy of John Dewey," *The Thomist* 18 (April 1955) 127-85. Cf. also the discussion of the practical intellect and the virtue of art in Jacques Maritain, *Creative Intuition in Art and Poetry:* Bollingen Series XXXV-1 (New York: Pantheon, 1953) 44-70.

138. *The Influence of Darwin,* 96-7. Note, however, that in the last chapter of his *Logic,* esp. on p. 514, he indicates that he is using *his* position as a standard for testing the validity of other philosophies of knowledge.

139. Arthur Child, *Making and Knowing in Hobbes, Vico, and Dewey:* University of California Publications in Philosophy, Vol. 16, no. 13. (Berkeley, 1953) 307.

IV

John Dewey and Progressive Education

SISTER JOSEPH MARY RABY, S.S.J.

Sister Joseph Mary Raby, S.S.J. is Professor of Education at Nazareth College, Rochester, New York. Sister Joseph Mary did her undergraduate work at Columbia University and, after entering the Sisters of Saint Joseph of Rochester, New York, her graduate work at the Catholic University of America. She has written A Critical Study of the New Education *and several articles on educational philosophy.*

Some Preliminaries

Lately I have been wondering whether there ever were any progressive schools.

This half-question comes from one who has taught in one of them, written something about them, who even as an undergraduate knew Dewey's educational ideas and Kilpatrick's tutelage. Why then such an unrealistic notion?

John Dewey has been acclaimed as the father of progressive education. He has been accused of it. He has been excused as not responsible for what went by that name.

Certainly, the Laboratory School at the University of Chicago, the enterprise of Dewey and described by him, was a progressive school? The famed story of the search for desks and chairs suitable for working, not just listening, Dewey told as far back as 1899, in the first edition of *The School and Society.* The "occupations," the activity, the freedom were all there. Only one year after the opening of the Laboratory School in 1896, the social situations, the continuous reconstruction of experience were worded in *My Pedagogic Creed.*

Why the wonder, then? What is the question? It is this: "What was Dewey really saying? What was his real design for education? Were progressive schools patterned on his design?"

One day in the 1920's, a visitor from Greece spent a day in a progressive school. It was the experimental school of a mid-west university. The director of the school remarked to me once that John Dewey, her former teacher, had said to her that the program of this school exemplified his idea of education. I was teaching there at the time. Out of Columbia University only a few years, in the school largely at the suggestion of my teacher, Doctor Kilpatrick, I was asked to take care of the visitor from far-off Greece. Thirty and more years ago, Greece was a faraway country.

Our guest stayed all day, saw everything, and then talked with me for some time after school. He asked many questions which I answered with, as I recall it, interest and high enthusiasm. Teaching in a progressive school was fun, and I enjoyed telling all about it.

Finally the man stopped asking questions. He sat back, nodded as if confirmatively and said very quietly, "Pragmatism." I remember my startled incomprehension; less vividly, my later comprehension. Perhaps any true understanding of Dewey that I may have was initiated that day.

The school in which this happened was known as a progressive school. In it we were living in social, in democratic situations; we were experiencing all the day long. We, in our third grade, all fifteen of us, were occupied in thoughtful purposing, in shared experience. That year, we were creating a mining community. There was a mine with real coal and, to transport it, a river with real water. Each morning in a group discussion we planned our work and then went about it zestfully and intelligently. We learned how coal is taken out of the earth and how it got in there in the first place. The way miners lived, their housing and wage problems, we discussed and read about. We even wrote a book about our project. In a coal mine conveniently opened practically in our school yard, we spent a dusty and fascinated morning.

Visits to learn about other kinds of work were part of our days. The trip to Heinz 57 Varieties was a favorite one, climaxed by the sampling of most of them. One day we were taken to a grain elevator and, going into one of the freight cars, walked about in the grain on the floor. Arrived at the school again, by delightedly emptying our shoes, we collected a good pile of grain. What use the mining community made of it, I do not remember.

Education was assuredly an "ongoing process." Conscience inspires me to mention that Dewey's commendation of the school had been made before the third grade and I had become engaged in the continuous reconstruction of experience. But in that third grade, education was incontrovertibly a process of living, whether or not any preparation for it. The visitor from Greece saw pragmatism there.

In all these "progressive" situations of that experimental school, I, not a pragmatist, simply taking for granted the design according to which the children had been made, rather forgot all the experimentalist principles I had, I suppose, learned more academically than functionally. All of us in that school were members of some church. Pat and I were Catholic, Billy and Janet Episcopalian, Mary Jewish, and the others belonged to some Christian church. In fact, one of the mothers saw to it that we said grace before lunch, we having gone graceless before.

In retrospect, I realize what could have been wrought through the social situations of that school had the teachers been pragmatist in conviction. As far as I can remember, no one of us was. Therefore we were not inhibited by the notion of how precarious knowledge might be. The idea that "there is no belief so settled as not to be exposed to further inquiry" [1] did not trouble us. We were, indubitably, a group committed to assorted absolutes. Nevertheless, both our guest from afar and the director of the school saw there Dewey's design.

At this point questions arise, several questions at once. What exactly is a progressive school? Was the movement called progressive education a logical consequence of Dewey's theory and teaching? Did progressive education make any contributions to educational thought and practice?

As suggested earlier, the necessary and basic question is this: "What was John Dewey really saying when he proposed his notion of a school and his design for education?" And to get back to first things: What was the principle from which Dewey's educational design proceeded?

To answer these questions, we shall begin with the last one, saying something about Dewey's foundational philosophy which may be properly called his design for living.

Dewey's Design for Living

The philosophy of John Dewey invites and challenges one-word characterization. It has been termed relativistic, evolutionistic, naturalistic; an experimentalist, instrumentalist philosophy, a pragmatic one. The invitation and challenge to distinguish this philosophy with one word I plan to accept. The word "democratic," in "my" Dewey, concenters all the others. In his philosophy, this word is summary. For his educational design, it sets the pattern, is architectonic.

Evidence for all and each of the interpretations of Dewey listed above may be found in his writings. Often in reading the many interpretations, I, like others, have concluded that only by asking Dewey could we know their correctness. Therefore, not calling at present on his formal works to account for my selection of the word democratic as summary, I turn to Dewey's autobiographical essay entitled, "From Absolutism to Experimentalism," written in 1929 at the time of his seventieth birthday and reprinted in 1949 for his ninetieth under the equally promising title, "Philosopher-in-the-Making." [2]

In this personal statement, a singular combination of detachment and dedication, he sketches with quiet reticence his odyssey through Hegel to (it seems only true to say) Dewey. Almost casually he gives "four special points that seem to stand out" in his intellectual development. We shall be particularly concerned with the first and second points. The first of these, "the importance that the theory and practice of education" had for him, we shall explore later. The second point affords us pertinent information and insight.

"A second point," he relates, "is that as my study and thinking progressed, I became more and more troubled by the intellectual scandal that seemed to me involved in the current (and traditional) dualism in logical standpoint and method between something called 'science' on the one hand and something called 'morals' on the other. I have long felt that the construction of a logic, that is, an effective method of inquiry, which would apply without abrupt breach of continuity to the fields designated by both these words, is at once our needed theoretical solvent and the supply of our greatest practical want. This belief has had much more to do with the development of what I termed, for lack of a better word, 'instrumentalism,' than have most of the reasons that have been assigned."

Dewey, writing this in 1929, was reviewing what he had not only long felt but had long been trying to do. He had long before undertaken the experiment of applying an effective method of inquiry to something called morals.[3] Indeed, as he declares, this has been the fundamental preoccupation of his instrumentalist enterprise.

In "Philosopher-in-the-Making" he recalls, "Social interests and problems had from an early period for me the intellectual appeal and provided the intellectual sustenance that many seem to have found primarily in religious questions." He refers to his known emphasis on "the concrete, the empirical and the practical." He opposes to this interest of his in the social and the concrete "a native inclination toward the schematic and formally logical." He says, "The formal interests persisted, so that there was an inner demand for an intellectual technique that would be consistent and yet capable of flexible adaptation to the concrete diversity of experienced things."

This essay thus repeatedly accents Dewey's interest in the social, the moral, the concrete diversity of experienced things and his interest in the logical. From these two principles, the social and the logical, has proceeded Dewey's "democracy." Dewey's democracy is the name for and the consequence of his experiment in the application of an effective method of inquiry to something called morals.

What is this democracy which we have said concenters all else in Dewey? It is a democracy of truths and of morals, a way of life in which the scientific method is the sole authentic mode of revelation. It is a creative quest, the shared seeking in the forum of experience of solutions for the problems of men. It is a moral enterprise, the progressive determination by conjoint inquiry of moral values in terms of the quality of experience generated by the experiences. In effect, it is a design for living.

A design for living? Dewey speaks of "the venture to which democracy has committed itself—the ordering of life in response to the needs of the moment in accordance with the ascertained truth of the moment." How complete a reversal this is of older and traditional designs for living is not at once apparent. "Democracy is possible only because of a change in intellectual conditions. It implies tools for getting at truth in detail, and day by day, as we go along. Only such possession justifies the surrender of fixed, all embracing principles to which, as universals, all particulars and individuals are subject for valuation and regulation." [4]

This democratic way is the way of tested thought. With the scientific method as the tool, it is the way of problems and hypotheses, of suggested solutions-tried-out-on-situations, with perhaps rejection and so more hypotheses and trying-out until consequences warrant acceptance of a solution, thus giving basis for verification or "making true" of some idea, itself an hypothesis, and—barely catching its breath—ready to go.

Is this frivolity or Dewey? It is Dewey, less gravely worded. Corroborative is a text from his *Logic* with its relevant subtitle, *The Theory of Inquiry*: "The attainment of settled beliefs is a progressive matter; there is no belief so settled as not to be exposed to further inquiry. It is the convergent and cumulative effect of continued inquiry that defines knowledge in its general meaning. In scientific inquiry, the criterion of what is taken to be settled, or to be knowledge, is being *so* settled that it is available as a resource in further inquiry; not being settled in such a way as not to be subject to revision in further inquiry." [5]

This may be Dewey's design for knowledge, his description of how we think, but is it his "democracy"? The answer to that question is a book. *Democracy and Education*, the book in which his earlier teachings are crystallized and his later ones largely implicit, reveals Dewey's democracy. In the preface we read, "The philosophy stated in this book connects the growth of democracy with the development of the experimental method in the sciences." [6] Democracy "is more than a form of government; it is primarily a mode of associated living, of conjoint communicated experience." [7] And in a summary paragraph of a summary chapter leading to his two final chapters, Dewey climaxes his review of the "previous discussions of the book" in these words: "In our concluding chapters we shall sum up the prior discussions with *respect first to the philosophy of knowledge,* and *then to the philosophy of morals.*" [8]

This recurring dual emphasis I think of as the "bifocal" character of Dewey's democratic philosophy. He was surely applying the method of inquiry—which is proper to something called science—"without abrupt breach of continuity" to something called morals: the result, "democracy."

In this whole "apostolate," Dewey is engaged in what he calls the "application of intelligence" to the problems of men. In *Intelligence in the Modern World,* Ratner's well-known volume of selections representative of all phases of Dewey's philosophy, the title is a deliberate accenting of this central idea. The democratic way as Dewey envisions it is essentially this life of intelligence.

Dewey, it must be noted, also seems to use the word democracy in the common meaning of the word. [9] The soul of Dewey's democracy in this usual sense, however, is his idea of "democracy" as we have been analyzing it. In the preface to *Democracy and Education,* he states that the discussion includes "a critical estimate of the theories of knowing and moral development which were formulated in earlier social conditions, but which operate, in societies nominally democratic, to hamper the adequate realization of the democratic ideal." [10]

The foundational papers in this volume will have explored the perspectives of Dewey's philosophy, and eminently. In a volume like this one, however, with the papers written independently of one another, a study of Dewey's educational theory must at least outline Dewey's foundational design. Therefore, I have given my statement of Dewey's design for living, knowing that in the other studies of this volume both corroboration and refutation may be available.

Before undertaking the examination of his educational theory, I wish to quote two studies of Dewey, one by a disciple of his, and one by a disciple of St. Thomas Aquinas. The first one provides a translation of the democratic way into the particular and the concrete; the second indicates the consistency, granted his premises, of Dewey's idea of democracy.

Jerome Nathanson's *John Dewey* translates Dewey into the concrete diversity of experience. His translation is authentic. Nathanson knows Dewey. Some of the examples he uses to make plain the implications of the democratic way might have given Dewey pause, but he could scarcely have disclaimed them.

"Is there any way," Nathanson asks, "to choose among different systems of morality?" [11] One example he uses to illustrate his point is the relative morality of monogamy and polygamy. The criterion to be applied is the satisfaction of needs. The decision must be made in terms of satisfaction of needs, not merely personal, but social as well. "The needs now to be considered, in a comparison of the two systems, would be those of the children as well as spouses, of families as units in relation to each other, of the community as a whole in its economic and civil life." And he says, "If it could be shown that all the relevant human needs were satisfied in one system as well as in the other, then, whatever our preconceptions, there would be no moral difference between them. If it could be shown, on the contrary, that the result of monogamous relations are decisively favorable to the human needs involved, then it would be evident that monogamy is *really,* that is, objectively, better than polygamy." [12] This criterion is then applied to "democracy and fascism, freedom and authoritarianism."

This book, I consider, is a correct presentation of the implications of Dewey's democratic idea. It should be noted that the satisfaction of needs, the quality of experience is to be judged not merely as personal, but as social also. Neither Nathanson nor Dewey is so naive as to suggest judging the morality of anything because it satisfies some people. A chapter from Dewey that might profitably be read in this connection is the one called "Social Inquiry" in his *Logic*. This chapter is an example of Dewey's application of intelligence to modern problems.[13] That is to say, it is an example of the implications of his democratic idea.

I have quoted Nathanson because his translation of Dewey confirms that the democratic way is truly a design for living.

The second study which I wish to use is one by Father Ferrer Smith, O.P. This article shows that Dewey's philosophy, by its rejection of the speculative, of absolutes, is thereby located in the order of the practical. This does not mean, of course, the merely utilitarian, but the order of doing and making. Father Smith emphasizes that the practical order, occupied with ends to be arrived at, has to do not only with truth but with the good as good. He reminds us that in the order of making and doing, the idea *is* a plan of action, the outlook is forward to consequences. Since the practical is concerned with operables and since the field of morals is properly that of operables, "Dewey," he says, "could and did invade the moral field and not in the spirit (at any rate) of destruction but with propriety." [14]

Therefore it is not surprising, it is consistent, that Dewey, operating in the artistic and prudential order, should verify ideas and even values by their consequences, should undertake his quest for the good life, embark on his enterprise related to something called morals and be constantly preoccupied with the concrete and the experienced. Dewey had actually put a lid on his universe by taking, as he saw it, the lid off the universe.[15] Both this article of Father Smith's and that of Jerome Nathanson give understanding of Dewey helpful in this paper.

The democratic design which I have been sketching was not, I believe, exemplified in the progressive school described earlier. Dewey's democratic design did, however, set the pattern for his educational theory. If, then, Dewey's democratic idea is for the educational design, architectonic, just what is the resulting structure?

Dewey's Design for Education

Under the "first point" in the account of his intellectual development, Dewey wrote, "A book called *Democracy and Education* was for many years that in which my philosophy, such as it was, was most fully expounded." Then noting that philosophic critics had seemed (at least up to 1929, when this essay was first published) not to realize this, he continues, "I have wondered whether such facts signified that philosophers in general, although they are themselves usually teachers, have not taken education with sufficient seriousness for it to occur to them that any rational person could actually think it possible that philosophizing should focus about education as the supreme human interest in which, moreover, other problems, cosmological, moral, logical come to a head." [16]

If Dewey believes that philosophy should focus about education, and if his philosophy was for many years most fully expounded in a book the title of which pairs democracy with education, Dewey is patently affirming a close relation between the two. Is this relation that of pattern to consequence?

I have said that for Dewey's educational theory, his democratic idea is architectonic. The statement requires instant qualification. An architect's design assumes a certain permanence and predictability. Dewey's democracy is architectonic in a very special sense. May I suggest that it will be helpful to recall the croquet game as Alice found herself playing it? In traditional croquet, things are more or less dependable. Wickets keep their shape, mallets don't twist into knots, and balls don't unroll themselves and move away. In the dynamic game in the Queen's croquet ground, flamingoes, soldiers, and hedgehogs served for mallets, wickets, and balls. To get three of these together for a strike was a problem Alice, a grave little traditionalist, did not solve. Nothing would stay put.

For Dewey, whose idea it is that no idea can be depended on to stay put, any so-called pattern or principle becomes hypothesis and a blueprint essentially for experiment. That Dewey's design for living is the pattern or principle or directive of his educational theory, must, I think, be so understood. Some texts will exemplify this point.

In the summary chapter of *Democracy and Education,* entitled "Philosophy of Education," Dewey recapitulates in a "critical review" the whole argument of the book. *Democracy and Education,* he says, falls into three parts. The first dealt with education as a social process, the desirable society being "democratic in quality." In this first part of the book, he points out, "the sort of education appropriate to the development of a democratic community was then explicitly taken as the criterion of further, more detailed analysis of education."

In the second part, "the analysis based upon this democratic criterion, was seen to imply the continuous reconstruction of experience" for social ends.

The third part, taking for granted the democratic criterion and its application in present social life, considered "the present limitations of its actual realization."

Although in these excerpts the lines between democracy and education are uncommonly fluid, the democratic pattern is seen to influence the design for education.

Later in the same chapter, Dewey says that philosophy cannot realize its purposes, cannot have any success in its tasks "without educational equivalents as to what to do and what not to do. Philosophic theory has no Aladdin's lamp to summon into existence the values it intellectually constructs." "Education," he goes on to say, "is the laboratory in which the philosophic distinctions become concrete and are tested." And again, "Philosophy is the theory of education as a deliberately conducted practice." [17]

In these texts, the relation of education to philosophic theory is that of educational equivalent, of a laboratory, of deliberately conducted practice.

This diversity of statements may perhaps be understood as the inevitable consequence of Dewey's exodus from the speculative. If it is correct that Dewey had deliberately constructed a universe of the practical, then by that very limitation, his will be an in-order-that philosophy. Not including in his postulates the necessary and the absolute, Dewey limits his theory to the order of the formally or speculatively practical. This points to a workshop world. And in a studio, as an example of a "practical universe," we know that making is a practical equivalent of the theory, it is the deliberately conducted practice, it is the laboratory or at least the experiment in which the theory is being tested.

Any confirmation from Dewey that he considers his philosophy of democracy to be the principle of his educational theory, has to be found in the characteristic variety of expressions which we have recorded. It is well to keep in mind the dynamics of the croquet game. That Dewey's democratic idea is for his educational theory architectonic has to be understood in terms of the dynamics of a Dewey universe.

Thus understanding the directive influence of Dewey's democratic design on his philosophy of education, we shall now examine the specifically educational works in order to distinguish the outlines of Dewey's design for education. We may expect that at the same time the shape of Dewey's pattern for the school will begin to appear.

Of the early works, four will be used; we shall scan *My Pedagogic Creed,* study at some length *The School and Society,* and glance at *The Child and the Curriculum* and *Moral Principles in Education.* Then *Democracy and Education,* Dewey's central work, will be given careful scrutiny. In *Experience and Education* we shall find Dewey's criticism of progressive education and the reiteration of his basic design.

MY PEDAGOGIC CREED

In his earliest essay on education, "My Pedagogic Creed," Dewey says on the first page, in the article, "What Education Is," "I believe that the only true education comes through the stimulation of the child's powers by the demands of the social situations in which he finds himself." The child is thus stimulated to act "as a member of a unity."

The child's powers give the starting-point for all education, but "we do not know what these powers mean until we can transform them into their social equivalent." Again, "If we eliminate the social factor from the child we are left with only an abstraction." [18]

It is in this Creed of Dewey's that he makes the famous declaration, "I believe that education, therefore, is a process of living and not a preparation for future living." He says this in reference to the school as "a form of community life," which must represent present life. Upon this conception of the school as a mode of social life, "I believe," he says, "that moral education centers." It is here that Dewey states that the discipline of the school should proceed from the life of the school as a whole and not directly from the teacher. [19]

Turning to "The Subject-Matter of Education," he believes that the true center of correlation is "the child's own social activities." And "I believe therefore in the so-called expressive or constructive activities as a center of correlation." [20] It is through the medium of these activities that the child's introduction into the more formal subjects of the curriculum should be made.

His reason for the teaching of science is significant. He says: "In reality science is of value because it gives the ability to interpret and control the experience already had." And language is "fundamentally and primarily a social instrument, the device for communication," not principally an expression of thought. [21]

Then in the same words used nearly twenty years later in his formal definition of education, "I believe, finally, that education must be conceived as a continuing reconstruction of experience; that the process and the goal of education are one and the same thing." [22]

These excerpts present a sampling of Dewey's *Creed*. Although an accompanying reprint of its twelve pages would be desirable, the quotations I have used give some idea of its potential.

THE SCHOOL AND SOCIETY

When in 1897 this educational charter of Dewey was published, the Elementary School at the University of Chicago had been in existence for one year. In 1899, the three lectures published a year later as *The School and Society* were delivered before an audience of parents and others interested in the Elementary School. The five other papers in this book were not added until the 1915 edition. In the preface to this later edition, Dewey expresses his satisfaction that "the educational point of view presented in the book is not so novel as it was fifteen years ago," and his "desire to believe that the educational experiment of which the book is an outgrowth has not been without influence in the change." [23]

Although the additional papers included in this 1915 edition had already been published in the *Elementary School Record,* it was the small and famous *School and Society* of 1899 which had helped bring about the change referred to.

To turn from the "charged" pages of *My Pedagogic Creed* to the first chapter in *The School and Society* produces a sensation of having slipped without warning into anticlimax. One way to estimate the import of *The School and Society* is to read the first two lectures, "The School and Social Progress" and "The School and the Life of the Child," with the deliberate purpose of finding in them none of Dewey's instrumentalism. Are these papers, as I once understood them, only fine common sense? [24]

His democratic idea is certainly less immediately evident here than in *My Pedagogic Creed*. This is perhaps because they were given as lectures to parents. Perhaps his personal interest in the school and its children accounts for the more informal and less explicit statement. Or is *The School and Society* simply the expression of a plan to utilize the characteristic activities of children? Is it just a description of the failure of the "traditional" school to meet the challenge of a new industrialized society, with the new education as a proposed remedy?

In the first essay, Dewey sketches convincingly the educational and moral values inherent in "the household and neighborhood system" of the pre-industrial world. He describes the good old days of responsibility for chores and charges, of the participation of the children in the life of the home and the neighborhood. "There was always something which really needed to be done, and a real necessity that each member of the household should do his own part faithfully and in cooperation with others."

"At present," he says (that "present" being 1899) "concentration of industry and division of labor have practically eliminated household and neighborhood occupations—at least for educational purposes." He then recounts some of the advantages of that present and asks, "How shall we retain these advantages, and yet introduce into the school something representing the other side of life—occupations which exact personal responsibilities and which train the child in relation to the physical realities of life?" [25]

He describes what happens in the Elementary School in which the "occupations" constitute the "articulating centers." "The difference that appears when occupations are made the articulating centers of school life is not easy to describe in words; it is a difference in motive, of spirit and atmosphere." He says that "the change from more or less passive and inert recipiency and restraint to one of buoyant outgoing energy is so obvious as fairly to strike one in the face." He speaks of the change in "social attitudes," of the development of "a spirit of social cooperation and community life." "They are doing a variety of things," he recounts, "and there is the confusion, the bustle that results from activity. But out of the occupations, out of doing things that are to produce results, and out of doing these in a social and cooperative way, there is born a discipline of its own kind and type." [26]

An example of an occupation, as Dewey calls it, later known as a "project," is the study of flax, cotton plant, and wool "as it comes from the back of the sheep." Dewey adds, "If we could take the children to the place where the sheep are sheared, so much the better." The combing, the spinning into thread, the comparison of the different qualities of the three fibers, the processes necessary for working the threads into cloth—all this is part of this "occupation." The children are introduced to each invention in historic order, "working it out experimentally, thus seeing its necessity and tracing its effects not only upon that particular industry, but upon modes of social life." He calls attention to the "science involved," the study of fibers, of geographical features, the great centers of manufacture and distribution. He speaks of the "historical side" and says, "You can concentrate the history of all mankind into the evolution of the flax, cotton and wool fibers into clothing." [27]

In the second lecture, "The School and the Life of the Child," he tells of his search for desks and chairs to use in the Elementary School and of the dealer, "more intelligent than the rest," who made this remark: "I am afraid we have not what you want. You want something at which the children may work; these are all for listening!" [28]

We have already seen something of the type of work done in the Laboratory School. In this chapter, Dewey compares the work and activity of the ideal school to the situation in an ideal home. The child learns through social converse, through participation. "Now if we organize and generalize all of this, we have the ideal school." [29]

The activities, starting with the child's interests, are not engaged in simply to humor those interests, Dewey explains, using cooking as an example of an occupation. "One of the children became impatient recently at having to work things out by a long method of experimentation and said, 'Why do we bother with this? Let's follow a recipe in a cookbook.' The teacher asked the children where the recipe came from, and the conversation showed that if they simply followed this they would not know the reasons for what they were doing." Dewey then lists all of the science they learned in connection with the simple occupation of cooking eggs.[30] Later he points out in reference to still another occupation that the instruction was not given ready-made. "It was first needed and then arrived at experimentally." [31] This second chapter shows examples too of the art work undertaken as a medium of expression in some of the occupations.

One statement may be used as summary. He lists as the "fourfold interests" of children, "the interest in conversation or communication; in inquiry or finding out things; in making things or construction; and in artistic expression." And he concludes, "We may say they are the natural resources, the uninvested capital upon the exercise of which depends the active growth of the child." This is followed by further description of the actual situations in the Elementary School.[32]

This chapter ends with the words: "When nature and society can live in the schoolroom, when the forms and tools of learning are subordinated to the substance of experience, then shall there be an opportunity for this identification (of individual and social interests), and culture shall be the democratic password." [33]

From the third lecture, "Waste in Education," I select this sentence from the concluding paragraph, "We do not expect to have other schools literally imitate what we do. A working model is not something to be copied; it is to afford a demonstration of the feasibility of the principle, and of the methods which make it feasible." [34]

This long presentation of quotations from *The School and Society* is necessary in order to give something of its content and spirit. The difference between the informality and descriptive character of this book and the concentrated and abstract *Creed* is very great.

I suggested that it is an experience to read *The School and Society* with deliberate intent of finding there nothing of Dewey's democratic idea; and I have deliberately presented excerpts which may give foundation for such an interpretation. I shall now list some additional statements—with the warning that they are being pulled out of context. Again, a reprint of the book would be helpful as a companion to our examination of it. These excerpts will simply be listed.

"It is radical conditions which have changed, and only an equally radical change in education suffices." [35]

"We must conceive of work in wood and metal, of weaving, sewing, and cooking as methods of living and learning, not as distinct studies." We must conceive them, "in short, as instrumentalities through which the school itself shall be made a genuine form of active community life, instead of a place set apart in which to learn lessons." [36]

"Upon the ethical side, the tragic weakness of the school is that it endeavors to prepare future members of the social order in a medium, in which the conditions of the social spirit are eminently wanting." [37]

"A spirit of free communication, of interchange of ideas, suggestions, results, both successes and failures of previous experiences, becomes the dominating note of the recitation." [38]

"But the school has been so set apart, so isolated from the ordinary conditions and motives of life, that the place where the children are sent for discipline is the one place in the world where it is most difficult to get experience—the mother of all discipline worth the name." [39]

"The great thing to keep in mind, then, regarding the introduction into the school of various forms of active occupation, is that through them the entire spirit of the school is renewed. It has a chance to affiliate itself with life, to become the child's habitat, where he learns through directed living, instead of being only a place to learn lessons having an abstract and remote reference to some possible living to be done in the future. It gets a chance to be a miniature community, an embryonic society." [40]

Although these quotations point to the influence of the democratic design, they are not conclusive. The total impression is, in effect, that of a new and informal pattern for the school in which the child's present powers and interests and experiences are to be used as starting points for social living and learning.

In spite of little unequivocal evidence in *The School and Society* for the influence of Dewey's democratic philosophy, I nevertheless consider that this book could not have been written by someone representing merely the contemporary ideas of the new education as they were emerging in the early 1900's. There is a unity of direction in *The School and Society,* which gives the impression of some directive principle more radical than any notion of child nature and its development in a social environment. To conclude, however, that there is such a directive principle and that this principle is Dewey's democracy needs evidence, I think, beyond that afforded by the text of *The School and Society.* Therefore we shall look to other sources for confirmation that this is so.

First, there are the articles of belief in *My Pedagogic Creed.* There the pattern of social inquiry is plainly indicated. It is improbable that the principles here enunciated would have had no influence on the experiment of the Laboratory School.

Second, in a previous footnote, I have mentioned Dewey's statement of the use of his theory of inquiry in the Laboratory School. In the preface to the 1909 edition of *How We Think,* Dewey expresses his indebtedness to his wife, "by whom the ideas of this book were inspired, and through whose work in connection with the Laboratory School, existing in Chicago between 1896 and 1903, the ideas attained such concreteness as comes from embodiment and testing in practice."

In the preface to his *Logic,* Dewey says, "This book is a development of ideas regarding the nature of logical theory that were first presented, some forty years ago, in *Studies in Logical Theory;* that were briefly summarized *with special reference to education* in *How We Think.*" He states that there has been modification during the years, but that "basic ideas" remain the same.

In relating these words of Dewey to the text of *The School and Society,* we must note his statement that the ideas were embodied and tested in practice in the Laboratory School; in the abstract wording of *My Pedagogic Creed* these ideas were expressed more or less explicitly, and in *The School and Society,* Dewey was describing the experience of feeling his way in the testing of these ideas in practice. The point is that the ideas were there, and so give basis for the impression of a radical unity of direction in *The School and Society,* the directive principle being the democratic idea.

Supplementary confirmation may be seen in some words from the biographical essay by his daughter, Jane Dewey, who tells us that during his Chicago years Dewey, through certain personal friendships, was "crystallizing his ideas of democracy in the school." She says that his faith in democracy as a guiding force in education took on a sharper and deeper meaning because of the influence of a friend who thought that "democracy is a way of life, the truly moral and human way of life, not a political institutional device." [41]

The Laboratory School, then, constituted a testing ground for Dewey's democratic philosophy of education, itself undoubtedly clarified and further defined in the testing. This, however, is not the picture Dewey paints. *The School and Society* does not, as we have seen, present an unmistakable picture of such a laboratory. The pattern sketched is that of education as a process of living, of a way of developing children's powers in social living and learning. The school is to be an extension of the home, in which the children's experience is to lead to an understanding of the new modern industrial world and its problems. Formal learning of the usual school subjects is to be integrated about the articulating centers of occupations or projects. Moreover, the democracy represented in these social situations appears nothing more than democracy in the usual sense of the word.[42]

This sounds so very familiar, so much a description of what we know as a progressive school. It could have been taken from a catalog of one of them. It is practically their pattern, particularly during the 1920's and 1930's. If this is all that is meant by a progressive school, I think there were many of them. If by a progressive school, however, is meant a "Dewey school," in the sense of a laboratory for the embodiment and testing of Dewey's democratic idea, then once more I am left wondering whether there ever were any progressive schools.

Of all Dewey's works, *The School and Society* was the most widely read and influential. This is commonly known and is verified by his daughter's statement.[43] It would consequently be most apt to constitute the charter of the progressive schools.

Ratner says in one of his analyses of Dewey that unless you accept Dewey's basic premises, you are left with "thises and thats"—items. Perhaps we may say that *The School and Society* is materially but not formally pragmatic. That is what I think the progressive schools were. The descriptions of the progressive school given at the beginning of this paper would corroborate this conclusion. And when you try to *define* such progressive 'education and evaluate its principles and practice, you find yourself dealing with "thises and thats." It is difficult to evaluate such education except by way of a *list* of criteria; it is frustrating to try to find any unifying principle for the "list." The reason, I believe, is that the original unifying principle, Dewey's democratic design, was not radically the directive principle of progressive education or progressive schools. Dewey apparently suspected the same thing, as we shall perceive when later we look into *Experience and Education.*

The Child and the Curriculum

Two excerpts will be given. "The fundamental factors in the educative process are an immature undeveloped being; and certain social aims, meanings, values incarnate in the matured experience of the adult. The educative process is the due interaction of these forces." [44] And, "Abandon the notion of subject-matter as something fixed and ready-made in itself, outside the child's experience; cease thinking of the child's experience as something hard and fast; see it as something fluent, embryonic, vital; and we realize that the child and the curriculum are simply two limits which define a single process." [45]

In this little book we find the notion of the child as an organism-in-interaction-with-the-environment, a notion which later became Dewey's "continuum of experience." *The Child and the Curriculum* has been influential in school practice and especially in the idea of subject-matter as experiencing. It has lent its name to a well-known sequence of courses in the preparation of elementary schoolteachers.

Moral Principles in Education

Dewey's *Moral Principles in Education,* published under that title in 1909,[46] should perhaps have been considered earlier. It first appeared, at least in its essentials, in 1897, but was more widely known in its later form. It is in this essay that we find Dewey's celebrated pronouncement: "Apart from participation in social life, the school has no moral end nor aim." [47] "The school," he says, "cannot be a preparation for social life excepting as it reproduces, within itself, typical conditions of social life." [48]

The concluding thoughts of the chapter, "The Social Nature of the Course of Study," are given in full: "In so far as the school represents, in its own spirit, a genuine community life; in so far as what are called school discipline, government, order, etc., are the expressions of this inherent social spirit; in so far as the methods used are those that appeal to the active and constructive powers, permitting the child to give out and thus to serve; in so far as the curriculum is so selected and organized as to provide the material for affording the child a consciousness of the world in which he has to play a part, and the demands he has to meet; so far as these ends are met, the school is organized on an ethical basis. So far as general principles are concerned, all the basic ethical requirements are met. The rest remains between the individual teacher and the individual child." [49]

To recapitulate, Dewey is saying in general terms in *My Pedagogic Creed,* by examples and instances in *The School and Society,* in relation to the environment and process of reasoning in *The Child and the Curriculum* and plainly in *Moral Principles in Education,* that "the democratic way" is the way of and for education.

DEMOCRACY AND EDUCATION

In *Democracy and Education,* given to the world in 1916, all that has gone before appears in its essence and implications. Of the structure of this book we have already given Dewey's outline in connection with his notions of the relation between democracy and education. This, the central book in Dewey's revelation of his democratic design, affirms what he has said in the earlier works of education and democracy. It develops and gives shape to what has before been only implied or partially expressed.

Here in this declaration of democracy we see in its details Dewey's pattern for living and for education. The index of *Democracy and Education* is practically a summary of Dewey. A few texts will be given, distinguished only by an identifying tag.

The thesis of the book:

"The philosophy stated in this book connects the growth of democracy with the development of the experimental method in the sciences, evolutionary ideas in the biological sciences, and the industrial reorganization, and is concerned to point out the changes in subject matter and method of education indicated by these developments." [50]

On communication:

"Communication is a process of sharing experience till it becomes a common possession. It modifies the dispositions of both the parties who partake in it. That the ulterior significance of every mode of human association lies in the contribution which it makes to the improvement of the quality of experience is a fact most easily recognized in dealing with the immature." [51] And, "We conclude that the use of language to convey and acquire ideas is an extension and refinement of the principle that things gain meaning by being used in a shared experience or joint action; in no sense does it contravene that principle." [52]

Dewey's famous words on the meaning of growth:

"Since growth is the characteristic of life, education is all one with growing; it has no end beyond itself. The criterion of the value of school education is the extent to which it creates a desire for continued growth and supplies means for making the desire effective in fact." [53]

On democracy:

"A society which makes provision for participation in its good of all its members on equal terms and which secures flexible readjustment of its institutions through interaction of the different forms of associated life is in so far democratic." [54]

On aims and mind:

"The net conclusion is that acting with an aim is all one with acting intelligently. To foresee a terminus of an act is to have a basis upon which to observe, to select, to order objects and our own capacities. To do these things means to have a mind—for mind is precisely intentional purposeful activity. . . . To have a mind to do a thing is to foresee a future. . . . Mind is capacity to refer present conditions to future results, and future consequences to present conditions. And these traits are just what is meant by having an aim or purpose." [55] Again, "Consequently, there has been indicated a philosophy which recognized the origin, place, and function of mind *in* an activity which controls the environment." [56]

Learning by doing:

"The most direct blow at the traditional separation of doing and knowing . . . has been given by the progress of experimental science. If this progress has demonstrated anything, it is that there is no such thing as genuine knowledge and fruitful understanding except as the offspring of *doing*. The analysis and rearrangement of facts indispensable to the growth of knowledge . . . cannot be attained purely mentally—just inside the head. Men have to *do* something to the things when they wish to find out something; they have to alter conditions.

This is the lesson of the laboratory method, and the lesson which all education has to learn." [57]

Democracy and knowledge:

"Since democracy stands in principle for free interchange, for social continuity, it must develop a theory of knowledge which sees in knowledge the method by which one experience is made available in giving meaning and direction to another." [58]

And the closing words of the book:

"All education which develops power to share effectively in social life is moral. It forms a character . . . interested in that continuous readjustment which is essential to growth. Interest in learning from all the contacts of life is the essential moral interest." [59]

These texts from the book in which Dewey said his philosophy "had been for some years most fully expounded" speak for themselves. Philosopher of experience, of change, of democracy—*Democracy and Education* shows Dewey to be all of these.[60]

Democracy and Education has a deceptively simply tone. Actually it presents Dewey's design for education in its totality; but the implications of the doctrine can be missed. This book might, one would think, have put "Dewey schools" all over the land.

During the 20's and 30's progressive education flourished. In 1919 the Progressive Education Association was founded. In 1932, in a study of the new education, I refer to one directory of American progressive schools which lists, admittedly a conservative estimate, one hundred and fifty such schools.[61] During these years, the influence of the ideas of progressive education in American elementary schools was very real.

Then in 1938 Dewey published *Experience and Education*. This work is usually quoted for its criticisms of the excesses of progressive education. Indeed if any but Dewey had made the charges, such a person might have been considered prejudiced, if not uninformed.

EXPERIENCE AND EDUCATION

Experience and Education is no mere critique of excesses. Rather, it indicates that progressive education was not really radical, that it was not realizing in practice a "philosophy of experience." Here is an insistent, a conscious summons to "a philosophy of education based upon a philosophy of experience." [62] In some ways, this is Dewey's clearest statement of educational philosophy. He is saying, in effect, that the excesses have been, rather, defects; not that progressive education went too far, but that it did not go far enough. In these pages, Dewey is really declaring that he has meant what he has all along been saying, what in the 1929 statement he said he had long felt, and what he had long been trying to do. If in any of his writings, here is the "democratic way."

The criticisms of progressive education that Dewey makes in this book have been cited so often that I shall merely refer to them. The newer schools, he says, "tend to make little of organized subject matter; to proceed as if any form of direction and guidance by adults were an invasion of individual freedom." They have tended to proceed negatively in reaction to traditional education instead of consciously expressing a philosophy of experience. Dewey warns that education and experience are not interchangeable terms, that some experiences, although enjoyable, may be mis-educative, may not lay a foundation for future and meaningful reconstruction of experience and thus not provide for a desirable quality of experience.[63]

He speaks of the "planless improvisation" of some of the progressive schools,[64] of the "absence of adequate intellectual and moral organization in the newer type of school." [65] "Unfortunate," he notes, "is the idea that progressive schools can to a very large extent ignore the past." [66]

These defects are the result of failing to build education on the philosophy of experience which Dewey had been teaching. Only by going to the root of the problem, by understanding what experience is, can the new education realize itself. "The central problem of an education based upon experience," he insists, "is to select the kind of present experiences that live fruitfully and creatively in subsequent experiences." [67]

In the third chapter, called "Criteria of Experience," which occupies more than one fourth of the book, Dewey recapitulates his whole teaching on the democratic way and its correlative expression in a democratic philosophy of education. The central idea is the continuous reconstruction of experience. This principle of the continuity of experience, the "experiential continuum," is involved in every attempt "to discriminate between experiences that are worth while educationally and those that are not." [68] Growth is one exemplification of the principle of continuity. The form of growth must create conditions for further growth.[69]

Finally, Dewey summarizes the connection of the scientific method with any educational scheme based upon experience. The three points, that ideas are employed as hypotheses, that they must be tested by their consequences, and that reflective review is directed to intelligent dealing with further experiences, are the ones he selects for this summary.[70] The only ground for anticipating failure in such an educational enterprise "resides to my mind," he concludes "in the danger that experience and the experimental method will not be adequately conceived." [71]

To understand what Dewey considers an adequate conception of education has been the preoccupation of this paper and the reason for the examination of six of his educational works.

Dewey's design for education may now be briefly summarized. The design requires a community of shared experience, of shared intelligence; an experiential continuum. In and through this community of living and learning will be developed a habit of mind which consists in the recognition and espousal of the democratic way as the life of intelligence: the way of problems and of conjoint inquiry for their solution.

A "Dewey school" would, therefore, in conjoint communicated experience and inquiry, nurture above all this habit of inquiry and the belief in its application without abrupt breach of continuity to science and to morals. In a Dewey school, the notion of the thorough (I had almost written "absolute") tentativeness of truths in morals or in science would be a leading and conscious principle. Children would learn not to expect too many settled conclusions.

The Progressive Schools

Immediately, one of the questions proposed for exploration rises before us: "Were progressive schools patterned on Dewey's design? Were they Dewey schools?" And another, "What exactly is a progressive school?" We have, early in this essay, spent a little time in one progressive school. I have spent time in a number of them. What were they?

Progressive schools, in their catalogs, and, allowing for individual differences, in their practice and the affirmations of the teachers, believed in social situations usually growing out of and centered about projects of one kind or another. In the school I have described the projects were cooperative (we called them community projects) and were the focus of work for some months. Some schools believed in individual projects more or less ephemeral. In most progressive schools these projects or centers of interest or units of work, starting with present child interests, led gradually to some understanding of the present-day world. Often a first grade "built" a town and visited the post office, bank, grocery store in their own community. A second grade, needing to know where the groceries and clothing and all the rest came from, might study the "farm," and make one. In these schools, with small classes, generous floor space was available for building. Building blocks, dolls, "meccano" were as plentiful as books, paints, pencils, paper.

In the development of any project, group planning, discussion, thoughtful purposing were in order. There was freedom to move about; activity was necessary. The design for progressive education was avowedly that of democratic living; but not, I emphasize, in Dewey's radical sense. If we analyze their programs, the attempt to get back to principles or to appraise the validity of their practice ends, as I have said before, in thises and thats.

Therefore I suspect that, unless the word "exactly" is deleted, the question, "What exactly is a progressive school?" is unanswerable. A progressive school is, from sheer frustration, described, not defined. It was not impossible, however, to say a few lines back quite exactly what I mean by a "Dewey school." [72]

Consequently, I think that the progressive schools were not in a proper sense patterned on Dewey's democratic design. This could have been the result of incomplete interpretation or understanding of what Dewey was really saying. It could have come (because the director of the progressive school I taught in certainly understood Dewey) from the exigencies of actual practice. Teachers and children were perhaps not pragmatists; they certainly were not merely Dewey's organisms-in-interaction-with-an-environment. In his design for man, Dewey had been anticipated by an earlier Creator. The children and the teachers—and, as I am not the first to note, Dewey—had not been fashioned according to Dewey's hypothesis. With such material, it is difficult to effect a Dewey school. Teachers and children may cling, without benefit of experiment, to certain conclusions and to assorted absolutes.

The idea that progressive schools were not Dewey schools helps explain some of their defects. One of the goals of progressive education was "learning democracy," the ordinary, every-day kind, by living it. By democratic living these schools meant participation in group living. This involved the children's sharing in planning the course of the day's work and the direction in which the project was to move. It implied the freedom and informality which is one of the first things to catch the notice of a visitor to a progressive school. I suggest that to pursue democratic living as a direct learning is unrealistic. Democracy is so very much a matter of relationships, based on and qualified by habits, intellectual and moral, natural and supernatural, that "learning democracy" must provide for learning what democracy really means and for the development of habits of mind and conduct which make up the very fabric of democratic living. Perhaps democratic living is consequent not primary. By not realizing this, the progressive schools incurred some merited criticism of defects in discipline and scholarship.

The project was the center of this democratic venture. In the "integrated curriculum," the usual school subjects were to grow out of the activities of the project. The mastery of subjects was often less than mastery. To learn the arithmetic, the spelling, the reading, as need arises in the pursuit of a project is an unrealistic undertaking. It would require angelic intelligence to see steadily and whole all the relations involved and the foundations for them. The human mind, and certainly a child's mind, has to proceed less totally, and step by step.

Note that with Dewey, democratic living and the occupations were part of the dialectical way, of the application of intelligence to modern problems. For Dewey, activity, freedom, discipline[73] were means to the formation of the habit of mind we have described. A Dewey school would have been a much more demanding enterprise than that of the progressive schools in which the freedom and discipline were not governed by Dewey's central and directive principle. A curious, uncoordinated quality of the progressive school, an air of going in several directions at once, was the result.

In the chief virtue of progressive education, however, Dewey's influence may be recognized. Problem-solving—and for scientific problems, the scientific method is a proper instrument—was daily fare in progressive schools. These schools really did direct the time and attention of children to thinking, to careful and well-directed gathering of evidence for the solution of problems. They provided the child with time to think and with practice in this interesting work. An environment for this thinking proper to man's very nature was provided in good progressive schools. There was an atmosphere of "We are all studying together" —with "we" including the teacher—which was a challenge to teachers and students alike. Such an atmosphere is not and never has been restricted to rooms with movable furniture and floor space devoted to projects. In this, however, the progressive schools I have known did give an example of value for all schools.

Dewey was, in one sense, the father of progressive education. He was one of its efficient causes, we may say; but progressive education was not strictly, formally, his child. Dewey's basic philosophy had its deepest influence, rather, on the thinking and teaching in institutions of higher learning. From various universities and colleges certain of Dewey's really basic ideas have flowed and trickled and seeped into some of the thinking and living in this country.

Doubts have arisen. In his foreword to the University of Chicago reprint of *The School and Society,* Leonard Carmichael uses the expression, "the intellectual counterrevolution," and says, "There can be no doubt that in our time a resurgent belief in the lifesaving character of a recognition of fixed and established values has at least begun." [74] Of many such current declarations, one of the most interesting is an article in *Modern Age* which, by way of contrasting the intellectual climate of Dewey's ninetieth birthday celebration with that of the farewell banquet held in honor of Herbert Spencer in 1882, accents the same resurgent belief in fixed and established values.[75]

Today progressive education is not in fashion. It was an experiment. Its defects were intrinsic. Its virtues can be cultivated in any good school.

Some Observations

Dewey's idea of shared experience from which, by the use of social inquiry, is to be fashioned a social-moral universe, stands primary. Society itself becomes the laboratory for the testing of the democratic hypothesis. This social enterprise is impossible of realization; it will not work. Man is more than organism and less than Providence. The continuum of experience will not be adequate. It is too limited; knowledge, not that univocal, will transcend it. The universe postulated is not spacious enough: a lid has been clapped on. If you try to envision yourself in a Dewey universe, absorbed in the continuing social quest, in what Maritain calls the rectilinear movement of problem solving, with no mystery, in the pursuit of truths, never of truth, you discover that you are in a world with the sky sliced off. There is no reach. The quality of experience is not satisfying. Man needs some magnificence.

Dewey's other laboratory, of education and the school, we have considered. There is one further point. Would a true Dewey school be practicable? Would it work?

As Dewey once said, "The case is of Child." In attempting to appraise the possibility of such a school, we have to consider the fact of the child. Dewey's hypothesis of an organism in interaction with an environment is basic for him, it is true. Dewey's account in *The School and Society,* however, of children and their activities depicts the kind of children everyone knows. Carmichael, in the foreword we have mentioned, refers to Dewey's "simple naturalistic psychology." Dewey in his crusade for intelligence in the modern world may have neglected the role of emotional factors in learning. Much research on the child has been done in fifty years, and much of it is valuable. There is truth in Carmichael's words that Dewey's theory of human nature must be evaluated in terms of present-day knowledge. Granted all this, and assuming perennial knowledge that the child is a rational being, a person, a doubt will arise. In a Dewey school, the leading principle of the tentativeness of all truths, moral included, would meet with difficulty in practice for two reasons. In the first place, the immaturity of a child, organism or person, would limit the application of such a principle in practice; the implications would be almost impossible for a child to comprehend. Second, if this principle were really to be exemplified in ways adapted to children's abilities, the result would be, I think, personal disorganization. We are all weary of the word "security," but children need what this word stands for. A serious, day-by-day program of continuous reconstruction of experience with the gradual realization by the child that this reconstruction is "of the essence" would have undesirable results. The quality of such experience is questionable. This child has deeper needs.

When we reflect on Dewey's real message, it is clear that he was establishing man as the measure of truth and morals, the designer. Dewey worked in the realm of the artist, of ideas. From his ideas flows a progressive blueprint for a progressive universe. The flux of Dewey's whole philosophy is palpable. Once in conversation with a professed experimentalist with whom I have for years been in friendly and radical disagreement, I asked, "How can any one with your intelligence think that this inquiry and experiment will solve these social problems and bring into being a better world?" The quiet answer was revealing: "I have never claimed that we shall solve any problems. I have only been saying that we must continue to inquire and to experiment."

Chesterton summed up for me long ago this rectilinear way: "A certain break or sharp change in history can hardly be sketched more sharply than by saying that up to a certain time life was conceived as a Dance, and after that time life was conceived as a Race." [76] Before that, was "the idea that one thing must balance another, that each stood on one side or the other of something that was in the middle, and something that remained in the middle. There might be any amount of movement, but it was movement round this central thing; perpetually altering the attitudes, but perpetually preserving the balance. . . . Now since that break in history, whatever we call it or whatever we think of it, the Dance has turned into a Race. That is, the dancers lose their balance and only recover it by running towards some object, or alleged object; not an object within their circle or their possession, but an object which they do not yet possess. It is a flying object; a disappearing object; and, as some hold, a disappointing object. But I am not concerned with condemning or commending either the religion of the Race or the religion of the Dance. I am only pointing out that that is the fundamental difference between them. One is rhythmic and recurrent movement, because there is a known centre; while the other is precipitate or progressive movement, because there is an unknown goal."

NOTES

1. John Dewey, *Logic: The Theory of Inquiry* (New York: Holt, 1938) 8. This sentence, although taken from the *Logic,* not published until 1938, represents Dewey's ideas as found in his earlier *How We Think* (1910) and as far back as the Laboratory School in Chicago, 1896-1903. This line of descent is indicated in the preface to the *Logic* and to *How We Think.*
2. "Philosopher-in-the-Making," *Saturday Review of Literature,* 22 (Oct. 1949) 9-10, 39-44.
3. Cf. "The Significance of the Problem of Knowledge," *University of Chicago Contributions to Philosophy,* 1897. Reprinted in *The Influence of Darwin on Philosophy* (New York: Holt, 1910) 298. Also "Logical Conditions of a Scientific Treatment of Morality" (1903) reprinted in *Problems of Men* (New York: Philosophical Library, 1946) 211-49. In the Prefatory Note to *Problems of Men,* Dewey says that this essay had not been previously reprinted (until 1946) and mentions that it seemed worth reprinting "as an anticipation of the direction in which I have moved during the intervening fifty years."

   These two references are typical of those that might be cited to show that Dewey had indeed long before 1929 been engaged in applying his logic to the domain of morals. Relevant, of course, is Morton White, *The Origin of Dewey's Instrumentalism;* in particular, 102 and 109.
4. "Psychology and the Philosophic Method." An address given at the University of California in 1899; reprinted in *The Influence of Darwin on Philosophy,* 267.

5. *Op. cit.* 8-9 (Italics his).
6. *Democracy and Education* (New York: Macmillan, 1916) V.
7. *Ibid.* 101.
8. *Ibid.* 387 (italics mine).
9. By the common "meaning" of the word, I mean democracy in the sense of a political order based on the possession by man of "unalienable" rights with which he has been endowed by the Creator. Democracy, in this sense, recognizes some absolutes.
10. *Ibid.* V.
11. Jerome Nathanson, *John Dewey* (New York: Scribners, 1951) 111.
12. *Ibid.* 112 (Italics his). Obviously, the measure and the judge is to be man.
13. *Op. cit.* 487-512. Again, although this point will undoubtedly be made elsewhere in this volume, it should be understood that Dewey does not mean that by the use of the scientific method in social-moral issues an actual experiment in, for instance, employer-labor relations is to be at once inaugurated. Thinking is to be done in advance: the "inquiry" is to be instituted. A typical Dewey analysis of a prudential problem in terms of the experimental method may be found in this chapter of the *Logic*. The very inclusion of such a chapter in a Logic is significant.
14. Ferrer Smith, O.P., "A Thomistic Appraisal of the Philosophy of John Dewey," *Thomist* 18 (April 1955) 146, 160.
15. Cf. *The Influence of Darwin on Philosophy,* 70.
16. "Philosopher-in-the-Making," 42.
17. *Democracy and Education,* 375-76, 384, 387.
18. *My Pedagogic Creed* (New York: E. L. Kellogg, 1897) 3, 5, 6.
19. *Ibid.* 7, 8, 9.
20. *Ibid.* 11.
21. *Ibid.* 12.
22. *Ibid.* 13.
23. The edition I am using is the University of Chicago reprint, 1956.
24. Cf. *A Critical Study of the New Education* (Washington: The Catholic University Press, 1932) 38.
25. *The School and Society,* 11, 12.
26. *Ibid.* 15, 16, 17.
27. *Ibid.* 20-2.
28. *Ibid.* 31.
29. *Ibid.* 34-7.
30. *Ibid.* 38-9.
31. *Ibid.* 53.
32. *Ibid.* 47-8.
33. *Ibid.* 62.
34. *Ibid.* 94.
35. *Ibid.* 12.
36. *Ibid.* 14.
37. *Ibid.* 15.
38. *Ibid.* 16.
39. *Ibid.* 17.

40. *Ibid.* 18.
41. Paul Arthur Schilpp, *The Philosophy of John Dewey* (Evanston: Northwestern, 1939) 29.
42. The sense in which this phrase is used has been indicated on page 90.
43. *Op. cit.* 28. "The most widely read and influential of Dewey's writings, *School and Society,* which has been translated into a dozen European and Oriental languages, consists of talks given to raise money for the Laboratory School."
44. *The Child and the Curriculum* (Chicago: 1902) 7-8.
45. *Ibid.* 16.
46. *Moral Principles in Education* (Boston: Houghton Mifflin Company).
47. *Ibid.* 11.
48. *Ibid.* 14.
49. *Ibid.* 43-4.
50. *Democracy and Education,* v.
51. *Ibid.* 11
52. *Ibid.* 19. This is an indication of what Dewey means by "learning by doing."
53. *Ibid.* 62.
54. *Ibid.* 115.
55. *Ibid.* 120. Dewey says elsewhere, "Mind is a verb."
56. *Ibid.* 377. (Italics his). Dewey's notion of the active nature of mind is mentioned in the "third point" of his philosophical development in connection with his debt to the ideas of William James. This conception of mind may, of course, also be traced to the "influence of Darwin on philosophy."
57. *Ibid.* 321. (Italics his). Note how much more radical this is than the popular notion of what Dewey means by "learning by doing."
58. *Ibid.* 401.
59. *Ibid.* 418.
60. In his *John Dewey,* Irwin Edman says that Dewey was more. As testimony from one who knew Dewey personally, I include for completeness of view his statement that for Dewey the life of intelligence was not the whole of life. He mentions the other aspects of life which Dewey called "consummations, to be sought where they are found; in love, in friendship and in art." (New York: Bobbs-Merrill, 1955) 33.
61. *A Critical Study of the New Education* (Washington: The Catholic Education Press, 1932) 12-15. Foreign schools are also given.
62. *Experience and Education* (New York: Macmillan, 1951) 19.
63. *Ibid.* 9, 10, 13.
64. *Ibid.* 18.
65. *Ibid.* 22.
66. *Ibid.* 93.
67. *Ibid.* 16.
68. *Ibid.* 24.
69. *Ibid.* 28-9.
70. *Ibid.* 109-10.
71. *Ibid.* 114.
72. See above, p. 107.

73. Cf. *Democracy and Education,* 352-53. Also *Experience and Education,* 105-7.

74. *Op. cit.* ix-x.

75. Francis Graham Wilson, "The Foremost Philosopher of the Age," *Modern Age* 2 (Winter, 1957-1958).

76. G. K. Chesterton, *Chaucer* (New York: Farrar and Rinehart, 1932) 158-59.

V

Dewey and the Problem
of Technology

JOHN W. DONOHUE, S.J.

Father John W. Donohue, S.J. teaches courses in the history and the philosophy of education at Fordham University. After graduation from Fordham he entered the Society of Jesus in 1939. He did graduate work at St. Louis University and at Yale University, obtaining his doctorate from the latter institution. He has published occasional articles as well as two books, Christian Maturity *and* Work and Education.

We must wrest our general culture from an industrialized civilization; and this fact signifies that industry must itself become a primary educative and cultural force for those engaged in it.

Individualism—Old and New

"A purely intellectual life," wrote John Dewey while still on the threshold of his enormously long and productive career, "is an unhealthy, one-sided life." [1] If these words are taken in a literal, quite obvious sense, they amount to a firm challenge of one of the most venerable traditions in both the East and the West, the tradition which elevates the contemplative life above the active and which has been impressively sustained from the Athens of Plato and Aristotle down to our own day. Dewey, however, was never notably intimidated by traditions and his own system owed much of its ascendancy to the characteristic coloration it derived from his central conviction that

117

thought should subserve the whole of life and action. There is a magnetism about the directness with which his philosophy establishes organic bonds between the most concrete recommendations for action and a total metaphysic and epistemology. From abstract theses about the nature of the universe, life, man and value there are made to issue, for instance, specific directives for the content and the method of elementary schooling. Moreover, these directives present themselves as the only defensible decisions. No forks divide that main road which leads from an analysis of man as an evolving element in a material and social continuum where crises can be resolved only pragmatically to the conclusion that education should, therefore, develop habits of instrumental thinking through problem-solving experiences. Not many other theories have quite this sort of commanding single-mindedness. Two sincere Christians, despite their basic agreements, can easily disagree about emphases in education. One of them may defend a curriculum of predominantly intellectual culture because he accents the scholastic portrait of man as an embodied soul, a spirit incarnated precisely because it needs a body as the medium for its own distinctively spiritual development. The other may be more preoccupied with the Biblical image and its somewhat different stresses on man as an animated body, on the primacy of charity and on action and moral choice in the irreversible historical process. This second perspective might then suggest a concept of education allowing more place than traditional Hellenic humanism does, to a concern for the individual person in his unique selfhood and for his essential complexity as a corporeal, affective, imaginative, social being whose spiritual maturation is itself profoundly conditioned by biological factors and social relationships. Divergencies in practice as striking as these, however, are not to be found among those who accept whole-heartedly Dewey's experimentalism. This is not to say, of course, that a philosophy is validated merely because it renders unilateral support to one particular course of action out of several, but only that if it does do so it is bound to be peculiarly influential for it will enter decisively into certain problematic situations and will cure all hesitancies even if this means banishing rather than confronting certain elements of the actual perplexity.

Although Dewey's educational theory is the best-known instance of his gift for connecting the general with the specific and for handling philosophically very immediate, down-to-earth affairs, it is not the only case of its kind. His reflections on the problems of work in modern times show the same method applied to another crucial contemporary concern. The curious blend of promise and threat posed by the highly mechanized work of our industrialized age makes a claim on everyone's attention and provokes more and more discussion. But since Dewey insisted so often that his own philosophy did, and all philosophies should, take for subject matter the stresses and strains agitating community life, should get all problems, as he said, from the world of action, we might naturally expect him to examine those questions which machine technology either symbolizes or exacerbates.[2] During the near-century which Dewey's life spanned, America was the scene of some of technology's most awesome exploits and he had an excellent chance to observe them as he moved from the Vermont of his boyhood, first to the Baltimore of his graduate student days, then to the inland states of his early teaching years at Ann Arbor and Chicago and finally to the New York City financial center of his later decades at Columbia. When he was born in 1859, many New England factories, as Lewis Mumford reminds us, still got their power from the water wheel invented in the third century B.C. But in the next 40 years, fourteen million immigrants were to come to the United States; tens of millions of acres of open country would be occupied by homesteaders and by Dewey's death in 1952 the general population would have doubled and more than doubled again, rising during his lifetime from 31 to 160 millions. Even before World War I the United States had become the leading manufacturing nation in the world, largely through the exploitation of enormous coal and petroleum deposits and the development of machines, electric motors and the techniques of mass production. The mechanical horse power available in 1952 was hundreds of times greater than that of 1859, and the yearly average of United States merchandise exports had mounted during this same period from some 239 millions to nearly 12 billions; the yearly production of corn from more than 800 million bushels to better than three and a half billion. A philosopher who thought of his task as that of interpreting the American culture to itself could hardly overlook so important an aspect as this one of technology.

Those who reject Dewey's system do not like to hear him called the philosopher of the American spirit for they naturally count themselves equally legitimate sharers of that spirit. It is possible, however, to accept certain distinctive attitudes in practice without generalizing them into philosophical positions. It is certainly true, for instance, that the American ethos includes an understandable preoccupation with the future. The first settlers had a virgin continent before them and their main business was to make something out of it. There was no local history demanding respectful consultation. Had they lived in a European cathedral town or a great English house, their chief interest might have been to preserve the past—the cathedral, the cloth hall, the yearly pageants like the Siena horse races or the great gardens. But, as it is conventional to note, Americans had less to preserve a past than to build a future. Still, one can share this dedication to the servicing of tomorrow's prospects without grounding it upon an explicit philosophy of futurism. Dewey, however, is at least *a* philosopher of the American spirit because he gave this whole dynamism a logical setting. He saw man as part of a world in process where puzzling alternatives are met on every hand and he conceived of intelligent activity as a matter of setting up programs for action on the basis of forecasts of the future. If the plan succeeds it is "true," or better yet, a "good" tool. This epistemological futurism is not, of course, the only possible intellectualization of American commitment to the forward movement of national history. The New England Puritans were also profoundly concerned with using the present to make a bright future for the glory of God. Here, however, we only want to note that when Dewey does, in fact, discuss the humanizing virtualities of man's work along with the opportunities and checks which it variously encounters at present, the argument moves out from a point close to the center of his thought and invokes most of his distinctive theses. But its strands must be gathered together from a number of places for they are not all bound up in a single book.

The Enigma of Machine Technology

Modern technology with all its astonishing brilliance and power is not yet so domesticated as to be taken wholly for granted nor so unquestionably friendly as to be accepted without any reserve. But there is no need here to echo in detail either the rhapsody over its achievements or the threnody aroused by its ambiguities. All this has been done often enough. There are still plenty of people alive who remember when the dynamo and the internal combustion engine were hardly more than toys; when the radio and television and atomic weapons were less conceivable than tours to Mars are now; when factory work itself was less mechanized than the procedures even of farms and offices are today. And we are all aware, if only unreflectively, that these developments have deep reverberations for the individual consciousness in a world where oceans are vaulted in a matter of hours and the news from Iraq, Ghana or

Burma is more significant for our town than events in the neighboring states would have been a century ago. "Technology," said Pius XII on Christmas Eve, 1953, "has in fact brought man's domination of the material world to a pitch of perfection never known before. The modern machine allows a mode of production that substitutes for, and multiplies a hundredfold, human energy for work, that is entirely independent of the contribution of organic forces and which ensures a maximum of extensive and intensive potential and at the same time of precision . . . nature itself seems to give an assent of satisfaction to what has been done in it, and to incite to further investigation and use of its extraordinary possibilities." [3]

This summary underscores certain important aspects of technology on which Dewey's own comments converged. There is, for instance, the fact that the impact of technology is felt most significantly less in the products of work than in its process, in the mode of production. Of course, many of the distinctive achievements of modern industry are not mere extensions of earlier inventions but are uniquely its own: aircraft, hydrogen bombs, skyscrapers. But no one would argue that mechanized production automatically and necessarily insures better goods than those once made by hand or by relatively rudimentary machines. It would hardly be possible to prove that the picture window is simply "better" than the stained glass of Chartres or that mass-produced crockery is superior to Wedgwood, or Wedgwood in turn to Cretan figurines, glazed Babylonian tiles or the neolithic earthenware of Susa. There is no doubt, however, that by technical innovations the process of fabrication has been expanded, transmuted and almost always made less burdensome. In the course of this development, new natural resources have been tapped and a powerful new "worker," the collective laborer who is the aggregate of many men has emerged. Alongside such an individual craftsman of classical times as the village cobbler stitching sandals there was to be found, it is true, a collective which built the mammoth tombs and ziggurats that no multitude of workers operating singly could have constructed. But for these works men were themselves the machines; there were simply thousands of hands and backs instead of one. Today the collective worker is armed with, or supervises, the most intricate mechanisms which do not merely multiply or enlarge human energies but bring under control the gigantic resources of water and electrical power and unlock the forces of fuel oils and the mysterious atom. As a result, the range of possibilities opened to corporate action runs from turning a car a minute off the assembly line to bridging harbors, driving submarines under the pole and compassing the moon. These great conquests, moreover, are the work of the collectivity as such. No one man could execute or perhaps even comprehend all the operations required to build and fly a transatlantic airliner. All these developments have also multiplied the number, depth and complexity of man's interactions with the material forces of the world and they lace him into an expanding network of relationships to his natural and social environments. Such factors of technology—the radical transformation of work processes, the explosive dilation of the industrial collective's power and the increase of man's instrumental transactions with nature—are much to the fore when Dewey takes up the problems posed by modern work.

For there are problems. A certain uneasiness, at least, envelops this ascension of technology and this mechanization of labor. This is acknowledged not only by such disenchanted observers as Eric Gill or Hannah Arendt, but also by a John Dewey or an Emmanuel Mounier who admit the weaknesses of "paleo-machinism" (as Mounier called it) but retain an optimistic faith in the possibilities of purification as opposed to rejection or radical alteration. The usual criticisms directed at the present situation are of several sorts. It is charged, for one thing, that the very success of modern technology has boosted the work phase of life into a position of unfortunate domination. Work absorbs too much of modern societies' time and energy. Even when the hours devoted to economically necessary occupations are relatively few, the culture remains work-oriented. People spend their leisure feverishly consuming the products of their industry lest the economy's wheels slow down, and they refresh themselves only to work some more. Technology, it is said, used to minister to art and religion and when it did so, it knew and kept its place. But nowadays work is becoming not a means of life but its very end. The notion of true leisure has disappeared, to be replaced by the vacuous concept of "free time." Dewey might have consented to some parts of this analysis although he would certainly resist all distinctions which having first sharply divided means from ends, go on to situate the latter outside of, rather than within the actual work experience. For he felt that distinctions of this sort, like that between the active and contemplative lives, are simply historical and social, not intrinsic and absolute.[4]

But it is precisely work experience itself, we are often told, which has been impoverished through the mechanization of production and the division of labor in the interests of efficiency. The individual is responsible now for only a minute and relatively meaningless fragment. Too much work, consequently, is reduced to routine toil, or labor, for it does not utilize a man's full personal capacities for thought and decision. Its intrinsic recompense has been snuffed out and the hours of work not only fail to humanize men but are often corrosive. The satisfaction an independent craftsman got when he personally planned and executed an entire project is lost when these procedures are lodged in the collective. By belonging to everybody they belong to nobody.

Two other criticisms of technology look more directly to its sombre effects on the relationships of men to nature and to one another. Despite the fact that man's interactions with natural resources have been multiplied, it is maintained that he has been divorced from direct contact with and consequent piety toward that natural world. Instead of mirroring in himself the harmony of cosmic rhythms in the cycles of night and day, season upon season, he is now attuned to the harsh percussive precisions of the machine which stands between him and nature and effectively alienates him from the world. Even if some machines seem, for a time, to restore his vision of nature and to heal these alienations— as early aircraft intensified the awareness of wind, space and stars— the "suicidal acceleration" of modern technics, to use Mumford's phrase, promptly upsets this balance and the jet pilot sealed in his pressurized cabin keeps his eye fixed on the instrument panel as he travels faster than sound. This same acceleration is also charged with having corrupted the social environment by polarizing it towards greed or frantic consumption. It promotes private neuroses by its competitive pace; it equips young people with high-powered cars while denying them a place in the economic order and thereby it spawns delinquents; it destroys esteem for the reflective mood and generally inflates a fatal *hubris*. Many of these complaints are hardly free of what Dewey once labelled the childish animism which blames everything on the machine.[5] The charges do become more formidable, however, when it is further argued that the very inner logic of technology spirals it inevitably towards such excess.

Dewey's own criticism of machinism and the contemporary situation of work concurs with some of this conventional indictment but significantly dissents from or ignores other elements in it. These dissents are themselves indications of the precise manner in which he visualized the problem and are therefore important; for, as Dewey once remarked, philosophical disagreements as to conclusions are perfunctory in comparison with disagreements as to problems—"to see the problem another sees, in the same perspective and at the same angle—that amounts to something." [6] What, then, was the precise nature of the difficulty as Dewey saw it, and what did he propose be done about it?

To begin with, he recognized that the trouble was real enough. A common and serviceable definition of technology equates it with applied science. But given Dewey's twin devotion to science and its method on the one hand and to the practical, progressive amelioration of social conditions on the other, it was to be expected that he should have welcomed all such scientific applications. Nevertheless, writing in his ninetieth year, after the Second World War, he noted that there was plenty of evidence suggesting that this application of scientific method and conclusions to daily life had produced "a mixture of things approvable and to be condemned; of the desirable and the undesirable." He added, somewhat obviously, that the problem was one of managing this technologization, this "return wave" of science upon our daily existence in such a fashion as to minimize its evil and intensify its good consequences. [7]

But if one had asked Dewey to specify these undesirable consequences, his answer would very likely have contrasted sharply with the more common arraignments of modern industrialization. Mechanized labor is, for instance, often criticized not so much for the routine or brutish character of the work process itself as for its shoddy or de-individualized products. Hannah Arendt suggests that *homo faber,* the genuinely creative man who truly "works," has now been replaced by the *animal laborans,* the man who simply toils. This means, concretely, a shift in focus from the fabrication of things of lasting worth and beauty to a preoccupation with method, production and the manufacture of impermanent consumptibles. "Processes, therefore, and not ideas, the models and shapes of the things to be, become the guide for the making and fabricating activities of *homo faber* in the modern age." [8] The same critique is expressed from a slightly different angle in her distinction between *labor* and *work,* the former a monotonous, slavish, repetitive activity like farming or housekeeping whose fruits are quickly exhausted; the latter a nobler affair whose fruits—building, fine furniture and artifacts—are relatively durable. Whatever is to be thought of these distinctions, it is pretty clear that those who accept them would not try to purify modern work or to redeem the machine by emphasizing the process still more.

In keeping with his characteristic metaphysical convictions, however, Dewey criticized modern technologizing primarily because it did not make enough of this very process, this industrialized work experience and did not exploit its intellectual and ethical reserves. No doubt he would have rejected a disjunction between labor and work, between a higher and a lower form of production as just one more of those miserable dualisms which are an unfortunate Greek heritage. Progress does not come, he would very likely have said, by disparaging human activities so basic as agriculture or the routine daily maintenance of the machinery of social institutions but rather by more fully unfolding and utilizing their inherent resources. "To exist," he wrote once, "is to be in process, in change." [9] Since this is the characteristic situation of all life, it ought to be a continually rewarding and instructive one. For it actually means involvement in a wealth of "experiences," a multitude of undergoings, as the human organism interacts with its environment. But these experiences always point beyond themselves and what we currently undergo is "a future implicated in a present." [10] We cannot, however, suppose that this future, toward which the present is evolving, will automatically be good, satisfying, pleasant or nutritious. It may turn out badly. Everything depends upon how wisely we control and alter the factors now at hand and how readily we learn to recognize the wisdom or error of the decisions we made in yesterday's affairs by noting their present results. For Dewey, of course, these decisions would only have been wise if they were grounded on an intelligent employment of scientific method. If life can lead, at any moment, to either good or bad issues it always has a problematic character and always confronts us with the necessity of selecting one of several alternatives. Such choice ought to be prefaced by an inquiry aimed at determining which avenue seems most promising. Dewey's central faith, as Sidney Hook calls it, was the persuasion that the only valid method of such inquiry is that which the triumphant advance of the natural sciences has perfected and publicized. In his "Introduction" to the 1948 reprint of *Reconstruction in Philosophy,* Dewey summed up the matter by remarking that the aim of the enterprise of reconstruction is "to carry over into any inquiry into human and moral subjects the kind of method (the method of observation, theory as hypothesis, and experimental test) by which understanding of physical nature has been brought to its present pitch." [11]

What is to be underscored here, though, is not this monism of method but rather Dewey's firm confidence in the power of processive and prospective experience to teach us what to do and provide us with the means for doing it. A statement he designed as a popular *credo* puts it all very succinctly: "Adherence to any body of doctrines and dogmas based upon a specific authority signifies distrust in the power of experience to provide, in its own ongoing movement, the needed principles of belief and action. Faith in its newer sense signifies that experience itself is the sole ultimate authority. Such a faith has in it all the elements of a philosophy. For it implies that the course and material of experience give support and stay to life, and that its possibilities provide all the ends and ideals that are to regulate conduct." [12]

Guided by such principles, Dewey would have expected to uncover the source of ambiguity in modern technology chiefly in some mismanagement of the work process or in its corruption by unhealthy social conditions and he would have hoped to dissolve the ambiguity by a wiser handling of the material of that work experience itself. Any attempt to reverse history and turn back to a pre-industrial age he would have judged impossible and undesirable. Impossible because our technological development is a reasonable phase of natural growth and to stop growth is to stop life. The vital nisus pervading cultural evolution has naturally carried it toward ever greater scientific understanding and mastery of the world through ever more effective technological elaboration. Were this course to be inhibited or checked, one would necessarily suspect the advent of decay and death. But even if that were not the case, it would be undesirable to halt technology's progressive application of science to daily life because the more power men achieve over nature, the freer they are to enter upon a fully rational existence. When all their energies are exhausted in painfully scraping a living from the surface of the earth they have no time to humanize themselves or their institutions. On the contrary: "The mechanization of nature is the condition of a practical and progressive idealism in action." [13]

It is worth noting, parenthetically, that this last theme is not the exclusive property of a naturalistic ethic. Technology, as Père Malevez, S.J. puts it, has also well served the aspirations and purposes of Christianity. Men immersed in the racking business of securing minimal subsistence cannot easily concern themselves either with worship or with the anxieties of their fellow men, either with the first or the second commandment. Malevez notes that certain of Bergson's pages are cited approvingly by those Catholic theologians who are sometimes called "Incarnationists." For Bergson argues that any authentic mysticism of charity (and Christian mysticism is pre-eminently such) finds its fulfillment in action. This is perhaps a way of saying that the best measure of affective love is effective love. But such a full flowering, Bergson continues, is only possible in a world which some industrialization has lifted above the level of brute toil. "En d'autres termes, la mystique appele la mécanique." [14]

The Dewey of mature reputation had put behind him his youthful religious *attraits,* but he would have certainly argued that a man's occupation ought to be the source of highly significant experiences directly contributing to his intellectual, moral and aesthetic growth. The chief weakness of industrialized work in American society today, he believed, follows from the fact that it is organized for profit with small regard for these educative values which it might and ought to have.[15] There has been an unfortunate segmentation of life, understood as the area in which experiences are valuable and instructive, from labor understood as the area in which they generally are not. This has certainly brought about a dehydration of work experience and its reduction to monotony, but machine technology is not itself to blame. "If the mass of mankind has usually found in its industrial occupations nothing but evils which had to be endured for the sake of maintaining existence, the fault is not in the occupations, but in the conditions under which they are carried on." For in themselves these occupations are able to "supply modes of experience which are intrinsically valuable; they are truly liberalizing in quality." [16] When he wrote those words Dewey was thinking explicitly of a school setting in which the occupations in question could be pursued for the sake of their content and not, as he put it, for pecuniary gain. But this content ought also, of course, to be apprehended in the regular economic situation; in the offices and plants and on the farm. Indeed, the central question about technology is just this: "Can a material, industrial civilization be converted into a distinctive agency for liberating the minds and refining the emotions of all who take part in it?" [17] To understand the answer, one must reflect on the nature of work itself and on the manner in which it is presently being warped.

The Concrete Logic of Action

It is generally acknowledged that the concept of experience is pivotal in Dewey's thought and at the same time somewhat ill-defined. He himself once described the term as general in the sense of vague. For our purposes, however, it is enough to note that work, particularly manual work, is for Dewey a very archetype of experience. For experience, as he noted in *Reconstruction in Philosophy,* is primarily a matter of doing.[18] It is a transaction between the organism and its environment; a trade in which each gives and takes. In his old age, when he wanted to emphasize again how inseparably man and milieu are linked in these affairs, Dewey borrowed an image from an eighteenth-century writer. The cooperative union between the two factors, he said, is like that between a fiddler and his fiddle in a fiddling.[19] Along with the insight here, there is perhaps some danger of blurring important distinctions in the enthusiasm for interrelatedness. As long ago as the fifth century B.C. a certain Epicharmus of Syracuse, examining the phenomenon of flute-playing, concluded that while the flute player is one who has mastered the instrument, "he himself is not his craft, but is the craftsman." Doubtless Dewey would have been less interested in this distinction between flute and musician than in their inseparability in actual music making. And in any event, human work is the best illustration of what he had in mind when he wrote, "that human life itself, both severally and collectively, consists of transactions in which human beings partake together with non-human things of the milieu along with other human beings, so that without this togetherness of human and non-human partakers we could not even stay alive, to say nothing of accomplishing anything." [20]

What makes work so significant is the precise character of the "doing" it involves. When a man works, he uses tools. Indeed, this capacity to make and use tools is fundamental, Dewey remarks, without raising the question of whether or not it really supposes an even more basic capacity. But to approach nature with tools, that is to say, instrumentally, is to open oneself to a transaction or experience of unique educative value. We are forced then to discover a basic principle of pragmatism, *viz.,* that "a thing is more significantly what it makes possible than what it immediately is." [21] The philosopher of classical tradition is the man who wants real knowledge, to be sure, but who goes about getting it in a self-defeating fashion. He imagines that he can understand the world by sitting back and studying it. For him, "the life of observation, meditation, cogitation, and speculation pursued as an end in itself is the proper life of man" and he condemns all practical, industrial activities as taking time from these loftier pursuits and unfitting man for the noble life since "means are menial, the serviceable is servile." [22] All this is the fatally delusive attitude of those misled by their quest for the wraith of certainty. Worthwhile knowledge is, on the contrary, scientific knowledge and its proper objects are exactly "nature in its instrumental characters." [23] The world that Darwin discovered is a world in which man makes his evolutionary climb by learning to handle tools; to use and read signs; to note the "sequential bonds in nature"; to say to himself, "If I do thus and so, this or that will follow," and hence to concern himself not with fancied forms but with the relationships of real means to real goals. Good intelligence simply *is* practical, workman-like intelligence. Its method is the pragmatic method of science which proceeds by hypothesis, test and observation. Now it was in work that man was first introduced to this method and compelled to observe and record nature's doings. If you want to find out something, said Dewey in a celebrated passage of *Democracy and Education,* you have to *do* something to things, you have to alter conditions. As a universal principle this has the effect, of course, of abolishing all questions not susceptible of solution through manipulation of material factors. But it is true that this is the chief avenue to practical knowledge for workmen. If one wants to know whether a chemical fertilizer will produce better results than animal manure (the example is Dewey's), he must experiment with both. Men at work are obliged to think pragmatically and to concern themselves with final causes, for to ask what a thing can do is to ask about its purpose and to be preoccupied with purpose is to be preoccupied with action for finalities.[24]

It is the very nature of a tool, in fact, to relate workmen to external things and activities as the hammer points towards nails to be driven or the plow towards soil to be turned. Work has, then, an outstanding intellectual value for it teaches what Dewey called in *The School and Society,* "the concrete logic of action." It cultivates the instrumental mentality and hence enlarges our store of meanings since "the character of intellectual meaning is instrumental." What does *chair* mean—something to sit upon; what does *cart* mean—something for hauling other objects.[25]

However, a great deal of modern industrialized work has unfortunately interfered with the achievement of these proper intellectual gains. For one thing, mechanization has become too complex to be readily understood and so workers cannot easily appreciate the concretization of science and the incarnation of pragmatic method in the processes which they uncomprehendingly share. A century ago when machines were relatively rudimentary and one could grasp imaginatively the whole procedure carried on in a small shop, people really did learn by doing. The work of the home, the farm or the factory was an authentic vocational education for everyone could see quite clearly how the products of his effort were the consequences of his activity. People perceived the means-ends relationships; they thought instrumentally and hence constructively and correctly. Nowadays, the men working in one corner of a great plant have little idea what goes on next door. Since they cannot understand the work process in which they have a key part they brace themselves to perseverance by the thought of their wages. Yet this unsatisfactory situation is not inevitable. It is hard to deal with, certainly, because when a task of manufacture is divided among many people no one of them, apparently, can hope to realize the joys that were once the solitary craftsman's as he did the whole job himself and thus understood and accomplished the total process from start to finish.[26]

Nevertheless, industrial operations today do represent the application of advanced engineering techniques and the discoveries of physics, mathematics, chemistry and bacteriology and therefore they "have infinitely greater intellectual content and infinitely larger cultural possibilities than they used to possess." [27] In fact, this theme of the mutual enrichment of science and work is not only common in Dewey but also basic to his whole scheme for humanizing industrial occupations. These occupations share with scientific enterprise the pragmatic methodology and just as science made progress once its implications for everyday life, for material devices and technological operations, were appreciated, so work, in turn, was wonderfully enriched once it was made scientific through mechanization. Science found its true experimental method by picking up, generalizing, and purifying the characteristic technique of work. Then, in gratitude, science liberated work from its former chancy condition and opened new perspectives for men at their occupations. Automation, for instance, gives the worker added leisure even while he is on the job for it can free his mind for a "higher order of thinking" and for thought upon other topics.[28] If his schooling has taught him to relish the scientific and social significance of his work, the hours at the machine will be intellectually rewarding. "There is nothing in industrial production which of necessity excludes creative activity . . . if men understand what they are about, if they see the whole process of which their special work is a necessary part, and if they have concern, care, for the whole, then the mechanizing effect is counteracted. But when a man is only the tender of a machine, he can have no insight and no affection; creative activity is out of the question." [29] Those whose education has not prepared them for such understanding will "inevitably sink to the role of appendages to the machines they operate." [30]

But a submersion of that sort will mean not only intellectual but also ethical loss for when work is all it should be, it is a prime shaper of character as well as of intelligence. There are three reasons for this. In the first place, work illustrates that basic bond between action and understanding which is one of the great and fundamental emphases in Dewey's philosophy. But just because work is a situation of this sort, calling for thought, choice and action it is pre-eminently a moral situation for the realm of choice is the realm of morality. Secondly, the supreme ethical ideal is itself that of a man alert and devoted to social interests such as those which work implies or nourishes. "There is an old saying to the effect that it is not enough for a man to be good; he must be good for something. The something for which a man must be good is capacity to live as a social member so that what he gets from living with others balances with what he contributes." [31] But work is always, save in bizarre cases, a cooperative enterprise ordered to social ends. Consequently, no better context can be found for drawing out men's social virtualities than that of sound work. Its moral value, Dewey said in *Democracy and Education,* lies in its development of sociality through its involvement of men in common, shared concerns. Christians will not deny that, for as one theologian has remarked, even when rivalries and greed have introduced inhibiting abuses, men at work must at least fraternize and that is the beginning of fraternity.[32]

Finally, Dewey would maintain that the method of valid ethical thinking is just that instrumental method which work inculcates and embodies. In his work a man is obliged to attend respectfully to the concrete conditions which the laws of matter impose on anyone who wants to exploit its resources for the upbuilding of individual and social existence. He must be concerned not only for the goals he seeks but equally so for the means to achieve them. But there is a special moral value in being obliged in this way to take matter seriously, to take finalities and instruments seriously. For the good society, as Dewey understood it, is a secularized Heavenly City, a social milieu which not only contributes to the comfort and health of its members but to their decency, creativity, and fraternal sense of responsibility. The good education is that which forms citizens for such a society. "For the ultimate aim of education is nothing other than the creation of human beings in the fullness of their capacities. Through the making of human beings, of men and women generous in aspiration, liberal in thought, cultivated in taste, and equipped with knowledge and competent method, society itself is constantly remade, and with this remaking the world itself is re-created." [33] The machinery for the production of this good society and these good citizens includes first-class schools, sound political institutions and social agencies together with expanding cultural opportunities at home and enlightened foreign relations abroad. But none of these things come by revery; only by carefully detailed action, since any policy is but the adjustment of apt means to the ends sought. The ideal of contemplation of eternal truths without reference to change and practice is "morally irresponsible estheticism." By contrast, work is just that kind of courageous practical activity which seeks its ends not by invoking luck or magic, not by sermonizing but by taking into reflective account the particular goals possible under these particular material conditions and the precise tools which will realize them. Work always requires a man to entertain a "whole" view which will embrace both ends and means. The carpenter approaches his materials with the aim of understanding the uses to which they can be put. For genuine advance in morals we must approach life in its problematic setting much the same way. "Education and morals will begin to find themselves on the same road of advance that say chemical industry and medicine have found for themselves when they too learn fully the lesson of whole-hearted and unremitting attention to means and conditions—that is, to what mankind so long despised as material and mechanical." [34]

But at this point we discover a good deal of work in our industrialized society failing again, failing this time to contribute to ethical maturation because it has been accidentally corrupted. Our economic and social life, for instance, as well as the education which prepares for it, is organized around and motivated by the ideal of self-regarding individual success. This naturally frustrates the socializing potential inherent in industrial activity, a potential that would be reduced to actuality were the individualistic accent to be supplanted by motivations derived from a sense of social purpose and service. The most powerful force for shaping character is always the social medium in which people live. Were that medium one of "unified action for the inclusive end of a socialized economy," clear ethical benefits would follow. For this would be a form of social organization "in which the new forces of productivity are cooperatively controlled and used in the interest of the effective liberty and the cultural development of the individuals that constitute society." [35]

The value of this socialized economy would consist in the fact that it gave individual workers a hand in assigning goals and selecting means and consequently called upon them to exercise their powers of pragmatic thought. But since any situation requiring this sort of thinking is, for Dewey, an ethical one, the workmen would find themselves morally matured in the very process of their labor. Like Marx and many other observers, Dewey noted that work experience is sadly impoverished when the workers do not themselves define its ends. They are engaged, too often, in an activity which divorces means from ends and instruments from what they achieve. The result is loss of interest, loss of the ethical insight which comes from a concrete appreciation of sequential bonds, loss of any sense of creative reward. Even the most routine or "humble" work, Dewey seems to say, can be idealized if one understands how it contributes to desirable social and cultural outcomes. Even the man who mops up and disinfects the lavatories after the day shift has left the plant, might get some satisfaction from the realization that his job in a small way helps the wheels of industry turn. And if those who direct industry from the front office were to guide it not towards profits but towards the construction of a more humane society for all, then both they and the lowly sweep would have the deeper satisfaction of regarding their work as, proximately or remotely, an application of means to the procurement of admirable human consequences.

One cannot help but see in this idealism, as so often in Dewey, the traces of that Protestant morality which nurtured him as a boy. For this glorification of occupations in terms of spiritual results has a real affinity with Luther's own theology of vocation which saw in the meanest callings, Providence's will for those who were following them as well as a prime vehicle of redemptive obedience to that will. For Dewey, to be sure, this spiritualization of work is not accomplished in terms of devotion to a personal, transcendent God. Yet he does not hesitate to describe the naturalist's devotion to social welfare as "religious" and even to use the word *God* as a symbol for the union of actual with ideal toward which that naturalist strains.[36] It is clear that if work life fails to support this sort of intellectual development and moral insight, because workers are little more than wage-earners, the situation appears more damaging in the perspective of instrumentalist ethics than it would be within that of Christianity where values are not simply promising tool-solutions to specific problems rising in the social context. Christians have not, however, been insensible to the harm done human personality when men have no voice in the direction of their own labor enterprise. Both Pius XI and Pius XII commended the modification of the wage contract by a partnership contract which would, as the former put it, permit workers to become "Sharers in the ownership, or the management, or in some way participate in the profits." [37]

Finally, in addition to its value for intellectual and moral growth work ought also to be esthetically satisfying. Yet here too, the "spiritual factor" seems crowded out in the contemporary industrial world. For Dewey, the artistic quality of an experience lies partly in the fact that while it points toward the future it also has certain elements making it enjoyable here and now. Many of his readers are left, in fact, with the strong impression that this theory of art is actually an attempt to re-enforce a weakness in his general philosophy. For it has often been remarked that the strong futuristic strain of that philosophy effects a devaluation of the present moment which appears to be esteemed chiefly for its role as a means of insuring better experiences tomorrow. By stressing what Geiger calls the consummatory aspects of Dewey's philosophy of experience, it is hoped that this objection will be effectively outflanked. Howsoever that may be, Dewey does seem to have admitted that the instrumentalist mentality which sees in nature only material for manipulation and control tends to be hard and aggressive and could do with some enlargement and softening by an injection of the esthetic attitude of enjoyment of things. "Surely there is no more significant question before the world," he wrote, "than this question of the possibility and method of reconciliation of the attitudes of practical science and contemplative esthetic appreciation." [38] This is one more aspect of the problem of modern technological work. The general tenor of Dewey's response to that problem is already clear but some concluding details may be added.

Reconstruction

Our over-all estimate of the technological revolution of the past few centuries ought to be, Dewey thought, basically favorable. That movement was a positive gain for reasons already indicated. It has resulted in greater control of natural forces and this, in turn, has meant greater possibilities of actualizing ideals. When men have been freed from the brute fear of starvation they have time for "the more gracious question of securing to all an ample and liberal life." [39] And in the essay from which this phrase is taken, Dewey goes on to observe that the industrial movement, itself the offspring of science, has restored to its central position in morals that very labor which the Greeks despised. This is its rightful position, not only because work develops the social dimension of individual personality and cultivates the habit of pragmatic thinking so significant for ethical life, but also because it creates the conditions needed for consistent moral behavior. It is axiomatic that political democracy succeeds best where an industrialized economy makes possible a relatively wide diffusion of ownership. But the moral value of democracy both as a political form and as a style of life lies in its gift of freedom with the consequent increase of opportunities for those responsible choices which mould men. By enlarging the area of that freedom, industrialism contributed to democratic advance. Dewey was certainly not unaware of the enslaving elements in our culture—the characteristic bondages imposed by assembly-line work or the pressure for conformity exerted by mass society. But he would doubtless have pointed out that these are less painful than the yokes borne by most people under slave or serf economies. Besides, current evils can be diminished if attacked intelligently. Broadly speaking, then, industrialized work experience can humanize those it employs because it is the actual and epochal application of instrumental, scientific knowledge and has highly important social uses. The precise problem is really that of releasing these intellectual, moral and esthetic potentials.

For that purpose one will certainly need a new theory and new practices. All the old philosophies, according to Dewey, were formed in and by the prescientific, predemocratic and pretechnological civilizations whose patterns they rationalized and reflected. But now that life has become scientific, democratic and industrialized, fresh values have emerged and we cannot expect that theories which articulated that old order should serve to intellectualize the new.[40] Experimentalism is the philosophy that will do that since a number of its main theses are especially useful for elaborating a new philosophy of work geared to the realities of a technological age. To begin with, two historic antitheses must be eliminated, *viz.*, that between theory and practice and that between ends and means in the sense of a distinction between fixed, absolute values good in themselves and nowise instrumental on the one hand, and certain practical, sheerly utilitarian activities on the other. It must be recognized, instead, that economic activities are, in their own order, quite as intrinsic, final and capable of idealization as anything else while all the so-called ideal ends are trivial unless *their* instrumental aspect is appreciatively understood.[41]

Dewey was suspicious of the opposition between theory and practice on both epistemological and social grounds. It was Aristotle, he thought, who had erected that caste division on the false supposition that the more solitary and self-sufficient an activity can be, and the less it has to do with practical affairs, the nobler it is. This makes philosophical contemplation supreme. For Dewey, on the contrary, the more an activity engages men cooperatively and the more significantly it is enriched by and enriches practice, the better. To his way of thinking, the solitary philosopher behaves undemocratically and unintelligently. His aristocratic isolation is as deplorable as his ignorance of the fact that theory and practice ought to fecundate one another. The history of science ought to have taught him how a borrowing of the technics of industry made possible advanced experimentation with the consequent invention of new theoretical constructs themselves. One may, indeed, distinguish two kinds of pragmatic inquiry: that whose concern is to know for the sake of knowing as in pure scientific research, and that whose concern is to know for the sake of advancing the necessary affairs of the work-a-day world.[42] But in both cases the knowledge is of the instrumental character of nature, not of essences. If work is to be fully redeemed, that sharp dualism of theory and practice must be scotched for it supports the mischievous notion that truly worthwhile pursuits are those that beguile leisure. Such a conviction naturally militates against efforts to enhance the prestige of work. Once it is understood that all authentically human activity means an interplay of theory and practice and that any honest means to an honest goal is as honorable as the next, we shall have gone a long way toward establishing the true dignity of human labor.

The positive side of the new theory will be familiar enough. Its basic interest is ethical. What is needed, said Dewey over and over again, is a new "scientific" morality which will harmonize rather than clash with the scientific character which already marks our culture. To realize this new morality we must enlarge our habit of instrumental thinking so as to construe not only nature but all human affairs in instrumental terms. So far as nature goes, this means mechanico-physical terms. So far as a moral problem like the humanization of technology goes, it means devising through operational inquiries a set of practices aimed at getting the most out of two reserves of this technological work—its distinctive mechanized process and its distinctive exaltation of the collective and cooperative character of contemporary industrial enterprise.

These practices are disposed into a three-step program. First, improve or "reconstruct" education. This will lead to a social reconstruction and that, in turn, to a reconstruction of work experiences so that the individual will become, to use a striking metaphor of Dewey's, an alembic through which the entire content of the funded social experience passes. This movement from school to society to occupations is not to be understood rigidly. The improvement of education, for instance, might itself be expedited by certain social enlightenments. But by and large the main flow of progress will be in the direction indicated.

Reconstruction of education is not at all a matter of accenting vocational or trade preparation. It means, indeed, the introduction into elementary schooling (which was the only level Dewey discussed in detail) of many characteristic work processes: hammering, sawing, folding, cutting, weaving and modelling. But the educator's aim will be to "utilize active and manual pursuits as the means of developing constructive, inventive, and creative power of mind." [43] He does not worry, therefore, if the school shops perform by hand the operations which industry itself has mechanized. The instrumental relationship of means to ends will be better grasped by a young child in these more rudimentary processes and hence formation in habits of operational thinking will be more surely secured. In after years, too, he will better appreciate the machine for knowing what operations it has absorbed. Older children can have direct experience, also, of scientific methods in the control of materials and processes in the laboratory and this too will contribute to the formation of "industrial intelligence." The more understanding of science a person has, the more rewards he can draw from technology confronted either at gainful work or in hobbies at his own tool bench. In all the school projects which prepare for such insight, there must also be decided emphasis on individual initiative and on personal selection of the aims, discovery of the solutions and execution of the plans devised. For this will introduce children to those inventive aspects of manual activity which are so valuable. It may also be wise to note here, that these work activities are not intended as the whole of the elementary school program. The traditional learnings will also be included although they may be acquired in a rather non-traditional fashion.

The school's purpose is not fulfilled, however, simply by drawing out the intellectual content of those social occupations which embody scientific gains and procedure. More vital still is the ethical dimension. "All education," said Dewey in the closing lines of his most celebrated educational treatise, "which develops power to share effectively in social life is moral." The work projects in school do this because they are group projects. But this is not all that must be done. The school should also emphasize the application of science more to social than to sheerly industrial ends. To put it naively: the building of public parks, theatres or hospitals is preferable to swelling dividends; thought and effort expended on care for the commonweal is preferable to the canniest administration of private capital. The school, of course, has no concern for economic profits and so it can easily underline these social values of responsibility and cooperativeness which anyone needs who would work willingly in a group but which industry at present neglects. Science, said Dewey, is not fulfilled until it issues in the management of affairs. But purely industrial objectives are the least of these. It is in socio-ethical affairs that the most valuable applications of scientific mentality and morality should be felt. He consequently expects the school to educate children to an appreciation of the "socialized disposition," or what he once called "state consciousness." [44] This state consciousness is weakened by any system of economic segregation which sharply opposes capital and labor as well as by a predatory, individualistic conception of economic life itself. The educator should, therefore, "aim at such a reorganization of existing schools as will give all pupils a genuine respect for useful work, an ability to render service, and a contempt for social parasites whether they are called tramps or leaders of 'society.' " [45] The wider objective of this training is, besides, to prepare for the eventual supplantation of "feudal" control of industry by "democratic."

Dewey himself often insisted that social idealism of this sort is, if not a religion, at least religious. And actually this whole concern for orienting technology toward service of the political community suggests not only that the work process is, after all, fully intelligible only when subserving goals beyond itself but also that this objective of a sacral idealism is the chief among those goals.[46] It is the dominant vision of that lay religion which Santayana once declared Dewey's philosophy to be. As if to restore, too, the other half of the ancient twofold ministry of work, Dewey would also direct it to the service of art. That is to say, he would enrich technology by drawing out its own inherent resources for esthetic satisfactions. After all, "Tools and their using can be directly enjoyed." [47] Once you have discovered the intelligible pattern of beginning, sequence and climax in your occupation, the process itself will be pleasurable and artistically nourishing. If a generation became accustomed to relishing this fulfillment in the work activities of school projects they would not permit themselves to be cheated of similar joys in the occupations of adult life. From the reconstruction effected by the school, therefore, one might expect a parallel social reconstruction.

The full details of that social reconstruction would involve all the lines of Dewey's social philosophy and there is no place to epitomize that here. It may be remarked, though, that the aim it envisions is that of progressive democratization of every level and phase of American life. This requires, as one of its catalysts, getting as many people as possible united in the attack on concrete problems through free inquiry. Dewey was convinced that intelligence had failed to manage social issues with anything like the success achieved by science, precisely because it had not made parallel applications of scientific method to those issues. His own political theories, though, have rather dissatisfied not only his critics but some of his friends because they seemed to deal more heavily in generalizations than in clear-cut policies. It is well known that he opposed the old-fashioned brand of liberalism which defended a *laissez-faire* economy in the name of freedom; that he advocated "planning" for a society that would be "socialistic" or, if that word has Marxist overtones, a "collectivistic democracy," and that he advised repression of any rebellious minority which would refuse to go along with these changes.[48] But aims so broad might be specified to their own satisfaction both by the Right and by the Left.

In *Liberalism and Social Action,* Dewey argued for such a purification of society as would result in its institutions affording to all the accumulated resources of social intelligence. This is unexceptional but still quite abstract. It is somewhat clarified by a recommendation and an analogy. The recommendation is for the creation of a civic organization in which the economy has been so socialized that each individual can lay hold for himself of "the accumulated wealth of mankind in knowledge, ideas and purposes," of the whole social intelligence incarnated in the machinery and institutions of his culture. It is a situation analogous to that of a mechanic of ordinary gifts who by mastering the pyramided skills in his own métier has expanded one phase of his intelligence beyond the point reached even by a genius several centuries ago.[49] Although he was not a Marxist, Dewey shared some of Marx's characteristic convictions and dreamed of a political community in which the destruction of economic caste barriers would make it possible for all citizens to enjoy the educative experiences involved in the direction of community affairs, the control of industry and the use of the fruits of the sciences and the arts.

This program seems rather uncertain, however, when applied to the specific problem of humanizing technology. It is easy enough to see that direct participation in public affairs was an educative experience which the citizens at a New England town meeting enjoyed and the slaves of the ante-bellum South did not. One readily understands that a civilization which provides workers with leisure for concerts and games in public parks, for hours with the books from the public library or before the pictures in the public gallery, is a more civilizing environment than nineteenth-century Manchester if it is brought about without damage to personal freedoms. But then one does not need to be an experimentalist to admire and defend all this. The instrumentalist does make distinctive comments on how to manage industrialized work so as to make it a humanizing medium but his recommendations are not wholly convincing. The invention of the telephone and the locomotive certainly stimulated the minds of their discoverers and, says Dewey, those who use these inventions now should derive certain similar benefits. If our economy were so reorganized that workers in the factory felt the same sense of freedom and responsibility as does the man using tools in his own home for his own purposes and if, in addition, they had the same scientific understanding of their machines that the original inventors had, then the stultification supposedly inseparable from mechanized work would be largely dissipated. If, besides, excessive individualism—characterized by Dewey as the setting up of human beings as "individuals" doing business on their own account—were to be superseded by the ideal of the individual as the "organ of corporate action," without delimitation of liberties, then all the phases of associative living would provide the ethical satisfactions which accompany a life of service.[50] Perhaps so. Thus far at least these hypotheses have never really been tested.

*   *   *

In September 1952, a few months after Dewey's death, Sidney Hook wrote a brief memoir of him for *Commentary*. Among other things, he recalled that Dewey used to grow irritated with those who wanted to absorb his insights into their own philosophical system. They should rather, he thought, adopt the basic Deweyan philosophy and then fit their particular intuitions into that. This reaction is understandable but Dewey must also have known, to take a single instance, that Christians will find naturalism fundamentally unacceptable. At the same time, many of Dewey's insights and analyses can awaken Christians to a renewed appreciation of certain virtualities in their own world view. His case for technology, pervaded as it is by perceptive and generous convictions, is an illustration in point. Dewey's serious reverence for the resources of our temporal life and for its natural setting will not seem unreasonable to those who recollect the primeval commission: "Increase and multiply and fill the earth, and make it yours . . ." (Genesis 1, 28). Nor will his insistence on the vital relationship between doing and knowing seem strange to those who remember the words: "He who does the truth comes to the light." (John 3, 21). And if it cannot be said that Dewey solved the great problem preoccupying him, *viz.,* that of unfolding and developing individual persons in terms of their social capacities and vocation—at least he recognized it, which is more than some twentieth-century descendants of Renaissance humanism have done. Here too, then, he may serve to remind Christians of one of the imperatives of their faith: "Each one looking not to his own interests but to those of others." (Phil. 2, 4).

NOTES

1. John Dewey, "The Obligation to Knowledge of God," *The Monthly Bulletin* of the Students' Christian Association of the University of Michigan, 6 (November 1884) 24.
2. The theme of philosophy's origin out of the context of current problems is pervasive in Dewey's thoughts. The phrases used in the text here will be found in *Reconstruction in Philosophy* (Enlarged edition; Boston: The Beacon Press, 1948) v-vi and *The Influence of Darwin on Philosophy: And Other Essays in Contemporary Thought* (New York: Peter Smith, 1951) 274. These books first appeared, respectively, in 1920 and in 1910.
3. Pius XII, "Christmas Eve Address: 1953," *The Catholic Mind,* 52 (March 1954) 176. The original text of this discourse is in *Acta Apostolicae Sedis,* Ser. II, XXI (1954) 5-16.
4. The attack on excessive separation of means from ends is another dominant motif in Dewey's writings. For the interpretation of this and similar distinctions as historical in origin see *Democracy and Education* (New York: Macmillan, 1916) 292-305.
5. *Individualism—Old and New* (New York: Minton, Balch, 1930) 96. This entire book bears upon the topics studied here. It is concerned with what Dewey called "the deepest problem of our times," *viz.* "the problem of constructing a new individuality consonant with the objective conditions under which we live." *Ibid.* 32. The two chief of these new conditions, it is further argued, are the corporate character of our civilization and the industrialization of our work. Both must be put to the service of the American democratic ideals of equality and freedom. Machine power may, at present, be harnessed "to the dollar rather than to the liberation and enrichment of human life," but this is neither a necessary nor an irremediable situation. *Ibid.* 96.
6. See the appendix, which is by Dewey alone, in John Dewey and Arthur F. Bentley, *Knowing and the Known* (Boston: Beacon, 1949) 314.

7. See the chapter, "Common Sense and Science," which is by Dewey in *Knowing and the Known*, 285.

8. Hannah Arendt, *The Human Condition* (Chicago: University of Chicago Press, 1958) 300. This unusually rich and subtle book is critical of much about modern technology. Its theses are insightful and brilliantly developed but not always completely persuasive. Consider, for instance, the notion that an activity is to be denominated *work* and a noble type of fabrication if it produces durable rather than consumptible goods. On that reckoning, the toil of the gangs that built the pyramids ought to count as *work* rather than as its supposed inferior, *labor*, although most people would consider it to have been slavish in the extreme. Or suppose that one decides to call *labor*, any painful and arduous fabrication and to distinguish it from the more humane activity of *work* on the basis of the physical exertion involved. In that case the efforts of Michelangelo under the Sistine roof ought to count as labor rather than as *work*. It may be argued that the elements common to both hard toil and creative production are at least as significant as the distinction pressed by Miss Arendt and entitle both to be subsumed under *work*.

9. "What I Believe," *The Forum* 83. (March 1930) 178. This essay is included in Albert Einstein *et al.*, *Living Philosophies* (New York: Simon and Schuster, 1937) 21-35.

10. John Dewey *et al.*, *Creative Intelligence* (New York: Holt, 1917) 13.

11. *Reconstruction in Philosophy*, ix.

12. "What I Believe," *op. cit.* 176 and also in *Living Philosophies*, 21.

13. *Reconstruction in Philosophy*, 72.

14. L. Malevez, "Deux théologies catholiques de l'histoire," *Bijdragen* 10 (1949) 237-38, quoting and commenting on passages from Henri Bergson, *Les deux sources de la morale et de la religion* (Paris, 1932) 242, 334.

15. Another recurring theme in Dewey's social philosophy. For a typical instance see, *Human Nature and Conduct* (New York: Holt, 1922), 122-24.

16. *Democracy and Education*, 234-35.

17. *Individualism—Old and New*, 124.

18. *Reconstruction in Philosophy*, 86. See also *Democracy and Education*, 163: "When we experience something we act upon it, we do something with it; then we suffer or undergo the consequences. We do something to the thing and then it does something to us in return: such is the peculiar combination."

19. "Common Sense and Science," in *Knowing and the Known*, 286, n. 8.

20. *Ibid.* 271. For the sentence from Epicharmus see Kathleen Freeman, *Ancilla to the Pre-Socratic Philosophers* (Cambridge: Harvard, 1948) 35, n. 3.

21. *Experience and Nature* (rev. ed.; New York: Norton, 1929) 128. For the comments on the importance of man's tool-making capacity see the whole fourth chapter of this book and also *Reconstruction in Philosophy*, 71-2.

22. *Democracy and Education*, 259-96. Dewey must have liked his homonymic pun for he repeated it in *Experience and Nature*, 124: "Means are menial."

23. *Experience and Nature*, 137. The phrase epitomizes one of the book's chief themes.

24. *Ibid.* 121-23 and also *Democracy and Education*, 321; *Reconstruction in Philosophy*, 71-2.

25. *Experience and Nature,* 128. See also *Democracy and Education,* 168.
26. For this analysis of the difficulties accompanying modern mechanization see *Education and the Social Order* (New York: League for Industrial Democracy, 1949) 4. This is the reprint of a pamphlet first published in 1936.
27. *Democracy and Education,* 367.
28. *Ibid.* 304. For the interconnections between work and science see *Experience and Nature,* 128 ff., 150 ff. and "Common Sense and Science," in *Knowing and the Known,* 280.
29. *Human Nature and Conduct,* 143-44.
30. *Democracy and Education,* 367.
31. *Ibid.* 417.
32. *Ibid.* 234-35 for Dewey's comment on the socializing nature of work. For the theologian's view see André de Bovis, "Le sens catholique du travail et de la civilisation," *Nouvelle Revue Théologique* 72 (April 1950) 365-66.
33. "Philosophy and Education," in Paul Arthur Schilpp (ed.), *Higher Education Faces the Future* (New York: Liveright, 1930) 282. This passage shows that Dewey's formulations could sound, at times, quite traditional—almost any educational theorist could subscribe to the broad aims enunciated here.
34. *Reconstruction in Philosophy,* 73. For the analogy of the carpenter and the indictment of irresponsible estheticism see *ibid.* 114-17. See also the whole fourth chapter of *Experience and Nature.*
35. *Liberalism and Social Action* (New York: Putnam, 1935) 91, 54. For the need of building up the motivating force of social ideals see also *Education and the Social Order,* and *Individualism—Old and New.*
36. *A Common Faith* (New Haven: Yale, 1934) 53.
37. Pius XI, "Encyclical on Restoring the Christian Social Order" (*Quadragesimo Anno*) in Joseph Husslein, S.J. (ed.), *Social Wellsprings:* II: Eighteen Encyclicals of Social Reconstruction by Pope Pius XI (Milwaukee: Bruce, 1942) 202. See also Pius XII, "Address to Catholic Employers: Address to 400 Delegates to the Ninth International Congress of the International Union of Catholic Employers, assembled at the Vatican, May 7, 1949," *The Catholic Mind,* 47 (July, 1949): "Why should it not be allowable to assign to the workers a just share of responsibility in the establishment and development of the national economy?" 446.
38. *Reconstruction in Philosophy,* 127. The description of the scientific attitude as having something hard and aggressive about it is found here.
39. "Intelligence and Morals," *The Influence of Darwin on Philosophy,* 58. In *Individualism—Old and New,* 29-30, Dewey wrote: "The world has not suffered from absence of ideals and spiritual aims anywhere nearly as much as it has suffered from absence of means for realizing the ends which it has prized in a literary and sentimental way."
40. *Reconstruction in Philosophy,* xxxvi-xxxix and 1-27; *Democracy and Education,* 294-98.
41. *Reconstruction in Philosophy,* 171-72.
42. "Common Sense and Science," in *Knowing and the Known,* 281-85. See *Experience and Nature,* 151: ". . . certainly in many cases the pursuit of science is sport, carried on, like other sports, for its own satisfaction."
43. "Learning to Earn: The Place of a Vocational Education in a Comprehensive

Scheme of Public Education," *School and Society,* 5 (March 24, 1917) 334. See also *The School and Society* (rev. ed.; Chicago: The University of Chicago Press, 1915), *passim.* A succinct summary is this from *Democracy and Education,* 231: "The problem of the educator is to engage pupils in these activities in such ways that while manual skill and technical efficiency are gained and immediate satisfaction found in the work, together with preparation for later usefulness, these things shall be subordinated to *education*— that is, to intellectual results and the forming of a socialized disposition."

44. "Religion and Our Schools," *Education Today* (New York: Putnam, 1940) 78-9. This essay first appeared in *The Hibbert Journal* for July, 1908.

45. "Learning to Earn," 334.

46. For the term *sacral* as a characterization of any system, theistic or not, which proposes some theory of ultimates, I am indebted to Charles Donahue, "Secularism," *Social Order* 5 (January 1955) 18.

47. *Experience and Nature,* 128: "Fortunately for us is it that tools and their using can be directly enjoyed; otherwise all work would be drudgery." And, on page 151, "Making and using tools may be intrinsically delightful."

48. *Liberalism and Social Action,* 87. See also George Raymond Geiger, "Dewey's Social and Political Philosophy," in Paul Arthur Schilpp (ed.), *The Philosophy of John Dewey* (New York: Tudor, 1951) 337-68. It is Geiger who calls our attention to the phrase of Max Lerner, "democratic collectivism," which appears also applicable to Dewey's system.

49. *Liberalism and Social Action,* 52-53, 54, 69-70.

50. For the description of individualism see Dewey, "Common Sense and Science," in *Knowing and the Known,* 285-86, n. 3. The phrase, "organ of corporate action," is from the essay, "The Problem of Knowledge," in *The Influence of Darwin on Philosophy,* 297.

VI

Dewey's Ambivalent Attitude Toward History

THOMAS P. NEILL

Thomas P. Neill is a professor of history at St. Louis University, the institution from which he obtained both his undergraduate degree and the doctorate. His studies at Notre Dame University led to his Master's degree. His field of interest is modern European history with special emphasis on the cultural and intellectual history of the late eighteenth and nineteenth centuries. He has a long list of distinguished books as well as a string of articles in both the popular and the scholarly Catholic periodicals to his credit.

Although John Dewey never treated history extensively in any single work,[1] he consistently used history in his attempt to reconstruct philosophy, and he can even be said to have given the "new history" of James Harvey Robinson, Charles Beard, and Carl Becker a philosophical foundation. Dewey was interested in history not for its own sake, but for the light he thought it threw on present problems and as a method of inquiry that was for social problems what the scientific method was for physical problems.

Something like half his writing is historical in character, and it reveals him to be widely though not always accurately informed about the past. Dewey received formal training in history when he took courses in the subject under Herbert Baxter Adams at Johns Hopkins University in the early 1880's. Moreover, in his early career he taught courses in the

145

history of philosophy, and he continued throughout life to write about many figures in the history of philosophy.

Dewey and the "New History"

The New History was the title of a book of essays published in 1912 by Dewey's close associate and admirer, James Harvey Robinson. In this work Robinson inveighed against the accumulation of useless information and against merely political and military history. Robinson's underlying thesis was that history is justified only if it helps solve present problems. "The one thing that it [history] ought to do, and has not yet effectively done, is to help us to understand ourselves and our fellows and the problems and prospects of mankind." Robinson complained that "the present has hitherto been the willing victim of the past; the time has now come when it should turn on the past and exploit it in the interests of advance." He also proposed the then revolutionary idea that history must "alter its ideals and aims with the general progress of society and of the social sciences." [2] Dewey had made this point several times before Robinson's essay on the "new history" appeared. In 1909, for example, he wrote: "Whatever history may be for the scientific historian, for the educator it must be an indirect sociology—a study of society which lays bare its process of becoming and its modes of organization." The aim of the study of history is "a deepening appreciation of social life." [3]

Robinson had collaborated with a younger colleague, Charles Beard, to publish *The Development of Modern Europe,* a two-volume text appearing in 1907 and 1908, in which the principles of the "new history" were followed. In 1908 Dewey combined with James Tufts to publish their *Ethics.* The similarity between these works, as Morton G. White has observed, "is remarkable. It appears not only in the attempt to combine history, theory, and practice, but also in the conception of the problems which faced the world in 1908. The last chapter of Robinson and Beard dealt with 'some of the great problems of today,' very much as Dewey and Tufts concluded their work with the world of action." [4]

The "new history" was given its classic expression in two presidential addresses to the American Historical Society: "Everyman His Own Historian" by Carl L. Becker in 1931, and "Written History as an Act of Faith" by Charles Beard in 1933.[5] Becker and Beard maintained that past events are meaningless until known or experienced by the historian or the reader, and in knowing an objective past event the knower contributes his own personal prejudices, principles, and presuppositions known as his "frame of reference" or "climate of opinion." One "cannot recall past events without in some subtle fashion relating them to what he needs or desires to do," Becker tells us. "In this sense all *living* history, as Croce says, is contemporaneous: in so far as we think the past (and otherwise the past, however fully related in documents, is nothing to us) it becomes an integral and living part of our present world of semblance." History, therefore, is an "imaginative creation, a personal possession which each one of us, Mr. Everyman, fashions out of his individual experience, adapts to his practical or emotional needs, and adorns as well as may be to suit his aesthetic tastes." [6]

Such a description of history, we shall see, could easily be attributed to Dewey. Although I have discovered no simple tutor-pupil relationship between Dewey and proponents of the "new history," similarities between them are striking. Both are hostile to what Dewey calls "the spectator view" of history and accept the instrumentalist view that the knower makes the truth rather than finds it. Both approach the past with the pragmatic purpose of subordinating it to present problems. Both agree that the changing present dictates a changing view of the past, and that the history written by each generation is true only for that generation. Both Dewey and the proponents of the "new history" present their argument psychologically, starting with the way an individual person recalls past autobiographical events, and then making the illicit transitions to folklore and to written history.[7] Moreover, both Dewey and the New Historians are more interested in social than in political history. "The men who invented the stationary and locomotive steam engine," Dewey wrote, "and the men who have since then harnessed both steam and electricity to all sorts of ends, have produced social changes by the side of which those produced by Alexander, Caesar and Napoleon are insignificant." [8] He was convinced that the only "living" or "dynamic" history is that which deals with social problems, with the way men master nature to enrich human life.[9] Robinson says essentially the same thing in *The New History,* where he inveighs against the "old" political history with its meaningless list of names, dates, reigns, and battles.

These similarities fall short of establishing Dewey's influence on the "new history." But we know that Dewey and Robinson were closely associated at Columbia University and in the New School for Social Research. Moreover, in his *Mind in the Making,* Robinson cites Dewey glowingly for his attack on classical philosophy, and he reveals his close

association with Dewey by quoting from the latter's essay on Darwin's
influence on philosophy shortly after its publication. Robinson gave one
of the addresses honoring Dewey on his seventieth birthday in 1929, in
which he acknowledges his indebtedness to him.[10] A study of the New
Historians' reliance on Dewey remains to be done, but the obvious evidence suggests that Dewey's instrumentalism and the "new history"
were two aspects of the same general intellectual development of the
first quarter of this century, that Dewey and the New Historians mutu-
ally influenced and supported each other, and that Dewey formulated
a philosophical apologia for the "new history" of which its proponents
were aware.

Dewey's Ambivalent Attitude Toward the Past

In many places Dewey has vigorously asserted the need for liberation
from the past, and yet many of his more substantial works deal with
thinkers of the past. His attitude toward the past is similar to Marx's:
he admired certain of its accomplishments as good for their time, but he
resented their champions not allowing them to die when they had performed their historical task. History comes naturally to man, Dewey
believed, for man is a creature who "remembers, preserving and recording his experiences." Indeed, nothing happens except as an echo
or reminiscence of what has gone before. This is man's distinctively human attribute. "Man differs from the lower animals because he preserves
his past experiences." [11]

Dewey frequently points out that the study of history is useful. One
of its greatest values is to liberate us from the past, an underlying thesis
in such studies as *Individualism Old and New* and *Liberalism and Social
Action,* and one stated bluntly in an early essay when Dewey told his
undergraduate readers that "if it takes a thief to catch a thief, it may
fairly be presumed that it takes a philosopher to catch a philosopher."
One must therefore study the origin of ideas in history, and "as we
draw them into the light of day, we free ourselves from them." [12] In
this same early article Dewey also suggested that some workable idea
or "neglected tool" might be found in the "storehouse of history" and
might be put to effective use in the continuing task of reconstructing
philosophy and society.

The greatest value accruing from the study of history is a practical
one—a conclusion which follows rigorously from the premises of
Dewey's instrumentalist theory of knowledge. An instrumentalist philos-

ophy must include a good knowledge of history, for "intelligent understanding of past history is to some extent a lever for moving the present into a certain kind of future." [13] Dewey believed that modern society differed from ancient in the way that each generation rewrites its history to obtain greater security and to control the present and the future. Social problems can be understood, and therefore resolved, only when they are put in their historical setting and studied genetically. In a brief essay on the social studies in 1938, Dewey observed: "It would probably be admitted on all hands that the present economic situation is a historical development, and that while present facts may be amassed in quantities, the information thus gained needs to be placed in an historic setting if it is to be intelligently grasped and used." [14]

Despite his concession that a knowledge of history is useful, Dewey is basically hostile toward the past and apparently afraid that history will be so studied as to become a hindrance to progress. Old ideas and ancient values persist long after social change has made them obsolete. "One of the main difficulties in understanding the present and apprehending its human possibilities," Dewey wrote in 1930, "is the persistence of stereotypes of spiritual life which were formed in old and alien cultures." [15] Eighteen years later, in his introduction to a new edition of *Reconstruction in Philosophy,* he similarly complained that any sound philosophical inquiry comes up against "the body of prejudices, traditions and institutional customs that consolidated and hardened in a pre-scientific age." [16] This is the past against which Dewey feels hostile, an attitude he voiced strongly as early as 1892 in the last sentence of his address to the Michigan University Students' Christian Association: "Remember Lot's wife, who looked back, and who, looking back, was fixed into a motionless pillar." [17]

Dewey's hostility toward the past resulted, then, from his belief that history imposes an intolerable burden on the present. He was convinced that advances in the scientific method and in industrial production had made the old ethical and metaphysical norms obsolete, and that the latter impeded both intellectual and social progress.

> If it [the scientific attitude] were generally applied, it would liberate us from the heavy burden imposed by dogmas and external standards. . . . It is the foe of every belief that permits habit and wont to dominate invention and discovery, and ready-made system to override verifiable fact. Constant revision is the work of experimental inquiry. By revision of knowledge and ideas, power to effect transformation is given us. This attitude, once incarnated in the individual mind, would find an operative outlet. If dogmas and institutions tremble

when a new idea appears, this shiver is nothing to what would happen if the idea were armed with the means for the continuous discovery of new truth and the criticism of old belief. To "acquiesce" in science is dangerous only for those who would maintain affairs in the existing social order unchanged because of lazy habit or self-interest.[18]

We may conclude that, although Dewey saw a value to the study of history, he was chiefly interested in studying it so as to free himself and his contemporaries from its imposition on our way of thinking, that he was interested in using history without being in any way burdened by it. Dewey would certainly have agreed with that Spanish dictum that history is a common meadow where everyone can make hay. The only justification for studying history, in his mind, was to make current hay, and this is the way he himself delved into the past.

Relationship of the Past and Present

Dewey had no interest in the past as an object of study in itself. To him the past as past was dead, devoid of interest, and unknowable. "If history be regarded as just the record of the past," he wrote, "it is hard to see any grounds for claiming that it should play any large role in the curriculum of elementary education. The past is the past, and the dead may be safely left to bury its dead. There are too many urgent demands in the present, too many calls over the threshold of the future, to permit the child to become deeply immersed in what is forever gone by." [19] He was interested in the past as a lever for controlling the present and the future, as we have seen, and he was therefore more interested in *how* things were done than *what* was done. As in philosophy, so in history Dewey was interested in epistemological and methodological problems rather than in being as such. His approach to both subjects was the same, and what he said of philosophy in 1892 can be applied to history: "The value of philosophy lies in its method, not in what it arrives at. . . . Philosophy as a method means interpretation of experience, or the full life of the race in all times and ages as far as we can get at it. . . . It does not create anything, but remakes what *seem* to be the facts. It remakes the facts *for us*. Any set of facts, in that sense, are never what they were before." In discussing the role of history in education, Dewey states that history is valuable for "teaching the *methods* of social progress." [20]

The study of history can reveal the main instruments in the discoveries, inventions, new modes of life, etc., which have initiated the great epochs of social advance; and it can present to the child types of the main lines of social progress, and can set before him what have been the chief difficulties and obstructions in the way of progress.[21]

Dewey condemned the "growing deification of history" among German scholars, but he admired the effective methods of research they had perfected so that "even mediocre men achieved respectable results."[22] Dewey believed that historical method was for the social sciences what the scientific method was for the natural sciences. The scientific method he considered "a method of inquiry so inclusive in range and so penetrating, so pervasive and so universal, as to provide the pattern and model which permits, invites and even demands the kind of formulation that falls within the function of philosophy."[23] Historical inquiry approximates this method for the social sciences. John Herman Randall, Jr., has aptly formulated this relationship in Dewey's thought:

> But if, as Dewey has learned from the social sciences, knowledge in general and science in particular are rather the ability of a society to do what it must and can, if they are primarily a matter of the intellectual methods whereby a culture solves its specific versions of the universal human problems, then the history of that culture and its problems, and the historical criticism of its methods of inquiry and application, become of the very essence of any philosophy with a claim to scientific inspiration. If science be an institutionalized method of trial and error, or, as James Harvey Robinson put it, of fumbling and success, then the trials, the errors, and the successes are equally instructive for the refinement and improvement and extension of scientific method, of experimentalism.[24]

In a long essay on "The Evolutionary Method as Applied to Morality," published in 1902, Dewey developed more fully than elsewhere the value of the genetic or historical method. His argument is that moral situations and values can be understood only in their historical development, that the experimental method in physical science is exactly duplicated by the historical method in social situations or morality. "I shall endeavor to point out," he tells the reader, "that there is more than analogy, there is an exact identity, between what the experimental method does for our physical knowledge, and what the historical method in a narrower sense may do for the spiritual region: the region of conscious values."[25]

Dewey believed that the value of the historical method lay in its centering, as experiment is supposed to do, on process rather than analysis, and therefore in studying antecedents and consequents as meaningful in terms of process. It is in this sense that he considers that history is "for the individual and for the unending procession of the universe, what experiment is to the detached field of physics." The historical method enables us to isolate any particular fact and to study it in terms of antecedents and consequents and thus to give us intellectual control over it. "Now," he concludes, referring to ideas and moral judgments, "when we see how and why the belief came about, and also know what else came about because of it, we have a hold upon the worth of the belief which is entirely wanting when we set it up as an isolated intuition." [26]

It is evident from what we have seen so far that Dewey subordinates the past to the needs and the interests of the present. This follows naturally from his interest in process and his concern with knowledge as power rather than apprehension of truth for its own sake. "In an experimental philosophy of life," he explains, "the question of the past, of precedents, or origins, is quite subordinate to prevision, to guidance and control amid future possibilities." [27] The past is also psychologically subordinate to the present, in Dewey's view, for the past as past is remote and dead. Its interest lies only in its connection with the present and its making the latter more understandable and more controllable.[28]

More important from the historian's and philosopher's point of view is Dewey's contention that the present dominates the past in such fashion as to reshape it each generation. As with philosophy, historical inquiry originates in a present problem which determines the purpose, the terms, and the direction of the inquiry. Moreover, the principles and conceptions prevailing at any given present time influence and color the historian's interpretation of what he finds in the past. And, "as culture changes, the conceptions that are dominant in a culture change. . . . History is then rewritten." [29] Thus as the present changes, Dewey holds, the significance of past events also changes. History will therefore "always be rewritten" since, "as the new present arises, the past is the past of a different present." [30]

Dewey treats what he considers the central problem of history in *Logic: The Theory of Inquiry:* since every act of knowing is a present act, we cannot really know the past. All the materials with which the historian works—manuscripts, inscriptions, coins and the like—have only present existence for the historian. He cannot know them in their past existence. From these materials he infers that past events happened, that certain values prevailed at a given time, that certain customs were practiced, and so on. Thus from the logical point of view history is never more than an inferential account of what seems to have happened.

Dewey's craving for unity and continuity affected his view of history and of the relationship between the past and present. Although in his *Logic* he sets up sharp cleavage between present and past, in other places he tends to merge them together. "The present is the true past," Dewey said in 1894. "It is the past in its fuller expression, in the revelation of its deeper meaning." [31] Dewey's idea of continuity excluded the possibility of "complete rupture on the one hand and mere repetition on the other." This craving for unity and continuity in history was an aspect of Dewey's hostility toward any dualism and any "spectator view" of historical knowledge, which, Dewey believed, implied a breach in the single continuous historical process. "The real existence," he writes, "is the history in its entirety, the history as just what it is. The operations of splitting it up into two parts and then having to unite them again by appeal to causative power are equally arbitrary and gratuitous." [32] Dewey's craving for unity did not lead him to the extreme "absolutistic block monism which, in behalf of the reality of relations, leaves no room for the discrete, for plurality, and for individuals." [33]

Dewey's demonstration that the present dominates the past and that the historian is in the historical process rather than viewing it from outside were valuable corrections to the nineteenth-century belief that history was truly "scientific" and that the historian can reconstruct the past with absolute objectivity and absolute verity. But Dewey was only one of many who rejected these extreme claims of Ranke's would-be followers. And in concentrating on such ancient and already discredited claims, Dewey overstated his case—although, of course, his views on history are consistent with his instrumentalist theory of knowledge. But the so-called "spectator view" of the historian-at-work does not assume that he views history with a time-glass from somewhere outside the historical process. It only assumes that there do exist things to be known—past events, institutions, persons, customs and so on—whose characters are not modified by the historian's cognitive processes. Historians are well aware that the present influences their search into the past, and they take precautions to remember this influence, to keep it in the open, keep it to the minimum, and make allowance for it. But few historians allow the present to "dominate" the past as Dewey thought it did. History as a meadow where everyone can make hay is the field of politicians, propagandists, and others. It is not the work of historians. While Dewey was making a good point against extremist claims of the so-called "scientific" historians, he fell into a trap of his own making in denying that knowledge of history has any function other than the instrumentalist function of controlling the present and plotting the future. Such a theory of knowledge logically reduces history to a tool in our intellectual engineer's work-kit for reconstructing and reforming society.[34]

History as a Method of Inquiry

In his *Logic* Dewey defines "history" as having two meanings. "History is that which happened in the past and it is the intellectual reconstruction of these happenings at a subsequent time." [35] This same distinction had already been made against a would-be objector to his advocacy of the historical method of studying moral values when he accused the objector of confusing "history as an objective succession of events with history as the rational account and interpretation of these events; history as bare fact and history as method." [36]

Dewey makes a further distinction between mere chronology or cataloging of events and history as an interpretative narration of past events. "Whatever deserves the name of history is more than an inventory of practices, beliefs, and opinions. It is concerned with the origin and development of these customs and ideas; and with the question of their mode of operation after they have arisen." [37] And again, thirty-six years later, Dewey wrote that "annals are material for history but hardly history itself." [38]

A final requirement of true history is that it have direction. "Since the idea of history involves cumulative continuity of movement in a given direction toward stated outcomes, the fundamental conception that controls determination of subject-matter as historical is that of a *direction* of movement." Changes acquire historical significance only "in terms of a direction *from* something *to* something." [39] The terms "from which" and "to which" are not in the nature of things, but arise from the purpose and problem of the inquiry. Thus for Dewey historical narration obtains one of its essential characteristics, its direction, from the present rather than finding it inherent in itself.

Dewey concedes in one place that objectivity is the ideal toward which historians should always strive. It is "a logical ideal which points the direction in which inquiry must move but which cannot be completely attained." [40] With this most historians would agree. They differ from Dewey as regards the degree of objectivity which is attainable. Dewey's view is practically identical with that of Becker and Beard who, accepting substantially the same theory of knowledge as Dewey, believed that every man must be his own historian and that history is an act of personal faith. Within the limits established by criteria of interpretation accepted by the craft of historians, they believe, each historian and each reader sees the past through personally distorted lenses. There is an objective past, they admit, but each historian will give his personal account of it just as each witness to an accident will give his personal version of what happened, depending on his point of view, his attentiveness, his accuracy of memory, and other subjective factors.

In the chapter on narration and description in his *Logic* Dewey offers a psychological account of history as a method of inquiry and narration, an account which reveals considerable psychological insight but suffers from his instrumentalist theory of knowledge. Thus he approaches historical narration as "an instance of judgment as a resolution through inquiry of a problematic situation." [41] He believes that "any and every historical inquiry about the course of the past events arises out of the need or desire to solve a problem or set of problems." [42] This contention is factually and psychologically unsound. As a matter of historic fact, many inventions and new ideas were not discovered because of social problems or needs, and many historical investigations have been started out of scholarly curiosity or "just to see what really happened." Good historians want to know what happened in the past, and more often than not they initiate an historical inquiry with no other purpose than discovering and explaining as well as they can what happened. The desire to know is a human characteristic which does not require a problem for its origin and development. Because Dewey thought of knowledge in terms of power rather than truth, he could not understand that historians frequently undertake inquiries without trying to "prove" anything or "clarify" a muddled question.

The first step in any historical inquiry, Dewey explains, is that of "controlled observations." Here he believes that historians and specialists in such auxiliary sciences as epigraphy and paleography have developed excellent techniques. These controlled observations furnish the material data for inferential constructions, which become what we call "history." But these data or controlled observations "are selected and weighed with reference to their capacity to fulfill the demands that are imposed by the evidential function. Consequently, they are relative to a problem. Apart from connection with some problem, they are like materials of brick, stone and wood that a man might gather together who is intending to build a house but before he has made a plan for building it." [43]

In describing the historian-at-work Dewey has reversed the first two steps of sound historical inquiry. He has described what the "historian" of a labor union or an automobile company might do if he were assigned the task of writing good advertising copy. But the good historian does not have the design of his house in mind—to keep Dewey's metaphor—before he gathers his bricks and wood. The design takes shape as the material is accumulated, sorted, and analyzed. To a certain extent the material imposes the design on the historian-builder, and to some extent, of course, it depends on the historian's abilities and aptitudes, as well as his theological, political, and other presuppositions. Dewey is right in insisting that each historian has a conceptual framework, whether he realizes it or not, but the whole bent of his writing—as with Robinson, Becker, and Beard—is to overweight this conceptual framework and to minimize the frequently overpowering role of the stubborn, and partly self-interpreting data. The followers of Von Ranke were naive in believing that history could be made as objective as physics, but Dewey's reaction to their naïveté goes too far in the other direction.

This leads to Dewey's claim—with which historians are in fundamental agreement—that written history is selective.

All historical construction is necessarily selective. Since the past cannot be reproduced *in toto* and lived over again, this principle might seem too obvious to be worthy of being called important. But it is of importance because its acknowledgment compels attention to the fact that everything in the writing of history depends upon the principle used to control selection. This principle decides the weight which shall be assigned to past events, what shall be admitted and what omitted; it also decides how the facts selected shall be arranged and ordered. Furthermore, if the fact of selection is acknowledged to be primary and basic, we are committed to the conclusion that all history is necessarily written from the standpoint of the present, and is, in an inescapable sense, the history not only of the present but of that which is contemporaneously judged to be important in the present.[44]

Dewey sees selection operating in a three-fold way: 1) by the people whose history is being written, for they have recorded some data for posterity and others they have obliterated; 2) by public memory, which retains some data and discards others; 3) by the historian himself. Therefore he concludes that "the notion that historical inquiry simply reinstates the events that once happened 'as they actually happened' is incredibly naive. . . . For historical inquiry is an affair (1) of selection and arrangement, and (2) is controlled by the dominant problems and conceptions of the culture of the period in which it is written."[45]

Conclusion

Dewey believed that all history could be divided into the prescientific age and the scientific age. He was incredibly naive in differentiating the way men lived, moved, thought, and had their being in the two ages. He was naive, too, in denying that any ideas or systems of thought could transcend the society in which they originated. This naive belief led him to consider the reconstruction of philosophy in the scientific age the most urgent task facing mankind.

In his own writing, Dewey practiced what he preached about history. In such works as *Individualism Old and New, Liberalism and Social Action,* and *Reconstruction in Philosophy,* Dewey uses history to explain how the present state of things came to be and to suggest solutions to present problems. And frequently his historical treatment of a subject helps considerably in clarifying the problem, as his showing the new form Liberalism took in the latter 19th century. In these works Dewey both uses and misuses history. Frequently his main theme is sound, and many of his insights into the significance of past events are penetrating. But the historian rightly complains that Dewey reads into the past what he wants to find to prove his thesis. Dewey seems not to have understood what ancient and medieval scientists did, for in his desire to make a strong case for the need of a new philosophy in the scientific age, he makes ancient and medieval science purely speculative and modern scientists purely empirical. A thorough study of the history of science shows that no such simple division is tenable.

This shortcoming is serious only on the presupposition that the historian's task is to discover and verify data about the past and then to use these data to reconstruct the past as accurately and completely as possible. If the historian had no obligation to the truth, as he does when he accepts the "spectator" view of knowledge, if the instrumentalist theory of knowledge were true, and if history were to be used only to elucidate present problems, then Dewey could be considered a good historian of ideas. For he labored many years in the meadow of intellectual history, and he cut much hay. In his works of an historical character, he offers many valuable insights which the historian cannot ignore. But neither can he accept them uncritically, inasmuch as Dewey's aim was intellectual power and control rather than truth—and we agree with him that an inquirer's purpose will set the limits within which he can consistently work. Because Dewey considered the past only as a lever to use in the present, both his writing about history and his use of history fail to achieve the end of historical research and writing—the discovery and elucidation of the truth about the past.

NOTES

1. Dewey's most important analysis of written history is Chapter 12 of *Logic: The Theory of Inquiry,* where he deals with the logical problem of inquiry into and narration of the past. He brings out the value of the "genetic" method in "The Evolutionary Method as Applied to Morality," *Philosophical Review,* 11 (1902), and he handles the problem of our knowledge of the past in his discussion with Arthur O. Lovejoy, "Realism Without Dualism or Monism," *The Journal of Philosophy,* 19 (1922). He also has a short article on the teaching of history, "History for the Educator," in the first volume of the short-lived *Progressive Journal of Education* (1909).

    Dewey's use of history is best seen in four well known works: *Liberalism and Social Action, Individualism Old and New, German Philosophy and Politics, and Reconstruction in Philosophy.*

    I have found only one study of Dewey's thought about history, the sympathetic treatment by Sidney Ratner, which relies heavily on Chapter 12 of Dewey's *Logic,* "Dewey's Contribution to Historical Theory," in the symposium edited by Sidney Hook, *John Dewey: Philosopher of Science and Freedom* (New York: The Dial Press, 1950). His relationship to the "new history" is indirectly presented in the excellent study of Morton G. White, *Social Thought in America: The Revolt Against Formalism* (New York: Viking, 1949).

2. James H. Robinson, *The New History* (New York: Macmillan) 17, 24, 25.
3. "History for the Educator," *The Progressive Journal of Education* 1 (March 1909) No. 5. 1, 2.
4. *Social Thought in Action: The Revolt Against Formalism* (New York: Viking, 1949) 55.
5. These addresses were published in the January, 1932, and January, 1934, issues of the *American Historical Review.* A reaction to the relativism of Becker and Beard quickly set in among historians, who, as a group, are not bothered by the epistemological problem of knowing a past event. See, for example, Samuel Eliot Morison's presidential address, "The Faith of an Historian," The *American Historical Review,* January, 1951, and Cushing Strout's recent *The Pragmatic Revolt in American History* (New Haven: Yale, 1958).
6. Carl L. Becker, *Everyman His Own Historian* (New York: Crofts, 1935) 242, 243.
7. See, for example, the first few pages of Dewey's *Reconstruction in Philosophy* and Becker's *op. cit.*
8. Essay entitled "Progress," in *Characters and Events* (New York: Holt, 1929) II 823.
9. See especially "History for the Educator," above, note 3, 1-4.
10. Published as "John Dewey and Liberal Thought," in *John Dewey: The Man*

and His Philosophy (Cambridge: Harvard, 1930). In this essay Robinson says of Dewey's *Reconstruction in Philosophy* that "there are probably no other 213 pages which cast so much light on the trail of past thinkers." (p. 155). Dewey's greatness lay, he believed, in weaning us from the "old body-mind ideas" and from "our old crude notions of morality." (p. 165).

11. *Reconstruction in Philosophy* (Boston: Beacon, enlarged edition of 1948) 2, 1.
12. "Why Study Philosophy?" *The Inlander* 4 (December 1893) 106, 107. This was one of Dewey's many minor publications at the University of Michigan in the last decade of the 19th century.
13. This point is well developed by George H. Mead, "The Nature of the Past," *Essays in Honor of John Dewey* (New York: Holt, 1929). Mead and Dewey were close associates at the University of Chicago and Dewey seems to have agreed with most of Mead's writing. In his essay in response to the essays mentioned above, Dewey puts Mead in the group with whom he agrees and who require no further discussion.
14. "What is Social Study?" *Progressive Education* 15 (May 1938) 367.
15. *Individualism Old and New* (New York: Minton, Balch, 1930) 149.
16. *Reconstruction in Philosophy,* xxxvi.
17. "Christianity and Democracy," *Religious Thought at the University of Michigan* (Ann Arbor: The Inland Press, 1893) 69.
18. *Liberalism and Social Action* (New York: Putnam, 1935) 156.
19. "History for the Educator," *loc. cit.*
20. *The Monthly Bulletin* xiv (January, 1893) 66. This was the journal of "The Relation of Philosophy to Theology."
21. *Moral Principles in Education* (Boston: Houghton Mifflin, 1909) 38.
22. *German Philosophy and Politics* (New York: Holt, 1915) 98.
23. *Reconstruction in Philosophy,* xxix.
24. "Dewey's Interpretation of the History of Philosophy," in Paul Arthur Schilpp (ed.), *The Philosophy of John Dewey* (2nd Ed. New York: Tudor, 1951) 83-84.
25. "The Evolutionary Method as Applied to Morality," *The Philosophical Review* 11 (1902) 113.
26. *Ibid.* 359.
27. *German Philosophy and Politics,* 127.
28. This point is most fully developed in a few pages from *Moral Principles in Education,* 36 passim., and in "History for the Educator."
29. *Logic: The Theory of Inquiry* (New York: Holt, 1938) 233.
30. *Ibid.* 239.
31. "Reconstruction," Address before The Students' Christian Association at Michigan University, published in *The Monthly Bulletin,* 15 (June, 1894) 155.
32. *Experience and Nature* (Chicago: Open Court, 1925) 275.
33. "Experience, Knowledge, and Value," Dewey's response to the essays in his honor edited by Paul Arthur Schilpp, *The Philosophy of John Dewey* (2nd Ed. New York: Tudor, 1951) 544.
34. Dewey's overstatement of the case in refuting the followers of Ranke is less justifiable coming in 1938 when their claims were no longer taken seriously by any competent scholars.

35. *Logic: The Theory of Inquiry,* 236.
36. "The Evolutionary Method as Applied to Morality," *The Philosophical Review* 11, 255.
37. *Ibid.* 355.
38. *Logic: The Theory of Inquiry,* 234.
39. *Ibid.* 238.
40. This is the only place I have found Dewey making this statement. All his writing tends in the other direction and, as regards history, casts doubt on the desirability as well as the possibility of attaining what most people regard as real objectivity.
41. *Logic,* 232.
42. *Ibid.* Also see pages 107-11 for a discussion of this point.
43. *Ibid.* 232-33.
44. *Ibid.* 235.
45. *Ibid.* 236.

VII

Process and Experience

ROBERT C. POLLOCK

Robert C. Pollock is Professor of Philosophy in the Graduate School at Fordham University. He holds B.S. and M.A. degrees from Harvard University, obtained his doctorate at the University of Toronto, and has taught at Bowdoin College and the University of Notre Dame. Coauthor with Don Luigi Sturzo of Del Metodo Sociologico *(1950) and editor of* The Mind of Pius XII *(1955), he has contributed essays and articles to various scholarly publications.*

An Incomplete Universe

We are hardly in a position to measure the full sweep of John Dewey's philosophical achievement if we isolate it from a whole new world which was rapidly taking shape before men's eyes. For the new world envisaged by men had extraordinary repercussions within consciousness, widening it in an unprecedented way and calling for an intellectual reorientation of a thoroughgoing sort.

John Dewey's philosophy is itself a powerful reminder of the intimate connection between the life of thought and the real-life situations which so vividly characterize the human story. And his philosophy contributes in no small way to an understanding of the way in which intellectual advances are bound up with crucial and vital experiences affecting the whole of life. Hence, it would betray extraordinary obtuseness to attempt an exposition of Dewey's thought without taking account of a fundamental transformation in human awareness which created a new cultural atmosphere and gave to consciousness itself a new orientation.

John Dewey's own words, written in his Foreword to a book dealing with what he calls the "Foundations of Pragmatism," leave no doubt as to how he would want us to deal with his philosophy. As he says, "One realizes the ineptitude of the method of pigeonholing classification of philosophical writings when one compares it with the method of placing them in the setting of a new and vital movement in culture which extends far beyond the confines of technical philosophy." [1]

A presentation of the cultural setting is beyond the scope of this study. Still, we feel bound to play up the cultural theme as much as possible in order to show that behind Dewey's philosophy lies a revolution in the world of thought, feeling and action. For unless we really get the "feel" of the new cultural movement, any attempt to interpret Dewey's philosophy will be confined to the surface of things. Yet what we want is a study in depth, one which will throw into relief the importance of Dewey's efforts in the face of an entirely new situation.

While touching on the cultural theme wherever possible, much will also be gained by placing before the reader the larger philosophical picture in which Dewey finds his place and which includes such figures as Peirce, James and Mead. While we can do little more than point to the larger picture, still even this should serve to keep attention focused on the dominant motifs which lead far beyond the domain of technical philosophy. Actually, the vision of things which alone gives meaning to Dewey's philosophical effort would be more surely grasped, could we broaden the scope of our study to include relevant matter from Royce and Whitehead. Still, the convergence of such differentiated minds as those of Peirce, James, Dewey and Mead bears witness to a rich experience shared in common, as well as to a common awareness of the need for a fresh appraisal of things.

What, above all, motivated these thinkers to inaugurate a fresh approach in philosophical thinking? In answering this, we can hardly do better than point to the new image of the universe which was taking shape in men's minds. In late medieval and early modern times man passed "from the closed world to the infinite universe." [2] Such a time of transition was crucial and fateful, and its repercussions within the depths of the human soul were immense. But we, too, are passing through a similarly crucial and fateful moment in history, for our picture of the universe is also undergoing a drastic transformation. Essentially, our own transition can be described as a passage from a complete to an incomplete universe, that is, to a universe in which the temporal dimension has come into its own, and with it the reality of growth and development.

Now this new image of the universe was especially congenial to Americans, for the whole American experience has made it second nature to take growth and development seriously. And in America the very notion of an unfinished world could stir men's souls and elicit the same sort of reaction which a great work of art can evoke in the very body of a true artist.

The need to reorient one's thinking in line with the new image of the universe was deeply felt by men like Peirce, James, Dewey and Mead. Hence, despite significant differences in their outlook, they yet managed to find a certain common ground in Pragmatism. Let us consider James and Dewey. No two men could be farther apart in essential genius and temperament, and even in sensitivity to different realms of experience. Yet they had no difficulty making common cause philosophically. Mead also stands out as an extraordinarily original thinker, especially in the crucial matter of interpersonal relationships. Nevertheless, he too, gravitated quite naturally to Pragmatism and for the reason that, like the others, he found the new image of the universe too challenging to be ignored. Or let us take Peirce. His scientific, metaphysical and historical interests put the stamp of universality on his thought. Here, surely, was a bold, soaring spirit who was not only in the vanguard of the modern discovery of the value of medieval Catholic thought, but who adhered to a metaphysics of a Platonic character. Yet it was he whom Dewey singled out as more than anyone else "the begetter in philosophy of an attitude and outlook distinctively American." [3]

We can appreciate the depth and power of Dewey's own particular response better against this background of an intense sensitivity to a new cosmic perspective on the part of brilliant minds. Indeed, so deep is this response to the new shift in cosmic awareness, that he can enter sympathetically into the earlier experience, when man passed from a closed world to the infinite universe: "One has only to read the authors of the transition period, say Giordano Bruno, to realize what a pent-in suffocating sensation they associated with a closed, finite world, and what a feeling of exhilaration, expansion and boundless possibility was roused in them by the thought of a world infinite in stretch of space and time. . . . That which the Greeks withdrew from with repulsion, they welcome with an intoxicated sense of adventure." [4]

It is important to note here that Dewey seemed unaware of the fact that Christianity changed the atmosphere of speculation with respect to infinity through its doctrine of an infinite creative God. The boundless universe of the Renaissance aroused deep emotion for the reason that men saw in it a more appropriate image of an infinite God. That is why the new picture of the universe was fashioned as much by poets, mystics and philosophers as by scientists. The old Christian vision of the world as a theophanic projection of divinity, a vision cherished in Augustinian and Pseudo-Dionysian currents of thought, was given a new cosmic shape. Hence it is not surprising to find a philosopher like Henry More celebrating the new universe as the production of a God of plenitude, Who creates with a lavish hand.[5]

If Dewey can describe with deep feeling an earlier change in cosmic outlook, it is surely because he himself knew what it means to find one's picture of the universe altered in a direction which leads to new frontiers in thought and experience. He, too, had been plunged into a new cosmic experience, and the world he gazed upon was "an open world, an infinitely variegated one, a world which in the old sense can hardly be called a universe at all; so multiplex and far-reaching that it cannot be summed up in any one formula." [6] To a mind as keenly perceptive as Dewey's this new view of an open world was bound to prove challenging in the extreme, as we can gather from the following words: "As against this common identification of reality with what is sure, regular and finished, experience in unsophisticated forms gives evidence of a different world and points to a different metaphysics. We live in a world which is an impressive and irresistible mixture of sufficiencies, tight completenesses, order, recurrences which make possible prediction and control, and singularities, ambiguities, uncertain possibilities, processes going on to consequences as yet indeterminate." [7]

Peirce likewise responded to the challenge of an open world, of a vast process in which we are all involved even down to our innermost feelings and instincts. But he insisted on relating that process to a personal God, creator of all, while seeking to render explicit a metaphysics which would enable us to accept this new world not only in our thinking but in the realm of conduct itself.

As for James, Santayana puts it concisely when he says that for James, "The universe is an experiment, it is unfinished." [8] And this great figure in the new philosophical movement understood the revolutionary implications of the new outlook, for, as he declared, "What we say about reality depends on the perspective into which we throw it." [9]

But what a drastic alteration in perspective when men can envisage a wide open world in which development, spontaneity and novelty are entirely at home! Here at last is a universe which no longer cramps man's style, a universe which makes it impossible for man to regard himself as "an unnaturalized and unnaturalizable alien in the world." [10]

Given this new image of the universe, experimentation and creativity are endowed with a new dignity, for they have gained a status within nature itself. Now looked on as essential aspects of a growing world, they speak with an authority to which man gladly responds. And indeed there are many today who feel a binding obligation to move along new and unexplored paths and to keep their minds open to new possibilities. Where the older imagination had been mastered by images conjured up by such notions as immobility, form and equilibrium, the new imagination is filled with images engendered by such notions as vital creative act, indefinite expansion, new horizons and breakthrough.

Thus was accomplished one of those decisive leaps which have marked human history, and which today we so easily visualize in thinking of jet-propulsion and nuclear fission. But the changes in man's life go deeper than these developments might indicate, for there has taken place a kind of 'nuclear fission' within the human soul itself. For if it can be said of earlier modern man that "The more imagination strove to grasp the astounding new universe, the more truly man realized his own potentialities. . . ." [11] how much more can it be said of the man of our own time!

In tracing the formation of the new image of the universe, we must give precedence, not to evolutionary theories, but rather to the burgeoning belief in linear and progressive history. True, this belief fostered a naive optimism concerning progress, but when this optimism is viewed in historical perspective, that is, when seen in connection with man's liberation from an ancient and depressing way of looking at things, it can be regarded with some indulgence.

Evolutionary theories gave to the notion of development a new standing in man's thinking by bringing him face to face with the most radical sort of change imaginable, since, as Dewey says, potentiality now means "the possibility of novelty, of invention, or radical deviation. . . ." Hence, even if evolutionary theories seemed at first to favor a naturalistic philosophy, they nevertheless assured victory to a developmental point of view as against an outlook which regarded the movement of things as "only the monotonous traversing of a previously plotted cycle of change." [12]

Due to evolutionary theories, the sense of an irreversible time was immeasurably deepened, and human history was viewed against the background of a process which includes the entire universe. In this way, there was formed a consciousness dominated by the idea of patterns and processes within an all-enveloping scheme. Consequently, we now feel so deeply implicated in a vast process that it is almost second nature to situate every human act, including the act of knowledge, within a temporal dimension.

Dewey observes that the first marked cultural shift in the attitude toward change took place in the late eighteenth and in the nineteenth centuries. "Under the names of indefinite perfectibility, progress, and evolution, the movement of things in the universe itself and of the universe as a whole began to take on a beneficent instead of a hateful aspect." [13] Where in early modern times only a mere handful of individuals could envisage a future different from the past, now great numbers of people were focusing their energies on a future viewed with expectancy and passion.

Change, Dewey tells us, was installed at the very heart of things by Bergson and William James, although they were animated by different motives and followed different methods.[14] But it is with the name of James that Dewey associates the idea of an open and incomplete universe. As he says, "and long after 'pragmatism' in any sense save as an application of his *Weltanschauung* shall have passed into a not unhappy oblivion, the fundamental idea of an open universe in which uncertainty, choice, hypotheses, novelties and possibilities are naturalized, will remain associated with the name of James; the more he is studied in his historical setting, the more original and daring will the idea appear." [15]

Elsewhere, writing of James, Dewey says this: "It may perhaps seem strange to the layman to learn that a new and vital movement could be launched in philosophy by insisting upon novelty, plasticity, indeterminateness, variety, and change as genuine traits of the world in which we live." Yet it looked as though men were not quite ready for so thoroughgoing a shift in viewpoint, for, according to Dewey, it took all of twenty years before James found an audience who responded to what Dewey describes a few lines further on as "his spirit of adventure into the unknown." [16]

How much James's world-view meant to Dewey himself can be seen in his vigorous defense of James against the rather strange accusation that he lacked a *Weltanschauung.* Dewey might have called attention to the fact that James himself had declared that the most important thing about a man is his view of the universe. However, he insisted that a *Weltanschauung* was present in "the idea of a universe which is not all closed and settled, which is still in some respects indeterminate and in the making, which is adventurous and which implicates all who share in it, whether by acting or believing, in its own perils. . . ." Moreover, he adds, it was "not only a *Weltanschauung,* but a revolutionary one." [17]

Dewey then goes on to say that even James's literary style was influenced by his leading idea. And, let us add, not only his literary style, but the very quality and range of his perceptiveness, to which his style is so strikingly adapted. For James's spontaneity of spirit could thrive to the uttermost in a universe which involves "a muddle and a struggle, with an 'ever not quite' to all our formulas, and novelty and possibility forever leaking in." [18] If he experienced a release of the spirit, it was because he faced a universe in which his most personal feelings were no longer alien presences. As Dewey puts it: "Are judgments in terms of the redistribution of matter alone valid? Or are accounts of the universe in terms of possibility and desirability, of initiative and responsibility, also valid?" [19]

In writing about the modern shift in attitude toward change, Dewey also tells us that a systematic assertion that reality is process had to wait until the twentieth century. Here, Whitehead of course, appears as the chief figure on the philosophical scene. However, we should not forget that in his great work, *Process and Reality,* Whitehead expresses his indebtedness to Dewey as well as to Bergson and James.[20]

In view of this new image of the universe, nothing could prevent a radical reconstitution of man's conscious and unconscious relations to his world. We can be sure that a new turning point in history has been reached when a philosopher can affirm that genuine time is all one "with the creative, with the occurrence of unpredictable novelties," [21] and when, again, he rejects the view that Reality is "neatly and finally tied up in a packet without loose ends, unfinished issues, new departures . . ." [22]

The more we widen our perspective on history, the more certain we become that Dewey was speaking with an authoritative voice on behalf of something new that was bursting forth within human consciousness, namely, the conviction that nature has its revolutionary as well as its conservative aspect. Dewey gave expression to this in a conception of nature which validates to the limit man's impulse to venture into the unknown. "Man," it is said, "has introduced the theme of a destiny which is open, ahead of him, directed toward the unforeseeable and the infinite, to replace a concept of a destiny already fixed, which he had, as it were, only to copy with application." [23] But it was Dewey along with others in the pragmatist movement who made a truly philosophical and disciplined response to this new theme of an open destiny, and in a bold pioneering spirit.

Granting that Dewey's 'time' suffers impoverishment in being detached from that which lies beyond time, he still has much to convey concerning a life that is lived within time and in full acceptance of the reality of process and development. "We always live at the time we live and not at some other time," [24] says Dewey, and, for him, this also means accepting the fact that our temporal moment finds its place in an ongoing process.

Unhappily, he seemed to be obsessed with the idea that belief in eternity lends itself to the survival of an attitude of antipathy to a world of changing things. And, doubtless, there are facts that would seem to justify his attitude. Yet the truth of the matter is that Christianity effected a radical transformation in the very structure of consciousness in creating a fruitful interplay between spiritual life and historical activity. But, obviously, such a transformation does not run its course in one generation or in a hundred generations, and even now we are feeling its effects more than at any other time in the past.

At any rate, we can applaud Dewey's statement that an "Eternity that is permitted to become a refuge from the time in which human life goes on may provide a certain kind of consolation. But emotion and comfort should not be identified with understanding and insight, nor with the direction the latter may supply." [25] Again, we can approve of Dewey's conception of a religious faith, which, in attaching itself to the possibilities of nature, would be manifesting "piety toward the actual," [26] a piety which, let us add, would engender an attitude which elsewhere he describes as "an imaginative insight into the possibilities of what is going on so assuredly although so blindly and crudely." [27]

A Real Future

The psychological gap between our own attitude to time and a much older mentality which barely tolerated time, is very great. In fact, the gap is more like a yawning abyss. Until we become intensely aware of it, we are hardly in a position to do full justice to Dewey's philosophy. Let us, then, consider for a moment this difference of attitudes.

If we take archaic man first, it would seem that he hardly lived in time at all, for real events were stripped of their time-character by being relocated within a mythological framework. From start to finish, his life was a sequence of repetitions, based on the archetypal actions and gestures which formed the substance of his myths. In short, he lived his life within a fixed pattern of behavior which nullified real time-experience.[28]

But even in the great cultures of East and West, the reality of time was brought into question through the device of the infinitely recurring cycle. The example of Aristotle is particularly instructive here, for, despite his profound concern to preserve intact the reality of change, his account of the universe is lacking in historical significance. And the cyclic mentality is evident in his statement "that the same opinions recur in rotation among men, not once or twice or occasionally, but infinitely often." [29] While some notion of a linear progressive evolution was present in the Greco-Roman world, it was associated with a rather bleak outlook. Besides, it made hardly a dent in the ancient way of life. The cycle view predominated, testifying, as it does, to a steadfast refusal on the part of man to accept himself as a historical being.

Christianity changed all this. And it is to St. Augustine that we turn, for it was he who asserted the temporalism of creation, while laying the foundation for a metaphysics of contingency and process. As to the ancient cycle theory, he declares that if it could not be refuted by reason, "faith would still smile at these argumentations." [30] Without showing how effectively St. Augustine broke with the ancient cycle mentality, it is enough to say that in him we clearly discern the figure of the new man arising, the new man for whom the course of events in time is characterized by the appearance of genuine novelty.

Naturally it took time for the new structure of consciousness to become operative in life. Habits persisting through eons of time are not easily broken. And even though the sense of history was installed at the apex of the Christian soul, it had yet to permeate the whole of man's being and even his feelings. Actually, it was not until the modern age that man began to feel at home in time, and to think in terms of a linear and progressive conception of history. Continuous time has become fully real, even when periodicities within social and cultural phenomena are recognized. Moreover, men are learning to look at history as developing according to internal principles. That is to say, they are now able to conceive the reality of an immanent process, even if, in the religious view, there can be no truly immanent process without a creative, transcendent principle.

Another great figure in the American pragmatist movement, Mead himself, expresses an attitude which is diametrically opposed to that of the ancients: "This present [that is, every actual present] is the scene of that emergence which gives always new heavens and a new earth. . . ." [31] The Biblical note struck by the phrase "new heavens and a new earth" is revealing, for it shows how thoroughly Christianity has molded our very language, in transforming our vision of history. Mead recognized the part played by Christianity in destroying the timeless universe of the ancients, for as he says, "St. Paul and Augustine ushered in the history of the world. . . ." [32]

But what we should note particularly is that with Mead, as with the great pragmatist thinkers, there was an earnest attempt to remain close to experience. As Dewey says, Mead's thinking "springs from intimate experiences, from things deeply felt, rather than from things merely thought out by him. . . ." And, Dewey adds: "He *felt* within himself both the emergence of the new and the inevitable continuity of the new with the old." [33] Thus, Mead's use of the phrase "new heavens and a new earth" was inspired by an attitude toward history which permeated his whole being, including his very feelings.

The contrast between our own situation and that of the ancients is spectacular. In his Meditations, Marcus Aurelius writes that the soul comprehends that "those who come after us will see nothing new. . . ." [34] But Whitehead has this to say: "I wish I could convey this sense I have of the infinity of possibilities that confront humanity— the limitless variations of choice, the possibility of novel and untried combinations, the happy turns of experiment, the endless horizons opening out." [35]

There is no doubt that we gain much-needed perspective in projecting the pragmatist movement against the background of our cultural and spiritual heritage. But we should not overlook the role of America in bringing to a head what is implicit in our religious heritage. In discussing the development of American pragmatism, Dewey makes the point that "the progressive and unstable character of American life and civilization has facilitated the birth of a philosophy which regards the world as being in continuous formation, where there is still place for indeterminism, for the new, and for a real future." "But," he adds, "this idea is not exclusively American, although the conditions of American life have aided this idea in becoming self-conscious." [36] Elsewhere, in quoting another author, Dewey calls attention to the fact that the American people had to do "with the unprecedented, the hazardous, the unpredictable . . ." He has no hesitation, then, in pointing to the similarity between the personal private experience of William James whereby his thought was nurtured, and "the free responses of the American people to the American scene." [37]

In America, as nowhere else, the notion of an unfinished world was indelibly fixed in the mind by everyday experiences. And an experimental temper was given free rein in an atmosphere formed by the belief in a wide-open future. Here at last was formed a mentality which in important respects represents the maturation of Christian consciousness. Certainly it is as different from the mentality of pre-Christian man as anything can be. How natural it was, therefore, that philosophers should appear who were resolved to take at full value what has been called the gift of Christianity, namely, the notion of a universe "opening out onto an irresistible adventure." [38]

Today, what Dewey calls the "universe of experience," as the precondition of the universe of discourse, has expanded into a very striking pattern. The settled boundaries of an older world have melted into an infinite horizon, and the historical drama exerts an irresistible fascination on man. Man is on the very threshold of a full acceptance of time and history, and his attitude is well expressed in the characteristically modern statement that history is "that in the 'direction' of which we have necessarily 'to be' under pain of not being at all." [39]

"The future rather than the past dominates the imagination," [40] says Dewey. And because, in a truly temporal world, the mind must ever face forward, he hails the pragmatic intelligence as the intelligence which is alone adequate to change, transformation and novelty. Moreover, in asserting that "a pragmatic intelligence is a creative intelligence, not a routine mechanic," [41] he is expressing the modern feeling for creativity in the face of an infinity of unrealized possibilities.

Given historical perspective and a sense of the unfolding human drama, one cannot resist the thought that thinkers like Peirce, James, Dewey and Mead were responding to a powerful trend within the depth of history itself. At least their thinking was well within the stream of history, and like all truly historical thinking that bears the stamp of genius, it faces forward to a future whose possibilities we cannot foresee.

In order to grasp to the full the inner motivation of the pragmatist movement, let us consider for a brief moment this new sense of an open future as it expresses itself within the world of the writer and the painter. A Catholic scholar, comparing Renaissance writers with modern writers, has this to say: "what was lacking to the Renaissance, from the twentieth-century point of view, was a sense of literature as exploratory, as facing into the unknown. A Gertrude Stein or a James Joyce, tinkering with the very structure of language to see what new and unexpected beauties it could be made to yield, would be rather unthinkable to the age of Colet and More, or even to that of Donne and Herbert. The notion that literature had before it indefinitely expanding horizons, and the related notion that the business of the writer was a kind of 'sincerity,' an objectivity in reporting which could lead to the discernment of issues previously unattended to or occluded, was hardly present."

The writer of these lines is fully aware that the Renaissance developed a sense of history, although "this sense was largely a feeling for perspective regarding the past," for, as he says, "There was little sense of the forward movement of history, of the present as a point on a trajectory traveling off into a future whose precise shape we do not know." It is true, of course, that already in the 17th century we find the beginning of linear and progressive views of history. But he is concerned with literature, and not with the development of such views. Continuing, he writes: "There is a feeling for what literature was or had been, not for what it might become or was becoming." Then he draws the conclusion: "The feeling for the future was defective, for the old pre-Christian cyclic view of history had never been effectively exorcised from men's minds." [42]

In our own day we find writers experimenting with word arrangements freed from associations derived from habitual and conventional ways of looking at things. They are experimenting with language so that it may become a better vehicle of expression, and, indeed, they are offering us subtle perceptions of reality quite new to man, opening new vistas of literary and poetic achievement.

Painters, too, are experimenting imaginatively and boldly with their medium, seeking new and more self-sustaining aesthetic experiences and fired with the conviction that in the arts there are no closed frontiers.

Dewey was concerned to give a larger meaning to whatever appears within the world's process, for, as he saw it, everything has its cosmic status. Having naturalized Hegel, this was the best he could do. But, just the same, the Hegelian vision of history had left its mark on him. Hence his powerful conviction of a great processual scheme, a cosmic drama, in which each individual plays his part. Indeed, in Dewey, there is the belief that each individual, so far from being a mere 'point' closed within himself, is woven into a vast and all-inclusive process, a process which is directed to "consequences yet indeterminate."

An All-Embracing Drama

Although Dewey's own premises do not leave room for the notion of the universe as an ethical drama, the notion, nonetheless, seems to hover in the background of his thinking. This sense of an ethical drama, cosmic in scope, was not at all foreign to the pragmatist movement. Peirce most certainly had it, and could give it free reign because of a metaphysics which takes us through Hegel right back to Christian traditions of thought. Thus he was able to view the entire cosmic process as an unfolding of God's purpose, and could even insist on linking living thought with a self-effacing love for the world.[43]

Dewey had little patience with such notions as universal progress or the inherent rationality of the universe. No one, it is true, could be more insistent than he on the fragmentary character of the world, its precariousness and its limitations. Yet it would seem that he himself was moved by a profound conviction of purpose at the heart of things that went beyond what his own philosophical premises would allow. Otherwise, how can we account for his view that the Golden Age lies ahead of us and not behind us;[44] and what meaning are we to assign to the following: "When we have used our thought to its utmost and have thrown into the moving unbalanced balance of things our puny strength, we know that though the universe slay us still we may trust, for our lot is one with whatever is good in existence." [45] Here, too, as in Mead's words, cited above, we find a Scriptural echo even if "naturalized."

Dewey, it would appear, was constrained to think about the world and its process in terms reminiscent of a religious tradition. Besides, his naturalism has elements which, so far from closing the door on religious feelings, can quite easily stir them up. After all, terms like 'faith' and 'piety' sprang readily to Dewey's lips, bearing witness to the persistence of a spiritual influence. And is it not likely that Dewey's feeling of being an active participant in a cosmic drama was the flowering of an irrepressible Biblical attitude in a mind which made a tremendous effort to take time seriously?

In placing Dewey's doctrine of experience in its proper context, it is necessary to hold before the mind the larger scheme in which the individual is rooted, and which, of course, must always be looked at as dynamic and processive. It is not to be wondered at, therefore, that Dewey was taken up with totality as well as with individuals, and with wholes as well as with parts and elements. In fact, his philosophy represents a form of consciousness which seeks to actively include within itself the whole universe. And, as we shall see, the very development of human experience is made possible by man's power to see events and objects within relational contexts which can expand to infinity.

Dewey's concern with the totality in which we live and have our being is evident when he calls attention to the fact that we sense "an enveloping and undefined whole" [46] which, in his view, springs from the feeling-part of man's nature and is nurtured by the imagination. This totality, or infinite whole, has been described by one writer on Dewey as the "all-embracing drama of life in its totality." The same writer is also communicating Dewey's outlook when he describes one's sense of inclusion in the universal drama as "a feeling of the wholeness of existence, as a 'history,' of the all conceived as a drama in which the individual has a part to play." [47]

"We are never wholly free," says Dewey, "from the sense of something that lies beyond." "We are, as it were, introduced into a world beyond this world which is nevertheless the deeper reality of the world in which we live our ordinary experiences. We are carried out beyond ourselves to find ourselves." Again, he writes: "We are citizens of a vast world beyond ourselves and any intense realization of its presence with and in us brings a peculiar satisfying sense of unity in itself and with ourselves." [48]

Dewey looked on a work of art as playing a key role in raising to clarity this sense of an enveloping whole. Since he seemed to regard an integrative immediacy as the aim of all developing experience, it was natural for him to play up the aesthetic experience. Actually, he considered it to be the "most direct and complete manifestation of experience as experience," [49] inasmuch as "esthetic experience is experience in its integrity. . . . For it is experience freed from the forces that impede and confuse its development as experience; freed, that is, from factors that subordinate an experience as it is directly had to something beyond itself." Hence the conclusion: "To esthetic experience, then, the philosopher must go to understand what experience is." [50]

If "the sense of an extensive and underlying whole is the context of every experience . . ." [51] we can see why Dewey regarded integral and integrating experiences as indispensable, above all, to the thinker. For a person untouched by the imaginatively engendered idea of "a thoroughgoing and deep-seated harmonizing of the self with the Universe (as the name for the totality of conditions with which the self is connected) . . ." [52] would hardly be in a position to think relevantly or vitally about anything. If the thinker plies his occupation it is because "he is lured and rewarded by total integral experiences that are intrinsically worth while." [53] Indeed, were he deprived of such experiences, he would not even know what it is to think and would be at a loss in trying to distinguish between real thinking and its imitation. It would seem, then, that from first to last, the thinker who is truly integrated in the universe is sustained by this primordial experience of the wholeness of existence. Or as Dewey puts it, "through the phases of perturbation and conflict, there abides the deep-seated memory of an underlying harmony, the sense of which haunts life like the sense of being founded on a rock." [54]

In this connection, it is interesting to note that Justice Holmes read Dewey's *Experience and Nature* and was impressed by the author's cosmic sense, for it seemed to him "to FEEL the universe more inwardly and profoundly than any book I know, at least any book in philosophy." [55] Coming from Holmes, this was high praise, since he too had a robust sense of the cosmic position of things, the law included. And in a tribute to him, Dewey took care to single out a passage of Holmes's which amply bears this out.[56]

Man Lives Forward—Experience is a Temporal Process

In the universe of Dewey, it is impossible to look upon man as an inert static being. If the whole of nature is in process of development, why should man be exempt, either in his thought or in his experience? Consequently, knowledge cannot be regarded as sundered from the process of man, the process by which his life is sustained and evolved in history. Nor can experience itself be thought of as having boundaries definitely ascertained and fixed once and for all. And we realize at once the truth of this when we consider the mighty convulsions within ex-

perience which have rocked history. It was Dewey's highly developed
awareness of an expanding experience within history which explains why
he could look upon the history of philosophy as "a chapter in the development of civilization and culture," while advocating that the story
of philosophy be studied in connection with anthropology, primitive
life, the history of religion, literature and social institutions.[57]

The preoccupation with process and development on the part of the
pragmatists threw into sharp relief the reality of an expanding experience, and, in addition, brought the realm of thought closer to the
experiential concrete. As James says: "The *full* facts of cognition, whatever be the way in which we talk about them, even when we talk most
abstractly, stand inalterably given in the actualities and possibilities
of the experience-continuum." [58] Manifestly, James spoke as one who
saw the world freshly, and who was fully aware that henceforth thought
must be viewed in its organic relation to the living, growing tissue of
experience.

Although the emphasis on concrete experience was entirely congenial
to James and Dewey, it was of course a broadly cultural phenomenon.
Justice Holmes expressed this new feeling for the concrete when he
affirmed that "The life of the law has not been logic: it has been
experience." [59] And today most of us look at things in pretty much
the same way, as, for example, in our preference for a deeply experiential rather than a merely abstract treatment of various matters.
Thus a study of the Greek mind or the Medieval mind does not appeal
to us nearly as much as the more revealing account of the Greek
experience or the Medieval experience. Even with respect to doctrines
like materialism or atheistic humanism, we feel we have failed to gain
depth in evaluating them until we come up against the actual experiences
with which historically they are bound up. A merely abstract confutation
leaves us cold.

While both James and Dewey raised their voices on behalf of the
rights of experience, James was much more thoroughgoing insofar as
he opened himself to a realm of experience beyond the bounds of the
visible world. Hence his observation that "our natural experience . . .
may be only a fragment of real human experience." [60] However, on the
horizontal plane, Dewey was most assuredly a pioneer of the first order
in opening wide the perceptive aperture on aspects of experience which
had been ignored.

"Faith in the possibilities of experience" [61] is a leading motif of
Dewey's philosophy. And here he is in complete accord with James,

whose attitude is stated by Perry when he says, "Whereas according to the traditional view experience *has* spoken, according to James experience has yet to speak. . . ." [62] Dewey could also speak with dedicated seriousness of "intellectual piety toward experience" as a "precondition of the direction of life and of tolerant and generous cooperation among men." Again, the same feeling for experience is expressed in the following passage: "If what is written in these pages has no other result than creating and promoting a respect for concrete human experience and its potentialities, I shall be content." [63]

Despite important differences in their approach to experience, James and Dewey throw a good deal of light on each other. So that when we set out to study Dewey, we should also apply ourselves to the study of James. Thus, something of the spirit of Dewey comes through to us when we see how supremely alert James was to the possibilities of experience. Or when we learn from James that experience does not come to us merely through the five senses but through "the total push and pressure of the cosmos," and in the white heat of moral action. Or when James insists that experience makes demands on us that we must fulfill if we are to remain within the path of our own experiential development. In short, James can deepen our appreciation of Dewey's desire to promote a respect for concrete human experience, and particularly for experience in its fresh and novel features. For no one was more open than he to the "effervescence of novelties" which "form the authentic stuff" of every person's biography, and no one was more ready to lend an ear, as Santayana says, to all sorts of persons, even cranks, quacks and impostors.[64]

James and Dewey certainly supplement each other with respect to experience taken as a process. "According to my view," says James, "experience as a whole is a process in time. . . ." Or as he says further on, "Our fields of experience have no more definite boundaries than have our fields of view. Both are fringed forever by a *more* that continuously develops, and that continuously supersedes them as life proceeds." [65] Dewey writes in a similar vein: "Experience as an active process occupies time and its later period completes its earlier portion; it brings to light connections involved but hitherto unperceived." [66] And a writer on Dewey tells us that for Dewey "an experience however unique in its own quality must be seen as containing 'something that points to other experiences.'" [67]

When we read James as well as Dewey it becomes impossible to overlook the tremendous sense of direction within experience itself

which came to life in the pragmatist movement. James had a keen
awareness of experience as a continuum. Which explains why he was
aghast at the view apparently held by some critics of Pragmatism that
experience is lacking in genuine continuity and therefore in direction.
Hence his rejoinder: "Such a shallow sense of the conditions under
which men's thinking actually goes on seems to me most surprising.
These critics appear to suppose that, if left to itself, the rudderless raft
of our experience must be ready to drift anywhere or nowhere. Even
tho [sic] there were compasses on board, they seem to say, there would
be no pole for them to point to. There must be absolute sailing-direc-
tions, they insist, decreed from outside, and an independent chart of
the voyage added to the 'mere' voyage itself, if we are ever to make a
port." [68]

Dominated as both thinkers were by so pronounced a sense of direction within experience itself, we can see how truly they expressed the
pragmatist feeling of involvement in a great temporal process. And
we can see, too, the extent to which Dewey was mastered by the need
to carry on within the stream of history. In him there was not the
slightest sign of mere cerebralism in his view of reality as a living
process, or in his insistence on a full commitment to life as against a
loosely wrought and irresponsible relation.

Consider, too, how the whole processive outlook of James sharpened
his awareness of the flow of experience: "We live, as it were, upon the
front edge of an advancing wave-crest, and our sense of a determinate
direction in falling forward is all we cover of the future of our path." [69]
Or take this: "Life is in the transitions as much as in the terms connected; often, indeed, it seems to be there more emphatically, as if our
spurts and sallies forward were the real firing-line of the battle. . . ." [70]

Dewey was also highly sensitive to the forward-direction within the
depth of experience itself, for "man lives forward" and "experience is
a future implicated in a present." [71] An accommodation on the part of
consciousness to what is new and fresh is written into its very nature,
—a fact, obviously, which would never have forced itself on the attention of man save within the newly envisaged universe. If nature were
finished, says Dewey, "the flickering candle of consciousness would
go out." [72] Elsewhere he makes the same point, but in asserting that
"sleep and waking would not be distinguished." [73]

Regarding the experiential process, Dewey states the matter simply
when he says that knowing is not initiated from "innocent sensory data,

or from pure logical principles or from both together," but involves received and asserted meanings which are deposits of prior experiences, both personal and communal.[74] Consequently, it follows that we cannot move forward experientially without remaining in continuity with what has been accomplished in the past. As Dewey himself asserts, present experience "can expand into the future only as it is enlarged to take in the past." [75]

Dewey insists that departure from the past solves no problems. For contact with the past is utterly essential. Nevertheless, when we establish connections with the past, we must do so not outside the body of present experiences but in and through it. If Dewey castigates the method of making the past the main material of education, it is because this method severs the vital connection of the present with the past, while tending to make the present nothing but a futile imitation.

Dewey, therefore, is compelled by the logic of his own position to play up our dependence upon the stream of culture, a dependence which "is an essential factor in original vision and creative expression." Speaking of the artist, he says that even if original in temperament, his work may be relatively thin and tend to the bizarre, "when it is not informed with a wide and varied experience of the traditions of the art in which the artist operates." And, for the reason that "each great tradition is itself an organized habit of vision and of methods of ordering and conveying materials." [76] Philosophers, too, are within the movement of history, for though they may perhaps be creators "in some measure of its future" they are also "creatures of its past." [77]

Unfortunately, Dewey was singularly lacking in power of penetration into the past. Given his doctrine of experience as process and of the "organized habit of vision" engendered within a tradition, this is quite surprising. Speaking of the deficiency of the historic imagination in America, Dewey claimed that Americans idealize the past egregiously, setting up "little toys to stand as symbols for long centuries and the complicated lives of countless individuals." [78] Dewey himself cannot be convicted of idealizing the past egregiously, but he surely indulged in generalizations which violated his own more empirical method of approach. And, in all frankness, it must be said that a good deal of what he says about the past seems hardly more than the little toys he himself held up to ridicule. However, Dewey's shortcomings should not obscure his deeper insights and the contributions he himself has made toward a better and more comprehensive understanding of the past.

Experience as Participation: Interaction

In the open, incomplete, temporal world of the pragmatists there is a marked gain in visibility with respect to the true setting of human experience. Given a world that is still in the making, and in which nature is gropingly and experimentally pushing forward, it would seem that, of necessity, a being capable of thought must play a more active part in the cosmic story. "We are not utter foreigners in the world," says Peirce. And, indeed, so truly do we belong within nature, that as rational beings our role can be nothing less than efficient and co-determining, if only through our capacity to remake our own lives and to adapt our environment to the immensities of the human spirit.

Such an outlook invalidates the spectator point of view. Moreover, if man is indeed capable of intervening freely and creatively within his life-process, his very experience must be seen as grounded, not in a merely passive recording of impressions, but in an active involvement and participation.

The pragmatist's stress on this primary dimension of experience, that of the interplay between beings and between the self and its environment, found its fullest expression in Dewey. Interaction is at the very forefront of his thinking, an interaction which at the human level and within the community is transformed into participation and communication. Dewey really took seriously the fact that apart from a specific concrete environment, the individual is a sheer abstraction. And by environment, Dewey does not mean only what lies immediately before us. For, as he explains it, the environment may consist of very different things, for example, persons or subjects discussed, or even toys or an experiment one is performing, or it may be just the book one is reading in which the environmental context is a certain country or an imaginary region.[79]

The changes in the self which follow upon its interactions with the environment is regarded by Dewey as but an aspect of a universal process in which all things undergo change and development through their countless transactions with one another. Every new relation or connection carries with it new possibilities of development,[80] and since there can be an indefinite number of new relations, nature is seen to be full of processes whose possibilities are beyond reckoning. It would seem, then, that for Dewey the very notion of 'being' implies the potentiality to establish relations with other things, since it is only through actual connections that each individual discovers, so to speak, its own form and possibilities.

In a doctrine like Dewey's, experience is clearly aligned with the actual processes of life, and is located in a specific life-situation in which the self is actively engaged. And it is only within this kind of situation that the self confronts a world full of meaningful and relevant beings. Thus through concrete, living relationships the world enters into man's life in a more intimate and internal way: "The world we have experienced becomes an integral part of the self that acts and is acted upon in further experience." Finally, what had seemed remote and alien "becomes a home and the home is part of our every experience." [81]

There is, then, no inert static relation between the mind and the things confronting it, but rather a relation grounded in interaction. And in its most mature form, this vital commerce with other beings leads to a "complete interpenetration of the self and the world of objects and events." [82] Or to put it another way, through the range and quality of its relations with the world, the self is drawn into the great community of life, and to a conscious realization of its role as "a cooperative part of a larger whole."

Nor can we forget for one moment that with which man's experiential growth is closely bound up, namely, a sense of the whole conceived as a "history." And it would appear that our sense of the whole conceived as a "history" underlies that ineffable consummatory experience which Dewey refers to as "that delightful perception of the world." Clearly, this perception has the finality of a value experience, and has, besides, and in a supreme way, that aesthetic quality which every experience has when had for its own sake. For this "delightful perception" is not to be identified with mere pleasure, inasmuch as it brings a fulfillment that reaches to the depth of our being, as "an adjustment of our whole being with the conditions of existence." [83]

Manifestly, a full concrete encounter with the world is at the very center of Dewey's philosophy. Therefore, he concentrates all his thoughts and energies on a conception of things which will dispel the illusion that man stands on the sidelines as a mere onlooker. In a world mechanistically conceived, man is easily induced into taking a false position in relation to nature. But not in the world of Dewey and the Pragmatists. Man is truly a functioning part of nature, and his experiences enjoy a genuine status in the universe. Thus, even if he finds himself frustrated by nature, the fact remains that he is also supported by nature. Hence his ideals have an anchorage in the existing world, despite the fact that a particular ideal may be an illusion.[84] Similarly, the imaginative processes have an existential reference inasmuch as they are not arbitrarily injected into the world by man. And the same is true of thought, for it, too, is most assuredly within nature and enjoys a cosmic standing.[85]

Dewey's view of experience as grounded in interaction implies a relational structure of being, but of a sort which leaves room for the individual seen as the ultimate source of what is unpredictable. Like James, Dewey holds that relations must be taken as seriously as things themselves, and, again, like James, he holds that relations as well as things are matters of direct experience.

James is most emphatic in his insistence that we experience relations: "There is not a conjunction or a preposition, and hardly an adverbial phrase, syntactic form, or inflection of voice, in human speech, that does not express some shading or other of relation which we at some moment actually feel to exist between the larger objects of our thought." [86]

Dewey owed to James his awareness of the fact that we experience relations, and in acknowledging his debt, he states that his own doctrinal position "is but a generalization" of what is involved in that fact.[87]

The desire to uphold both individuality and relations is an interesting aspect of pragmatist thinking. Dewey is a particularly good example of this two-fold desire, for he not only makes the most of relations, but he also highlights the importance of the individual as "the carrier of creative thought" as well as "the author of action and of its application." [88] Consider, also, the following: "The mystery of time is thus the mystery of the existence of real individuals. It is a mystery because it is a mystery that anything which exists is just what it is. . . . We can account for a change by relating it to other changes, but existences we have to accept for just what they are. Given a butterfly or an earthquake as an event, as a change, we can at least in theory find out and state its connection with other changes. But the individual butterfly or earthquake remains just the unique existence that it is." [89]

Nothing can be more vexatious, philosophically, than the attempt to take full account of both individuality and relations. Thus, although in modern philosophy the category of relation has come into its own, it has done so, more often than not, at the expense of individuality. Dewey, at least, was bent on achieving a balance between individuality and relation even if, metaphysically, his doctrine of the individual, especially at the human level, is far from adequate.

However, what especially interests us here is that Dewey's double emphasis is a distinct echo of the Christian intellectual tradition as it took shape in Augustinian and Pseudo-Dionysian currents. Contrary to Aristotelianism, the trend in these currents was toward a primary accent on relations. Alerted by the relational structure of the Trinity, Christian thinkers were naturally disposed to take a closer look at the category of relation, especially in dealing with personality. Accordingly, it came about that religious faith and deep religious feeling were instrumental in inducing the habit of relational thinking.

Taken in a relational scheme, the Christian doctrine of man as image of God threw into bold relief the fact that an actual concrete relationship of the human person to God is crucial in the very formation of selfhood. The contact with God was, hence, taken as intrinsic to the being and life of each individual person. As we may readily imagine, such an attitude invited the more general position that the entire process of experience and knowledge belongs integrally within the pattern of actual living relationships.

Considering Dewey's fidelity to both individuality and relations, it would appear that his thought here is indeed an offshoot of that "organized habit of vision" formed through centuries of Christian experience and Christian thinking. Furthermore, Dewey was advancing at a new level the ancient Christian habit of viewing experience and knowledge within a concrete relational scheme, despite the ultimate restrictiveness of his naturalistic framework. And his awareness of the fact that the face-to-face relationship is intrinsic to the life of thought most assuredly has its roots in the Christian heritage. "Logic in its fulfillment" says Dewey, "recurs to the primitive sense of the word: dialogue. Ideas which are not communicated, shared, and reborn in expression are but soliloquy, and soliloquy is but broken and imperfect thought." [90]

Obviously, Dewey's doctrine of interaction implies an emphasis on the individual as such, as against relation. But the individual, as seen by him, is a focal point of spontaneity and initiative. Consequently, even if he cannot offer us a satisfactory portrait of human personality, he has still provided us with new dimensions in which to view the human subject in a more concrete and dynamic fashion.

As we have seen, Dewey's individual is very much a participant in an incomplete world. For each individual self acts as well as undergoes,[91] and what he undergoes is not stamped upon him as though he were inert wax. Both undergoing and doing are essential aspects of one balanced life, and, while inseparable, each depends for its quality on the way in which it is related to the other.

Experience, then, for Dewey, is a patterned structure in which undergoing and doing occur not in mere alternation, but in a far more integral way. For that reason, experience can be limited by all the causes which interfere with one's perception of the relations that bind undergoing and doing together. There may be interferences because of an excess either on the side of undergoing or on the side of doing. That is why, as Dewey says, "zest for doing, lust for action, leaves many a person, especially in this hurried and impatient environment in which we live, with experiences of an almost incredible paucity, all on the surface." The individual never allows an experience to complete itself, for he is forever hurrying off on a new line of action, with the result that he develops a preference, conscious or unconscious, for just those situations in which the most can be done in the shortest time.[92]

That Dewey felt his own approach to the human subject was far more realistic than that of traditional education can be seen in his attack on the older system of education on the ground that it pays little attention to the internal factors in the individual's relation to the subject-matter of education.[93] Unquestionably, he contributed much to a more realistic conception of the human subject, notwithstanding the ultimate inadequacy of his conception of personality.

Dewey's realism with regard to the human subject stands out still more vividly when placed within the context of the larger pragmatist movement. Take, for example, Mead's philosophy of the social self. Here we have an "ego-alter dialectic" which exhibits what has been called a "strange parallelism" to Martin Buber's reflections upon the I-Thou relation.[94] Thus, in Mead, we discover once again the fact that the pragmatist movement has accomplished a great deal in the sphere of the human subject.

Consider also what Perry says of James: "To read James is to recover the natural unities of the human mind, as a being that perceives, attends, reasons, wills, imagines, has sensations, forms habits, feels emotions, and acquires self-consciousness; and as an individual being in which these several modes of activity act and react on one another." [95]

In the final analysis, if Dewey stresses inward as well as outward factors in man's relations to his world, it is because they are both found in an unanalyzed totality in life and history. On one hand, life signifies a comprehensive activity which embraces at once organism and environment. On the other, history not only has to do with deeds enacted and tragedies undergone, but it also takes in rivers, mountains, laws and institutions. In the concrete of life and history, we have, then, a totality of experience which defies every dualistic interpretation of man's relations to his world.

Insisting as strenuously as he does on life-experience, Dewey refuses to grant a monopoly to knowledge. Knowledge, as we shall see, plays its role in the improving and developing of primary experiences, that is to say of experiences that occur chiefly in modes of action and undergoing. But it must not be glorified as the exclusive avenue to the real world. "For things are objects to be treated, used, acted upon and with, enjoyed and endured, even more than things to be known. They are things *had* before they are things cognized."

The philosopher must be sensitive to the need for experience, and while recognizing no "fatal chasms" in experience, he should never forget that knowing cannot be taken as primary without cutting the cord that binds experience and nature together.[96] From first to last, the knowing process is grounded in a real world, where experience signifies not simply observation but active participation. For experience includes *"what* men do and suffer, *what* they strive for, love, believe and endure, and *how* men act and are acted upon, the ways in which they do and suffer, desire and enjoy, see, believe, imagine . . ." [97] And all phenomena must be respected, whether they have to do with magic, myth, politics, painting or penitentiaries.[98]

Religion too is also revelatory of existence.[99] And the affections can claim a place long denied them, for "Our affections, when they are enlightened by understanding, are organs by which we enter into the meaning of the natural world as genuinely as by knowing, and with greater fullness and intimacy. . . ." [100]

The Emancipation and Enlargement of Experience

In relocating experience within a nature which is not denied a truly temporal character, Dewey has raised the requirements of concreteness in the handling of experience. Unfortunately, he remained impervious to certain inner experiences which yield intelligible necessities with respect to truth and value. They, too, have their place within experience conceived as "a moving whole of interacting parts," [101] and, by their very nature, occupy a privileged position.

The fact remains, however, that despite the deficiencies of his philosophy, Dewey was yet able to gather in a good many insights which no one can afford to ignore. Moreover, he widened our conception of empirical method, while throwing open new vistas of experience. Then, again, he did more than his share in showing the futility of treating man as though he were segregated from history and process and as though he were incapable of exercising a truly creative function in his own process. And here, of course, he can help us orient our thinking in a world in which things exist in some genuinely temporal sense. Perhaps, too, he can even help us form a more realistic attitude toward those intelligible necessities which are a part of the given of experience, even if unacknowledged by him. For, despite their transcendent character, or rather because of it, they, too, are in time, manifesting themselves and unfolding their implications within a definite course of events. The reality and efficacy of truth and value in terms of a temporal process need to be given more serious philosophical consideration. But here, too, we have much to learn from that other great figure in the pragmatist movement, Peirce, who like Dewey was determined to take growth and development seriously, and who could also declare that the "ideas of 'justice' and 'truth' are, notwithstanding the iniquity of the world, the mightiest of the forces that move it." [102]

In drawing this study to a close, we shall consider briefly man's creative role in the world, and, this of course, in experiential terms. For nothing emerges so clearly from a study of Dewey's thought as the single-mindedness with which he drove home the fact that man can shape the experiential foundations of his own life.

In this connection, let us recall that, in accepting a relational system, Dewey also upholds the reality of the individual. Dewey is referring to this kind of scheme when he says that "Only if elements are more than just elements in a whole, only if they have something qualitatively their own, can a relational system be prevented from complete collapse." Thus, without the infinitely plural and irreducible qualities found in nature, the relations which are the subject-matter of knowledge "would be algebraic ghosts, relations that do not relate." [103]

These immediate qualities form the basis for what Dewey calls a "having" experience as against a "knowing" experience. In the "having" experience, we come up against the immediacy of existent things, and since they are indescribable and undefinable we have to accept them as they are. "Empirically, things are poignant, tragic, beautiful, humorous, settled, disturbed, comfortable, annoying, barren, harsh, consoling, splendid, fearful; are such immediately and in their own right and behalf." The unique and ineffable character of these data are such that they must be taken as absolute rather than comparative. Moreover, such experiences include not only things, events and persons, but also situations inasmuch as they, too, have an immediate, final or self-enclosed quality.

As to the "knowing" experience, this is made possible because things are not isolated from one another, for they are involved in a continuity of interactions and changes which render them a potent means of new experiences. All knowing, for Dewey, always proceeds by taking things out of their isolation and seeing them as related parts in some larger whole.[104] Or, as he tells us, philosophy has but to note that every bare occurrence, whether in the way of having, being or undergoing, is an invitation to thought to seek and find unapparent connections.[105]

Through the agency of knowing, that which James refers to as "the advancing front of experience" brings with it the widening of experiential coherence and unity. This movement toward concrete unification is the story of our process, even if that unification is always meager and partial. And the story has its source in the infinite relationships already existing between men and their fellows and between men and things. Yet "the enduring and comprehending whole" touches our consciousness insofar as we sense "these encompassing continuities with their infinite reach." Moreover, "This meaning even now attaches to *present activities* because they are set in a whole to which they belong and which belongs to them." [106] (My emphasis.)

Knowledge, then, has to do with the process by which we bring things into a larger pattern of relationships. For each thing or event takes on stable meanings through its reference to something extrinsic, but connected. The result is a "knowing" experience, "the product of deliberate art, of which relations rather than qualities are the significant subject matter." And, Dewey insists, the "connections are as much experienced as are the qualitatively diverse and irreducible objects of original natural experience." [107] Putting the matter in experiential terms, "An experience is a knowledge, if in its quale there is an experienced distinction and connection of two elements of the following sort: *one means or intends the presence of the other in the same fashion in which itself is already present, while the other is that which, while not present in the same fashion, must become so present if the meaning or intention of its companion or yoke-fellow is to be fulfilled through the operation it sets up.*" [108]

With respect to the immediate objects of existence, our knowledge of "sequences, coexistences, relations" "constitute a memorandum of conditions of their appearance." [109] In other words, by acquiring such a "memorandum" we can procure by "intentionally performed operations" the kind of experience we consider desirable. That is to say, we can procure the finalities required, in regulating the date, place and manner of their emergence.

Knowing is itself a way of interaction by which we bring under control other interactions. Thanks to a directed activity, we can so modify the empirical situation that objects are differently related to one another. Knowing is, therefore, experimental inasmuch as it is intrinsically bound up with overt doing, or the making of changes in the environment, or in our relation to it. Ideas are entirely indispensable. Nevertheless, they are regarded by Dewey as worthless unless they are indivisibly one with overt actions which "rearrange and reconstruct in some way, be it little or large, the world in which we live." [110]

According to Dewey, "the function of intelligence is . . . not that of copying the objects of the environment, but rather of taking account of the way in which more effective and more profitable relations with these objects may be established in the future." [111] Unquestionably, in a processual scheme where there is real growth and development, ideas must be viewed dynamically and as means of leading us deeper into reality in some sort of teleological way. Dewey tells us that "The identification in modern thought of ends with ends-in-view, with deliberate purpose and planning . . . is in effect a recognition that the teleology of nature is achieved and exhibited by nature in thinking, not apart from it." If this implication has often escaped modern theories, says Dewey, if modern thought has been content to deny all teleology, "the reason is adventitious; it is found in the gratuitous breach of continuity between nature, life, and man." [112]

The purpose of the concept is to redirect us back into experience, so that through our constructive control of the environment experience is modified or developed. Thus there is a real process of experience because reason is able to make the world other than it would have been without it. Reason's function is directive with respect to the course of experience, and, accordingly, the meaning of the concept is tied in with its applicability to a world of existing things. Hence, the concept always faces forward, since, in making possible a creative handling of relations, it is oriented to the expansion of experience.

In his approach to knowledge, Dewey was generalizing at a philosophical level the mode of thinking that experimental science brought to life. That experimental thinking has a good deal to say with respect to the life of thought is beyond question. And, like Peirce, Dewey understood this and was attempting to open up a new frontier in philosophy. But concerned as he was with the immediacy of existence and the finalities grounded in such immediacy, Dewey also paid heed to "experience in the form of art." As we already know, he insists that the philosopher must go to aesthetic experience in order to understand what experience is. And among the things to be learned from "experience in the form of art" is the falsity of any division between overt and executive activity on one side and thought and feeling on the other. "In creative production," he says, "the external and physical world is more than a mere means or external condition of perceptions, ideas and emotions; it is subject-matter and sustainer of conscious activity; and thereby exhibits, so that he who runs may read, the fact that consciousness is not a separate realm of being, but is the manifest quality of existence when nature is most free and most active." [113]

Although Dewey has much to say regarding knowledge as a means of gaining control in a troubled situation, nonetheless it is with the modification and development of experience itself that he is, above all, concerned. Knowing is primarily for the sake of a consummatory experience, for we know in order more satisfactorily to have. If our thinking is inviscerated in a real world of objects and events, it provides us with an experience of that phase of objects which is constituted by their connections with one another. Reflective thought is, in fact, transitional. That is to say, it stands in an intermediate and mediating position within experience, in carrying us from a relatively casual and accidental experience of existence to one relatively settled and defined.

Dewey is tireless in his insistence that the course of experience can be directed and that we should have faith in "the varied possibilities of diversified experience." [114] To him nothing could be more certain than that man has reached a new stage in his development precisely through his power to enter boldly into the world of concrete experience, instead of fleeing from it in the mistaken notion that it represents mere flux and confusion. Consequently, he raised his voice against those non-empirical philosophies which have cast aspersion upon the things of everyday experience, and have helped to solidify an attitude whose very essence is 'deviation from concrete experience.' As he says, "The serious matter is that philosophies have denied that common experience is capable of developing from within itself methods which will secure direction for itself and will create inherent standards of judgment and value." [115] Here, Dewey would have been on firmer ground if he had but recognized a deeper level of experience, of which we have already made mention, where we come face to face with realities apart from which we should be hopelessly adrift in an absolute relativism.

As we have seen, in Dewey's doctrine, thinking always begins and ends in experience, but, in the process, experience itself is transformed. "Development," he says, "does not mean just getting something out of the mind. It is a development out of experience and into experience that is really wanted."[116] Therefore, we can deliberately set about making experience our teacher, through our power to qualify its course and to turn it in the direction of a specific goal. As Dewey declares, "at every level there is an expanding development of experience if experience is educative in effect. Consequently, whatever the level of experience, we have no choice but either to operate in accord with the pattern it provides or else to neglect the place of intelligence in the development and control of a living and moving experience." [117]

Discussing Dewey's contribution to the notion that experience itself is educative or pedagogical, a writer has this to say: "It is experience that is directive, it is experience that teaches and while the entire American tradition is characterized by the acceptance of experience as pedagogical, it is nowhere more explicitly stated than in the following passage from John Dewey's *Reconstruction in Philosophy:* 'Now, old experience is used to suggest aims and methods for developing a new and improved experience. Consequently experience becomes in so far constructively self-regulative. What Shakespeare so pregnantly said of nature, it is 'made better by no mean, but nature makes that mean,' becomes true of experience. We do not merely have to respect the past, or wait for accidents to force change upon us. We *use* our past experiences to construct new and better ones in the future. The very fact of experience thus includes the process by which it directs itself in its own betterment.' " [118]

Dewey's penetrating insight into the way in which man plays a creative role in relation to his own experience explains, of course, his constant preoccupation with the field of education. For the whole process of education can be made to exemplify in a highly conscious way the truth that experience itself is pedagogical. Since "the business of education might be defined as an emancipation and enlargement of experience," [119] it was quite natural for Dewey to view his educational theories as a handle to his entire philosophy. It is not surprising, then, to find Dewey fully prepared to grant a pre-eminent role to the philosophy of education: "The philosophy of education is one phase of all philosophy in general. It may be seriously questioned whether it is not the most important phase of general philosophy . . . the whole philosophic problem of the origin, nature, and function of knowledge is a live issue in education, not just a problem for exercise in intellectual dialectic gymnastics." [120]

Again we must emphasize that Dewey's philosophy was motivated by an intense desire to take seriously the fact that knowing is inside, not outside, the life-process, and to follow through with the implications. His highly disciplined thinking with regard to experience as pedagogical cannot for a moment be separated from his view that man is deeply involved in a great processual scheme. Like James, he looked on experience as a continuum, and not at all as a "rudderless raft." As he saw it, man does not live his life amidst events which are indifferently neutral to him, for these events are taken up into an integrated scheme which forms a more or less coherent story. Dewey describes this temporal process as an integrated series of episodes whose wholeness imparts to each episode a meaning it would not have if it were part of another story. Hence human consciousness has a dramatic quality which cannot be ignored when we view man in the full concreteness of life and history.

Man is actively engaged within a growing process involving the whole world, and through his active participation, the story unfolds. And meaning itself takes shape within the unfolding story; each moment contributes to a "continuum of *meaning* in process of formation."[121]

It is clear, then, that Dewey's conception of thought as instrumental is in line with his desire to maintain the closest ties between the life of thought and the developing story. And, as we have seen, this unification is possible because of man's power to reshape the whole of his existence in order to liberate and develop his experience. The dynamism of man's life is found in this very effort to expand his experience, for as Dewey says, "Nothing but the best, the richest and fullest experience possible, is good enough for man. The attainment of such an experience is not to be conceived as the specific problem of 'reformers' but as the common purpose of men." [122]

Because we are able to reconstruct continuously our environment, we can make our experience abound in meaning and value. Thus Dewey has given us insight into the fact that we are indeed participants in the unfolding drama of the onmoving world. Moreover, he has made us see the need for establishing an intimate and even creative connection between the life of thought and the world, inasmuch as experience is capable of endless development. Action is given new dignity in its more intrinsic relation to thought. And everything that adds to man's power to shape his environment takes on an enlarged significance. Consequently Dewey can say: "Every discovery of concrete dependence of life and mind upon physical events is therefore an addition to our resources." [123]

The growth of experience is a communal affair, even if the person plays a primary role. It implies, therefore, the joint activity of individuals as well as the indissoluble unity of thought and deed. In building up his social life, man is at the same time giving more amplitude to the world of his experience. And even his body plays an indispensable role in making meaning and value triumph over the instability of events. Obviously, then, creative activity with respect to the environment has implications far beyond the merely practical.

Given such an outlook, nothing could be more repugnant to Dewey than the view that institutions, as such, are the enemy of freedom and that all conventions are but slaveries. But everything in his outlook also made him react strongly against any form of society which failed to keep pace with the human process. As he insisted, social institutions have for their purpose the liberation and development of the individual's capacities. But the individual that Dewey had in mind is the real individual of history who is in process of growth, and who is discovering the whole world of inner experience, and is even now entering into "the new age of human relationships." [124]

Man is always in process of growth, and the developments in our own time clearly call for a fresh reconstruction of the social world, in order to strengthen the bonds which hold persons together in the "immediate community of experience," that is to say, in the face-to-face relationships of the local community. For the human spirit will not return "to seek calm and order within itself" save "in the vital, steady, and deep relationships which are present only in an immediate community." [125]

Inspired by the conception of a universe which is still "in the process of becoming," Dewey built his philosophy around the notion of thought as creative and constructive, and as oriented to the task of making the world more reasonable in actual fact. Through the experimental reshaping of his world, man is able to achieve a "securer, freer and more widely shared embodiment of values in experience. . . ."[126] Because he has the power to develop and organize his experience, man is capable of filling his world with meaning and value, and consequently, of bringing it into accord with his ideals. And today, more than ever before, man must make full use of this power. For as Dewey says, "Never have the 'real' and the 'ideal' been so clamorous, so self-assertive, as at the present time. And never in the history of the world have they been so far apart." [127]

This doctrine which lays so much emphasis on the "embodiment of values in experience" also finds expression in Peirce in his doctrine of the ultimate good as the furtherance of concrete reasonableness. Dewey cites Peirce's own words concerning this doctrine, when, in referring to his view that generals [universals] are real, he writes, that for Peirce, "the pragmaticist [Peirce's own version of pragmatism] does not make the *summum bonum* to consist in action, but makes it to consist in that process of evolution whereby the existent comes more and more to embody those generals. . . ." (My insertions.) [128]

In his account of the thought of James Marsh, early American philosopher, Dewey brings out a conception of Marsh's, which, in spirit at least, is not unlike the pragmatist view under consideration. Dewey is showing how Marsh was under Christian influence in developing a conception of reason and its relation to the world which was far from that of Aristotle. ". . . Aristotle," says Dewey, "held that reason could be actualized in contemplative knowledge apart from any effort to change the world of nature and social institutions into its own likeness and embodiment. Following the spirit of Christian teaching, Marsh denied any such possibility. He held that Reason can actualize itself and be truly aware or conscious of its own intrinsic nature only as it operates to make over the world, whether physical or social, into an embodiment of its own principles. Marsh constantly condemns what he calls speculation and the speculative tendency, by which he means a separation of knowledge and the intellect from action and the will. By its own nature, reason terminates in action and that action is the transformation of the spiritual potentialities found in the natural world, physical and institutional, into spiritual realities." [129]

If Dewey had had a first-hand acquaintance with the traditions of Christian thought, his own cast of mind would have brought to focus doctrines which, like Marsh's, clearly show the influence of Christianity in their emphasis on action. Nor would he have missed the new love for the concrete among Christian thinkers, as well as a strong desire to stay close to experience. Above all, he would have learned that the incarnation mentality, fostered by Christianity, made it entirely inevitable that men should strive to bring truth and value down to earth. In short, he would have discovered how truly these Christian traditions brought forth an "organized habit of vision," whose influence has been felt in philosophy right down to the present, and even in Pragmatism itself.

NOTES

1. Philip H. Wiener, *Evolution and the Founders of Pragmatism* (Cambridge: Harvard, 1949) viii.
2. *Problems of Men,* (New York: Philosophical Library, 1946) 156.
3. Alexandre Koyré, *From the Closed World to the INFINITE UNIVERSE* (Baltimore: Johns Hopkins, 1957).
4. George Santayana, *Winds of Doctrine* (New York: Harper, 1957) 208.
5. *Experience and Nature* (Chicago: Open Court, 1929) 47.
6. *Reconstruction in Philosophy* (New York: Holt, 1930) 66-7.
7. Marjorie Hope Nicolson, *The Breaking of the Circle* (Chicago: Northwestern, 1950) 139.
8. *Reconstruction in Philosophy,* 61.
9. *Pragmatism* (New York: Longmans Green, 1907) 246.
10. *Experience and Nature,* 24.
11. Nicolson, *op. cit.* 180.
12. *Reconstruction in Philosophy,* 58.
13. "Time and Individuality," *Time and Its Mysteries* (Series II; New York Univ., 1940) 87.
14. *Ibid.* 89.
15. *Characters and Events,* Joseph Ratner, Edit. (New York: Holt, 1929) II, 440.
16. *Ibid.* I, 116-17.
17. Ibid. II, 439.
18. Ralph Barton Perry, *The Thought and Character of William James* (Boston: Little Brown, 1936) II, 700.
19. "Does Reality Possess Practical Character?" *Essays in Honor of William James* (New York: Longmans Green, 1908) 63.
20. A. N. Whitehead, *Process and Reality* (New York: Macmillan, 1930) vii.
21. "Time and Individuality," *op. cit.* 106.
22. "Does Reality Possess Practical Character?" *op. cit.* 56.
23. Emmanuel Mounier, *Be Not Afraid* (New York: Harper, 1954) 19.
24. *Experience and Education* (New York: Macmillan, 1938) 51.
25. *Problems of Men,* 12.
26. *The Quest for Certainty* (New York: Minton, Balch, 1929) 306.
27. *Characters and Events,* II, 499.
28. Cf. Mircea Eliade, *The Myth of the Eternal Return* (New York: Pantheon, 1954).
29. *Meteorologica,* I, 3. (Loeb edition, Cambridge: Harvard, 1952) 13.
30. *De Civitate Dei,* XII, 17, *Basic Writings of St. Augustine,* Edited with Introd. and Notes by Whitney J. Oates (New York: Random House, 1948) II, 198.
31. George H. Mead, *The Philosophy of the Present* (Chicago: Open Court, 1932) 90.
32. *Ibid.* 89.
33. "Prefatory Remarks," Mead, *op. cit.* xxxix.

34. XI, 1, *The Stoic and Epicurean Philosophers,* Edited with Introd. and Notes by Whitney J. Oates (New York: Random House, 1940) 571.
35. Whitehead, *Dialogues of Alfred North Whitehead,* as recorded by Lucien Price. (Boston: Little, Brown, 1954) 163.
36. *Philosophy and Civilization* (New York: Minton, Balch, 1931) 33.
37. *Characters and Events,* I, 119.
38. Mounier, *op. cit.* 20.
39. Denis de Rougement, *Man's Western Quest,* R. N. Anshen, Edit. (New York: Harper, 1957) 95.
40. *Reconstruction in Philosophy,* 48.
41. "The Need for a Recovery of Philosophy," *Creative Intelligence* (New York: Holt, 1917) 64.
42. Walter J. Ong, S.J., "Renaissance Humanism and the American Catholic Mind," *The McAuley Lectures* (St. Joseph's College, West Hartford, 1954) 65.
43. *Collected Papers,* Charles Hartshorne and Paul Weiss, Edits. (Cambridge: Harvard, 1931-1935). Six volumes. 5.119; 6.479; 5.354.
44. *Reconstruction in Philosophy,* 48.
45. *Experience and Nature,* 420.
46. *Art as Experience* (New York: Milton Balch, 1934) 195.
47. Folke Leander, *The Philosophy of John Dewey* (Goteborgs Kungliga Vetenskapoch Vitterhets-Samhället. Handlingar, 1940) 112.
48. *Art as Experience,* 193, 195.
49. *Ibid.* 297.
50. *Ibid.* 274.
51. Ibid. 194.
52. *A Common Faith* (New Haven: Yale, 1934) 19.
53. *Art as Experience,* 37.
54. *Ibid.* 17.
55. Cited by Wiener, *op. cit.* 186-87.
56. *Characters and Events,* I, 101. Cf. *Experience and Nature,* 417-19.
57. *Reconstruction in Philosophy,* 25.
58. W. James, *The Meaning of Truth* (New York: Longmans Green, 1914) 151-52.
59. Oliver Wendell Holmes, *The Common Law* (Boston: Little Brown, 1881) 1.
60. James, *A Pluralistic Universe* (New York: Longmans Green, 1916) 306.
61. *Forum* 83 (March, 1930) 180.
62. *The Thought and Character of William James,* I, 558.
63. *Experience and Nature* (1925, 1929) 39.
64. Santayana, *Winds of Doctrine,* 205.
65. James, *The Meaning of Truth,* 111, 117.
66. *Democracy and Education* (New York: Macmillan, 1916) 92.
67. William O'Meara, "John Dewey and Modern Thomism," *The Thomist* 5 (Jan. 1943) 315.
68. James, *The Meaning of Truth,* 71.
69. *Ibid.* 116.
70. *Essays in Radical Empiricism,* Ralph Barton Perry, Edit. (New York: Longmans Green, 1912) 87.

71. "The Need for a Recovery of Philosophy," *op. cit.* 12.
72. *Experience and Nature,* 349.
73. *Art as Experience,* 17.
74. *Experience and Nature,* 428.
75. *Experience and Education,* 93.
76. *Art as Experience,* 265.
77. *Philosophy and Civilization,* 7.
78. *Characters and Events,* II, 515.
79. *Experience and Education,* 41.
80. Cf. "Time and Individuality," *op. cit.* 101-2.
81. *Art as Experience,* 104.
82. *Ibid.* 19.
83. *Ibid.* 17.
84. *Experience and Nature,* 62.
85. *Ibid.* 421, 420.
86. *Psychology,* Briefer Course, Introd. by R. B. Perry (New York: World, 1948) 162.
87. "Experience, Knowledge and Value: A Rejoinder," *The Philosophy of John Dewey,* P. A. Schilpp, edit. (New York: Tudor, 1951) 533, n. 16.
88. *Philosophy and Civilization,* 33-4.
89. "Time and Individuality," *op. cit.* 105-6.
90. *The Public and Its Problems* (New York: Holt, 1927) 218.
91. *Experience and Nature,* 8, 22.
92. *Art as Experience,* 44-5.
93. *Experience and Education,* 39.
94. Paul E. Pfuetze, *The Social Self* (New York: Bookman Associates, 1954) Foreword, 7.
95. James, *Psychology,* Introd. ix.
96. *Experience and Nature,* 21, 23.
97. *Ibid.* 8.
98. *Ibid.* 20.
99. *Philosophy and Civilization,* 9-10.
100. *The Quest for Certainty,* 297.
101. Cited by Jerome Nathanson in John Dewey: *The Reconstruction of the Democratic Life.* (New York: Twentieth Century Library, 1951) 18.
102. Charles S. Pierce, *Collected Works,* 5. 431.
103. *Experience and Nature,* 87, 86.
104. *How We Think,* (New York: Heath, 1933) 138.
105. Cf. *Experience and Nature,* 326.
106. *Human Nature and Conduct,* (New York: Holt, 1922) 330.
107. *The Quest for Certainty,* 125.
108. *The Influence of Darwin on Philosophy and Other Essays in Contemporary Thought,* (New York: Holt, 1910) 90.
109. *Experience and Nature,* 86.
110. *The Quest for Certainty,* 138.
111. *Philosophy and Civilization,* 30.
112. *Experience and Nature,* 352.
113. *Ibid.* 393.

114. "What I Believe," *The Forum* 83 (March 1930) 179.
115. *Experience and Nature,* 38.
116. *The Child and the Curriculum* (Chicago: University of Chicago Press, 1902) 18.
117. *Experience and Education,* 112.
118. John J. McDermott, *Experience is Pedagogical: The Genesis and Essence of the American Nineteenth Century Notion of Experience.* Unpublished Doctoral Thesis, Fordham University, New York, 1959, p. 229, (text cited, pp. 94-5).
119. *How We Think,* 202.
120. Cited by Gunnar Myrdal, *An American Dilemma.* (New York: Harper, 1944). Vol. II, pp. 882-3.
121. *Experience and Nature,* pp. 306-8.
122. *Ibid.* 412.
123. *Ibid.* 263.
124. *The Public and Its Problems,* 109.
125. *Ibid.* 214.
126. *The Quest for Certainty,* 37. Cf. Manford George Gutzke, *John Dewey's Thought and its Implications for Christian Education.* (New York: King's Crown Press, Columbia University, 1956). ch. VI.
127. *Reconstruction in Philosophy,* 128.
128. Peirce, *Chance, Love, and Logic,* With a Supplementary Essay on the Pragmatism of Peirce, by John Dewey. Morris R. Cohen, ed. (New York: Harcourt, Brace, 1923) 304.
129. *Problems of Men,* 369.

VIII

Dewey's Influence in China

THOMAS BERRY, C.P.

Father Thomas Berry, C.P., is associated with the Institute of Far Eastern Studies at Seton Hall University. After ordination in 1942, he studied history at Catholic University, where he obtained his doctorate. In 1948 he studied in China and from 1951 to 1954 was engaged in work in different European countries. He has contributed articles on Asian studies to Catholic periodicals and has published one book, The Historical Theory of Giambattista Vico.

Among the most interesting but least known phases of the life and work of John Dewey is his intimate association with recent Chinese history. His devotion to China, even his fascination with that country, mirrored somewhat the experience of the French thinkers of the Enlightenment. Yet, unlike the writers of this earlier period, Dewey did not so much learn from the Chinese as teach them. Many Chinese came in the first two decades of this century to study under him at Columbia University. Then in 1919, while in Japan giving a series of lectures on philosophy, he was invited by some of his former students to extend his travels to China and to lecture in the greater universities of that country. He accepted the invitation. In June of that year he arrived in Shanghai.

At this time Dewey was approaching his sixtieth birthday. A year younger than the Chinese patriarch, K'ang Yu-wei (1858-1927), he was older than most of the other distinguished leaders of China's intellectual life, among whom, to mention a few, Ts'ai Yuan-p'ei (1867-1940), Liang Ch'i-ch'ao (1873-1928), and Ch'en Tu-hsiu (1879-1942) were leaders of the older generation. They were followed by such men as Chiang Monlin (b. 1885), Chang T'ung-sun (b. 1886), Carsun Chang (b. 1886), Li Ta-chao (1888-1927) and Li Ta (b. 1889). Hu Shih (b. 1891) and Fung Yu-lan (b. 1895) were still in their twenties. All of these were at one time considered progressive, even revolutionary, in relation to the traditions of the past. In relation to the present they represented in their ideological and political views a range of thought that extended from the nominal Confucianism of K'ang Yu-wei to the incipient Marxism of Ch'en Tu-hsiu and Li Ta-chao.

The year of Dewey's entry into the intellectual circles dominated in part by these men may be considered among the most critical years of modern Chinese history. The more westernized elements in Peking were taking control. Confucius, and his greatest modern defender K'ang Yu-wei, under the assault led by Ch'en Tu-hsiu and Hu Shih, had just retired from the scene. At this moment of transition from the old to the new order of things, Dewey was called upon to speak before the professors and students of the new Chinese universities, to make his suggestions concerning the best intellectual approach to reality and to indicate just what adaptation China should make in order to survive nationally and internationally in the new world order into which it was passing. As the first foreigner invited by Chinese officials to lecture at a Chinese university, Dewey had at this moment an opportunity seldom given to any philosopher.

It came at the right moment in his own life. He had for many years been, in his own country, a teacher of teachers. He had acquired a feeling that his special mission in life was to teach men how to live and think in the new age of science, technology and democracy. By now he had published his most influential works on education: *School and Society* (1899) and *Democracy and Education* (1916). His philosophy had come to its newest expression in his recent lectures in Japan which were being published that same year, 1919, under the title, *Reconstruction in Philosophy*. These works, his general experience in educational affairs, his age, and his dedication to the establishment of a new mental orientation for man in the new world order, all these gave him the confidence that marked his appearances in Peking and elsewhere throughout China. In Dr. Hu Shih, a former student of his at Columbia, he had an excellent interpreter.

That he understood the importance of the moment is evident from his observation: "Simply as an intellectual spectacle, a scene for study and surmise, there is nothing in the world today—not even Europe in the throes of reconstruction—that equals China. History records no parallel." [1] To his own question: "Can an old, vast, peculiar, exclusive, self-sufficing civilization be born again?" he answered: "Made over it must be or it cannot endure." [2] As vividly as any western observer, Dewey saw what was involved in the modern awakening of China. A "new mind" was being formed there. It was an event not only for China but for all the world. The important thing was that it be properly orientated to the world of reality, that it attain effective political form, and that the educational program be adjusted to the realities of the present rather than to the conditions of the past. As he saw the situation: "China has the alternative of perishing, to the disturbance of the world, as well as itself, or of condensing into a century or so the intellectual, scientific, industrial, political and religious progress for which the rest of the world has taken several centuries." [3] If existing disorders were to continue for five or ten years, the world, he thought, would have a China under Japanese military domination or all Asia would come completely under Bolshevik rule.

The Student Crisis

To understand these statements of Dewey we must remember that Dr. Sun Yat-sen, the revolutionary leader of the period, had thus far been unable to unify his country. Sectionalism was tearing China apart. Yüan Shih-k'ai, a military figure and protégé of K'ang Yu-wei, sought unsuccessfully in 1915 to restore the Empire as a Constitutional Monarchy. Disorder seemed too great for either Monarchy or Republic. The period of decline which extended throughout the entire 19th century had so weakened the foundations of social order that immediate remedy was impossible. Men as capable as Yen Fu and K'ang Yu-wei considered that the best hope for the future lay with a restored monarchy. But the general sentiment among the students and the advanced intelligentsia was in violent opposition to such a restoration. The ideals of liberal democratic government were too attractive, the corruption of the Manchu dynasty too obvious. Yet in 1919, eight years after the first efforts to establish a republic, no effective instrument of government had evolved. Order was kept more by memory of the past than by realities of the present.

In spite of all the political unrest, however, the rising generation of Chinese intellectuals was enthusiastic about the new developments and gave expression to their revolutionary enthusiasm in terms similar to those of European writers during the corresponding years of the previous century. The new ideals which earlier had been expressed in phrases such as "Change and Reform" and the "New Learning" were now expressed in terms such as "New China" and a "New People." Even the term "Young China" became popular in imitation of Mazzini's "Young Italy" movement.[4] Sun Yat-sen, by whom the various movements for political revolution had been coordinated during the early part of the century, understood how deeply responsive men in the new age were to nationalist ideals. This provided his basic hope that the Chinese people, now "a sheet of loose sand," would attain the unity necessary for survival. The difficulty was that in rejecting the Empire the traditions of the past had also been rejected and no satisfactory basis of public order had been established. There was need of replacing not only a political institution but a form of living, a set of values, a vision of reality, a social discipline. Political structure was difficult to replace. But to replace Confucian Humanism and its corresponding individual and social virtues— that was the real challenge.

In former times the scholars had been the fundamental support of the social order. They advised the ruler and administered the affairs of the people. It was natural then that they should play an important part in the changes that were taking place. The most capable were at the moment in Peking. Advances in modern learning led by Confucian scholars such as Tseng Kuo-fan (1811-1872), Chang Chih-tung (1837-1909), K'ang Yu-wei, T'an Ssu-t'ung (1865-1898) and Liang Ch'i-ch'ao, had in 1898 brought about the establishment at Peking of a new center of intellective life known as the National University of Peking. This university had survived the political changes of both Empire and Republic and now had as its Chancellor Ts'ai Yuan-p'ei. At the invitation of Ts'ai, Ch'en Tu-hsiu had become Dean of the Faculty of Arts and Letters. Chiang Monlin was also there along with Li Ta-chao, Hu Shih and a number of other very capable scholars.

This group in Peking was at the time carrying out the amazing literary revolution that had begun among the Chinese students in America under the leadership of Hu Shih. The language of the classical tradition was considered by these men as too artificial to carry the more genuine thought and emotions of the new age and the new people. The popular spoken language, they argued, should become also the written language. The arguments presented were so effective that their program of linguistic reform was accepted. Within four years this new written language had become the language of the schools and the re-education of China was begun in earnest. Politics, language, thought and education, all were to become democratic at the same time. One important result of this linguistic change was that communication between the scholars and the people was now more complete and more immediate than at any time in Chinese history.

Such revolutionary changes produced among the people, but particularly among the writers, scholars, professors and students, a spirit of boundless enthusiasm. The new freedom of thought and expression was even more exhilarating than political freedom as such. New disorders appeared throughout the country as the social patterns of the past were shattered. Yet this new situation had great possibilities, for leading scholars remembered well that the most glorious days of ancient philosophical development in China had taken place in the disorderly period between the Chou and the Ch'in dynasties (between the sixth and third centuries before Christ). So now a period of disorder seemed a normal and necessary condition for the new creative effort being made in every sphere of Chinese life. The most impressive scholars at this time were those most decisive in rejecting the past order of Chinese life and most determined on establishing an entirely new way of life. "The new intellectual leader of the period, Mr. Ch'en Tu-hsiu, advised the youth of the nation to worship only two gods: Science and Democracy." [5] This attitude resulted from the belief, common at the time, that science and technology alone had produced the much-admired civilization of the West. There was no doubt in the minds of these men about the relative values of Chinese and Western cultures. "They wanted people to recognize frankly the superiority of Western Culture and the decadence of Chinese learning." [6]

To communicate their thought to each other and to the people, the intellectuals founded a number of new periodicals, a type of publication highly developed in China at the turn of the century. It was a medium well adapted to the Chinese who traditionally had written in short essay style. Now through new printing processes and more extensive distribution to university students in the main cities of China, periodical literature became increasingly effective in the intellectual and political life of the nation. At one time there were over four hundred periodicals being put out by Chinese students in China and Japan, responsible to no government, no person, no tradition. The most outstanding of these publications during the second decade of this century and the one which

attracted the most capable writers was the *Hsin-ch'ing-nien,* founded
and edited by Ch'en Tu-hsiu, who was later joined by Chien Hsuan-
tung, Hu Shih, Li Ta-chao and Shen Yin-mo.

Much vigor and brilliance was displayed during these years, but no
program appeared which could do for China what Confucian Humanism
had done. The general impression created by these writers is that they
wished an immediate and complete westernization of Chinese life but
that they had only a limited understanding of just what this involved.
This led to a sense of awkwardness, confusion, loss of balance and loss
of direction. Few realized just how deep the social unrest had become
until May 4th, 1919, when the dissatisfaction of the students came to
violent expression in Peking. This movement, both political and intellectual in nature, made clear to everyone that the central doctrine of
Confucianism, filial piety, was no longer an acceptable basis of social
order. Henceforth student unrest was a continuing thing in the university
life of China. It reflected and further increased the need for new principles of order. This first success gave the students the assurance they
needed. Neither those concerned with university administration nor
those with the office of teaching were able to control the situation. "It
was beyond their power or any other power in the country to stop, for
the root of discontent lay deep in the political, social, and intellectual
soil of China." [7]

Learning from the West

The Chinese for the past twenty years had been learning much from
Japan, England, France, Germany, Russia and the United States. This
enlargement of knowledge, while a most satisfying thing, was no luxury;
it was a strict need for survival at this period of Chinese history. Already the advances in science and technology were impressive. But
something more was needed. A choice had to be made from the conflicting doctrines learned in these countries of some basic principles of
intellectual and social order that would save China from the rising tide
of unrest and establish the new set of values. The Confucian difficulty
had been settled, at least for the present. Yet when this traditional
humanism was set aside something else had to be inserted in its place.
It was taken for granted that this new pattern of life would be taken, at
least in large part, from the West. The fundamental quest was for a pattern of life that would provide power, power for inner self-strengthening
and for resisting pressures from abroad.

So far as the Chinese intellectuals could judge, the power of the West lay not in any spiritual or humanist tradition but in its understanding and control of the material world and in its democratic institutions. The best hope of China seemed to be in following the West in these areas of national development. The spiritual traditions of the West had not been communicated to the Chinese intellectuals with any great success in the past century so that they had little awareness of the profound spiritual discipline that had given the West its inner form of life and which still determined, to a large degree, the course of Western development. Only a few men, such as Liang Ch'i-ch'ao in his later years, came to understand how much of Western greatness lay in its spiritual formation by Christianity and in its classical intellectual heritage. K'ang Yu-wei had less insight into these sources of Western culture, but he did see very clearly that neither science nor democracy could supply the moral and humanist foundations needed for the new order of life in China. Neither these men nor any of the other outstanding leaders of China's intellective life saw where the spiritual and cultural traditions of the West could make any serious contribution toward solving China's problems, though the need for a spiritual dynamic did lead to a movement to make Confucianism into a religion. This movement had no success. Chinese intellectuals generally who had studied in Europe and America, with a few exceptions such as the eminent jurist, Dr. John C. H. Wu (Wu Ching-hsiung), came back either with no idea of the religious nature of Western society or with a definite antagonism toward religion. We cannot be surprised at this since the West at this time was in its period of extreme secularization. Western intellectuals themselves had only disdain for their own heritage.

It seemed therefore that the advanced intelligentsia of both China and the West, forgetful of the past, could work together in the further development of the new secular-scientific world order. China had rid itself of its ancient humanism and of the political order that it sustained as the West had rid itself of its Christian Faith and the authoritarian regimes with which it had been associated. The West had first formed the new conditions of human life by its development of scientific knowledge and democratic institutions, but there was yet time for New China to learn these things and to find the place in the world that it deserved. The New Age was still in process. Advanced Chinese scholars already were far ahead of the backward groups of the West.

Yet just at this time a new development had taken place in Russia. Another pattern for the universal society of the future was emerging.

These two patterns, that of Western liberal democracy and that of Marxist Communism were finding their most dynamic expression in two countries, America and Russia, both opposed to Europe, both pregnant with tremendous possibilities for the future. America had achieved in the political order a more democratic society than had thus far been known to the world and was rising rapidly to a dominant position in world affairs. Russia was still in the agony of its revolutionary period. Yet it was already proclaiming a new age of man and a more equal distribution of wealth than had yet been attempted by the most democratic societies of Europe or America. This stirring new gospel was receiving wide acclaim, especially among the rising groups of intellectuals in every country who professed a universal concern for the future of man. In China, too, this new gospel was finding a receptive mentality.

It was essential at this time that China establish cultural and political relations with outside Powers. The question was: with what people and with what political and intellectual traditions should China align itself? In the year 1919 the trend of thought was definitely toward the liberal democracy of America and its pragmatic philosophy. These seemed to be the chosen substitutes for the traditions of her own past, although a group of Chinese intellectuals would welcome the Russian Comintern agent, Voitinski, in 1920 and begin a course of training under him in the Communist program of thought and political action. In 1922 another Comintern agent, Joffe, would be welcomed in Peking where he would give lectures at Peking University on developments in Russia. Michael Borodin and other Soviet advisers would assist the reorganization of the Kuomintang in 1923 according to the model of the Communist Party in Russia. Still in these early decades of the 20th century America was quite closely associated with China, particularly after the Boxer Rebellion when the United States set up a special fund for the education of Chinese students in China and in America out of her share of the Boxer indemnity. The past efforts of America to protect China from occupation by European Powers, the position of America across the Pacific Ocean, the economic ability of America to aid China—all helped to determine the special intimacy that was developing between these two peoples. The supreme moment of intellectual communication between China and America was about to take place when Professor Dewey, among the most renowned of American philosophers, arrived in China. Emotionally and intellectually the Chinese were keyed to hear and to give serious consideration to the thoughts that he would present to them.

Dewey was well received at the National University of Peking where he gave his five most important lectures: Social Philosophy and Political Philosophy; Philosophy of Education; Ways of Thought; Three Philosophers of Our Times (Bergson, Russell, James); On Ethics. During the next two years he travelled throughout the country speaking in most of the university centers on substantially the same subjects as those covered at Peking. He was so successful that two years later when he was leaving China, Dr. Hu Shih said of him that no one since the beginning of East-West relations "had so profoundly influenced Chinese thought." [8] His lectures were reprinted many times. Translations of his other writings were also published: *Reconstruction in Philosophy; How We Think; The Sources of a Science of Education; Schools of Tomorrow; Democracy and Education.*

Influence on Political Development

The great hope of Dewey for a democratic China appears constantly in his lectures to the Chinese and in his writings about the Chinese. He found that America was at the time idealized by China because the Chinese saw in America "a projection of China's democratic hopes for herself." The personal interest shown in Dewey was even more clearly founded on a basic attraction toward democratic ideals. He concluded: "Although this democracy is articulately held only by a handful who have been educated, yet these few know and the dumb masses feel that it alone accords with the historic spirit of the Chinese race." [9] The instinctive attraction of the Chinese for a democratic order was sufficient evidence that "for Bolshevism there is no preparation and no aptitude in China." Among the students who had been trained in the West he found no attraction toward Communism. The more radical among them were those who had been trained within China itself and who spoke and read only Chinese. The exceptions were among those who had been trained in France and who had picked up certain anarchistic ideas that came down from the French Revolution. [10]

The lecture given by Dewey in Peking entitled "Social Philosophy and Political Philosophy," must be considered of special significance. It made a deep impression upon Ch'en Tu-hsiu, who had already become interested in Marxism and who soon would become the founder and, for some years, the intellectual and political leader of the Chinese Communist Party. Dewey's presentation of the democratic idea "delayed by a strong counter-influence" the movement of Ch'en toward the Marxist-

Leninist position, as Benjamin Schwartz, an eminent student of modern China, has asserted. The main idea of this lecture was that democracy in any true sense of the word must begin on the local level and rise from there through successively wider application to the higher realms of political authority. Schwartz considers that these ideas of Dewey led Ch'en to his conviction, at least temporary, that "Democracy must have a grass-roots social basis. It must be part of the fabric of the lives of people and begin in every village and in every city block. Discussions concerning cabinet organization, parliamentary organization, even about centralism versus federalism, are unreal so long as the people as a whole are not thoroughly imbued with democratic attitudes and do not participate in the processes of a democratic life." [11] But however great the influence of Dewey on Ch'en, it did not succeed in bringing his intellectual and political abilities into the service of liberal or social democracy of a European or American style, for in 1921 Ch'en joined with Li Ta-chao to found the Communist Party, the dynamic center of a movement that would first be the opponent and later the conqueror of all other political forces and doctrines in mainland China. The modern destiny of this country was to a large extent determined in the person of Ch'en.

As a distinct political party, the democratic movement envisaged by Dewey was never successful in China. As an ideal it has remained a constant influence there and has seriously affected the political life of the country. Sun Yat-sen had always been doubtful about the success of democratic government in China. Particularly in his later years he considered that authoritarian government was the only type of government that could satisfy the political needs of China and attain those essential aims which were the object in other countries of democratic institutions in the proper sense of the word. After the Revolution of 1911 and the resultant overthrow of the Imperial Manchu government, efforts toward a parliamentary regime had been made—without success. Sung Chiao-jen had at the time of the Revolution drafted a constitution providing for an elected Parliament to which the new government would be responsible. Internal Party dissension among the revolutionists and the military difficulty of establishing rule over the country led to negotiations with Yüan Shih-k'ai who had been recalled by the Regents of the Manchu government to suppress the Revolution. A settlement was made providing for the abdication of the Manchu dynasty in favor of the Republic which was to be under the Presidency of Yüan Shih-k'ai.

In the elections of 1913 the newly formed Kuomintang attained a majority in the first Parliament which then came under the leadership of Sung Chiao-jen. Sung's influence grew rapidly. But at the same time antagonism developed between himself and Yüan Shih-k'ai. Tension increased until on March 20, 1913, Sung was assassinated by arrangement of Yüan's government. This ended the first efforts to establish in China a republican government responsible to a freely elected parliament. The Kuomintang remained out of power for some years but after it was reorganized in 1924 with the help of Russian agents, it regained its hold over the country and ruled as an authoritarian institution. In the future the legislative Assembly, although consisting of elected members, would be responsible to the government, not the government to the Assembly.

This background of Chinese political life must be understood to appreciate the difficulty faced by Dewey during his stay in China. The contest for power was still going on. The Kuomintang had not yet begun effective operation as the ruling power. A democratic regime was not an immediate possibility. Yet liberal ideals were already a dynamic factor in the political life of the country, especially among the professors and students who manifested more enthusiasm than practical ability in political affairs. It was from these intellectuals that Dewey absorbed his conviction that the Chinese had an instinctive attraction to a democratic political order. If these liberals were consistently unclear about the practical measures necessary to establish a democratic order, they were quite clear about their opposition to the Manchu dynasty, to the warlords, and to every type of authoritarian regime. The weakness of successive governments, their inability to meet the rising threat from Japan, corruption among government officials, repressive measures against liberal opposition—all tended to produce a deep cleavage between those most committed to the liberal democratic program and the existing government.

The choice faced by Chinese liberals in recent decades was whether to support the government and to foster liberal and social developments within the existing political order or to foster resentment against the government in the hope that this would in some way or other bring about a transition to a truly democratic structure. A few of the more outstanding liberals such as Ts'ai Yuan-p'ei and Chiang Monlin became associated with the Kuomintang government, but the larger number maintained an attitude of antipathy. This was the attitude of Hu Shih until his later years. Dewey, at the time of his stay, was on intimate terms of acquaintance with those associated with the government and with those in opposition, but he was in no position to influence practical politics in a direct way. His work was to encourage democratic and liberal thought among the advanced intellectuals, while at the same time he set forth an educational program that would prepare future generations for a more effective participation in political life. The greatest benefit of the Kuomintang, as envisaged by the liberals generally, was that it preserved public order which permitted the free exercise of writing and teaching of the principles of a democratic society. Having themselves no direct responsibility for public order or public welfare they could freely indulge in criticism. There was no lack of material to criticize.

Liberal intellectuals in China have since 1920 spanned the entire range of political life, from intimate association with the government to sympathetic cooperation with Communist opposition. Definite areas of agreement have existed between the liberal and the Communist intelligentsia, particularly among those in Peking. Both had the same complaints against the existing regime. Both were anti-Confucian, were thoroughly materialist in their conception of reality, and in general shared in a common world of thought. They understood and respected each other. Division, but only limited opposition, came about through the action of Ch'en Tu-hsiu. When Ch'en and Li Ta-chao committed themselves to the Marxist-Leninist position, we may consider that "This trend in the direction of the Russian Revolution led to the fundamental split, in which Hu Shih as an apostle of Dewey and pragmatism represents the other line of development." [12] Hu Shih was too much the scholar and professor to enter as profoundly into the play of practical politics as Ch'en had done. He was also much less certain about his opposition to the program sponsored by Ch'en than Ch'en was about his opposition to the Liberalism sponsored by Hu Shih. It is clear that despite the division and difference there was on the whole a minimum of opposition between Liberals and Communists during this period. Both were obviously more intensely preoccupied with the faults of the Government than with their own mutual differences. The liberals consistently underestimated the Communist threat. This became another reason for the fatal end that came to both the Kuomintang government as an institution and to liberalism as an intellectual tradition on the mainland. The classical triangle of modern political tensions—authoritarian Government, irreconcilable Liberalism, and aggressive Communism—reached one of its possible resolutions.

Philosophy

Dewey's influence in the philosophical order might be described as a further development of the Positivism that began to dominate the intellectual life of China after Yen Fu published his translation of Thomas Huxley's *Evolution and Ethics* in 1898, a book which became extremely popular with the young students of the period. We can follow the later development of this Positivism, especially in the years just preceding Dewey's arrival, in the pages of the periodical *Hsin-ch'ing-nien,* which began publication in 1915. Before Dewey's arrival in 1919, its pages had carried studies on such men as Adam Smith, Nietzsche, John Stuart Mill, Tolstoy, Thomas Henry Huxley, Darwin, Spencer, Rousseau, Montesquieu and Kropotkin.[13] Also at this time Wang Kuo-wei (1877-1927) was giving the Chinese a wide acquaintance with modern European thought with special attention to the 19th-century German philosophy. Yet it was Positivism from English sources that held the leading position.

Henri Bernard has given us a description of the influence of 19th-century Positivism on Chinese thinkers: "The first books which were made available to the Chinese public pertained exclusively to this school. The translation of Huxley's *Evolution and Ethics,* published by Yen Fu in 1898, had been acclaimed by the Chinese intellectuals as the remedy for the evils of the country. They thought that the Darwinian theory, especially in its social and political applications would be the stimulus needed by a nation that suffered from a centuries-old stagnation. 'Survival of the fittest' became the proverbial formula and they began to compare the evolutionist hypothesis with the naturalist views of many thinkers of ancient China, such as Lieh Tzu and the Taoists." [14]

These works, particularly those of Spencer, Huxley and Darwin, provided excellent preparation for the Pragmatism of Dewey with its avowedly empirical approach to reality with no Kantian subtleties, no structured synthesis such as that of Hegel, no spiritual insights such as we find in Bergson and James, and none of those subjective preoccupations found in Husserl. Already by the time of Dewey's lectures in Peking, Chinese intellectuals were fully committed to Comte's outline of man's development from the religious and mythical understanding of the earliest period, through the metaphysical to the scientific age of true knowledge. Dewey had consistently explained his own thought by reference to these stages of development, though the main purpose of his reference to the classical philosophies of the past was to destroy their grip on the intellectual tradition of the present. In true pragmatic fashion, after his attack on philosophies concerned with man's knowledge of trans-material being, he tells us plainly that he was less concerned with the logic of his attack than with its practical effectiveness: "Common frankness requires that it be stated that this account of the origin of philosophies claiming to deal with absolute Being in a systematic way has been given with malice prepense. It seems to me that this genetic method of approach is a more effective way of undermining this type of philosophic theorizing than any attempt at logical refutation could be." [15] With his sense of the immediate problems of life, Dewey proposed that intelligence be considered an instrument for meeting and mastering the new social environment confronting it. Such a "reconstruction" of the meaning of mind would effectively remove all former illusions about transcendent truths.

This rejection of the past heritage of Western culture was attractive to the Chinese intellectuals as was its counterpart, concern for immediate issues of individual and social life. They too were in the mood to reject their own past, especially the ethical, artistic and social conformism which had limited their country's development in recent centuries. Yet even with this mutual sympathy and a common background of Positivism, Dewey attracted only one outstanding exponent of his philosophy, Dr. Hu Shih. Others of minor importance did take up Dewey's position, and it might even be said that many Chinese thinkers in the last four decades have come under his influence. Yet they were more caught in the general influence of Western Positivism than formally attached to Dewey's Pragmatism. Counterattractions existed in Confucianism, in Kantian Criticism, in Hegelian Idealism, and in Bergson's Vitalism, all recent imports from Europe. Yet special attention should be given to one counterinfluence that has seldom been presented in its full force, the aesthetic type of Humanism represented by Ts'ai Yuan-p'ei. He agreed with Dewey in many things. Yet Ts'ai had too much depth and breadth in his intellectual life to be overly influenced by Dewey's Pragmatism. One of those impressive scholars of the transition period, Ts'ai had obtained a thorough training in both Chinese and Western thought. He was deeply sensitive to the realm of beauty in both its emotional and intellectual aspects. Man's responsiveness to the beautiful he considered the highest of human accomplishments, even a worthy substitute for religion. Dewey's Pragmatism provided no enrichment to this type of Humanism. The origins of Ts'ai's Aesthetic

Humanism were in the very substance of the scholarly and artistic life of China. It had a present as well as a traditional appeal. Now as in the past, it gave to Chinese scholars a higher mystique that supplied in part their relative lack of metaphysics and religion. Hsü Ch'ing-yü, in his *Philosophy of Beauty,* proposed an attitude similar to that of Ts'ai. While this type of Humanism was, in China, frequently associated with Positivism, it did provide a certain refined modification in a spiritual direction that prevented it from being absorbed into the Pragmatism or Instrumentalism proposed by Dewey.

Hu Shih was much younger than Ts'ai and from his earliest years as a student responsive to the attraction of Western materialist philosophy. He saw in science and technology something more spiritual than material. He developed the religious enthusiasm for Dewey's Pragmatism that Mencius had for Confucian Humanism. A writer of exceptional ability, Hu Shih was in close contact with the intellectual life of China during the critical years of its transition. Through him the new conception of the human mind as the instrument of pragmatic adaptation to reality was transplanted to China. Yet even in Hu Shih the unfruitfulness of Pragmatism as a formal philosophy can be seen, for his early promise was never fulfilled in philosophical speculation. He turned toward the history of philosophy and there made his greatest contribution to the intellectual life of modern China.[16] For the first time, in his work, the ancient schools of Chinese philosophy were studied by a Chinese scholar with the scientific care and critical analysis proper to contemporary Western standards of scholarship. Hu Shih sought especially to relate Chinese philosophical systems to their historical and social setting. What he began has been further developed by a large number of more recent scholars in the history of Chinese thought, Fung Yu-lan and all succeeding writers on the subject being greatly indebted to him. One important though regrettable result of this positivist approach to Chinese thought traditions is the tendency to read modern positivist conceptions into the early thinking of the Chinese, a tendency that can be seen in the work of Hu Shih and also in the first volume of Fung Yu-lan's *History of Chinese Philosophy*. It can, perhaps, also be seen in a recent translation of the *Analects* wherein the Chinese word *T'ien* is translated as "Sky" rather than "Heaven," apparently to avoid the spiritual connotations of the latter word.

To trace Dewey's influence on other Chinese writers would be possible but of little value, for there has been a continual shifting of position by the more important figures and the major influence of positive thought was already present before the time of Dewey. In the field of philosophy, properly so called, other traditions have been stronger than that of Dewey and Hu Shih. As a special school of philosophy Pragmatism was vigorous for only a few years. The verdict of a careful student is that "Since the middle 1920's, Pragmatism as a system has been overshadowed by other Western philosophies. Pragmatists, including Hu, turned their attention to educational reform, social reconstruction, and political revolution. The philosophical arena was taken over by Neo-realism, Rationalistic and Idealistic Neo-Confucianism, and finally, Marxianism." [17] To this summation of the career of Pragmatism in China we might add that of Homer Dubs who wrote in 1938: "The golden period of Hu Shih's influence in China was about 1923-1924. Since that time his influence has declined very considerably. He has failed to attract disciples, and today pragmatism is the smallest of the groups I shall mention." [18]

Education

The greatest influence of Dewey in China as in the United States has been in the field of Education. He more than anyone else has made of Education a special field of advanced study in its own right. His influence on political and philosophical thought was part of a larger trend. His influence on Education was original, decisive, lasting. Not only in China but on a universal basis it is doubtful if anyone in this century has had as extensive an influence on the educational programs of the world. If this influence has been delayed in making itself felt in Europe, in Asia it arrived much earlier. Its greatest impact was in China.

The main contacts of Dewey in China were with the university professors and the students. An ideal situation existed for his work as educator, a situation much more favorable, in some ways, than the situation in America, for Chinese students had a sense of political and social involvement lacking among students in America. Detached intellectual speculation was as impossible and as undesirable for them as for Dewey. "Education for living" had a welcome meaning to students anxious to make their contribution to the welfare of their society.

They were, in fact, caught up in the dramatic student movement at the time of Dewey's arrival in the country. By violent protest against the conduct of the national government they had forced upon it some important political decisions. Dewey was as thrilled with their action as the students themselves. To him it marked the awakening of China from a state of passive waiting. "A sharp blow has been given the idea that China itself is helpless and must be saved from without." It was a revelation of what educated China "can do and will do in the future. . . . The spell of pessimism has been broken. An act has been done, a deed performed." There now existed a better and healthier movement for the salvation of China than at any time since the Revolution. There was yet much to be done, "But in no other country could moral and intellectual force accomplish so quickly and peacefully what was effected in China in the last five or six weeks. . . . If the present organization persists and is patiently employed for constructive purposes, then the fourth of May, nineteen hundred and nineteen, will be marked as the dawn of a new day. This is a large If. But just now the future of China so far as it depends upon China hangs on that If." [19]

Other forces for the correction of political disorder existed in the country, Dewey conceded, "but in the schools, in the Student Movement, now grown politically self-conscious, are the forces making for a future politics of a different sort." [20] While this appears as a simple statement about the general influence of the schools on a country, it has a depth of meaning for Dewey that is not generally possessed by ourselves. In all his thoughts about man Dewey went instinctively to the young mind and its formation in the centers of education from the most elementary to the most advanced levels. The school was especially important as an instrument of social change. Thus he sensed a certain inevitability in the development of democracy in China when he saw the university students so attached to the ideals of liberalism. Here were the men who would later control the entire society and who would eventually resolve the basic political problems of contemporary China. He found that the Chinese themselves, more than most peoples, were aware of the social function of education. "There is nothing which one hears so often from the lips of representatives of Young China of to-day as that education is the sole means of reconstructing China." Yet the vastness of the problem was appalling. The numbers of the people, the stiff traditionalism that had marked recent centuries, the political turmoil, all these things led him to reflect that "the difficulties in the way of a practical extension and regeneration of Chinese education are all but insuperable." [21] The whole affair was now of more than academic concern. It was of utmost importance to China and China was of utmost importance to the entire world.

Modern educational efforts prior to Dewey's arrival in China had been dominated by German educational ideals and programs which the

Chinese had learned from Japan. Noteworthy advances had been made within this pattern. Now, however, with the coming of Dewey, American aims, methods and materials became dominant. The entire system of American educational research was transferred to China. Experimental schools and programs of training in educational theory and practice were set up.[22] At the Educational Conference in China in 1919, the purposes of education were redefined according to the views of American progressivism: students should learn by doing; their abilities should be developed according to their capacities; the school, as a society, should be run as far as practicable by students themselves.[23]

Dewey's influence was particularly strong in the Educational Conference of November 1922. This can be seen in the statement of aims agreed upon by the Conference, which were: "1) To adapt itself to a new and changing society; 2) To promote the spirit of democracy; 3) To develop individuality; 4) To take into special consideration the economic status of the average citizen; 5) To adjust education to the needs of life; 6) To facilitate the spread of universal education; 7) To make itself flexible enough to allow for local variation." [24]

Dr. Ou Tsuin-chen, who has for several decades been associated with the Ministry of Education in China, has recently, in 1958, published a second edition of a study on Dewey that originally appeared in 1931. He has consistently been critical of extremist tendencies found in many followers of Dewey; yet he remains of the opinion that "there is in the real teaching of the Master very little for reproach." [25] Such has been the prevailing attitude toward Dewey among educators in China. There have been extravagances there as elsewhere in applying some of the principles taught by Dewey but these are explained as based on incorrect understanding of Dewey's thought. Ou Tsuin-chen is generally correct in saying: "The influence of Dewey on Chinese education is general and even total. It was brought about by conferences with educators while Dewey was himself in China, and also by his publications, almost all of which have been translated into Chinese, and by his outstanding students who are the leaders of Chinese education. Among these are Monlin Chiang, ex-Minister of Education and Rector of the National University of Peking; Hu Shih, an ardent Pragmatist, who inspired the movement for a New Culture and who was also a Professor there at the time and P. W. Kuo, the ex-Rector of the National University of Nanking. The renown and activity of these men have been very influential in bringing about popular acceptance of Dewey's teaching and putting it into practise." [26]

In 1925 and again in 1928 the need of creating a national spirit among the Chinese led to a different statement of aims. These put greater emphasis on society and less on the individual. The entire educational program was put into a severely nationalist context.[27] Yet Dewey's influence remained. The less desirable features have been considerably modified in time by a renewed awareness in educational circles of the values of Chinese Humanism. Within this context the main features of Dewey's program—education for living, child-centered instruction, the school as a society—have their own proper and permanent place. These ideas have a certain universal validity and have been used in both Nationalist and in Communist China no less than in the democratic world of America. In each case a reappraisal of Dewey's work has taken place and the more general context of education, its final orientation, has been provided by more ultimate views on the nature and destiny of man.

Opposition to Dewey

In all these areas of Chinese life—political, philosophical and educational—the influence of Dewey has been widespread and to some degree permanent, despite the fact that even during the years of his greatest appeal, 1919 to 1925, his influence on political and philosophical thought was so much a part of more extensive movements that his specific contribution is not easily identified. So also the opposition to his influence was part of a general opposition to an over-assertive Positivism. Except for the Marxists there was much less opposition among the writers of the period to his social and political ideals, though opposition to Dewey and Hu Shih specifically and to the general trends which they represented did exist.

First came the opposition from Confucian scholars who objected to the iconoclastic attitude adopted toward the cultural traditions of the past. All serious-minded men of the time, except a few extremists such as Ku Hung-ming (1875-1928), wished an extensive degree of modernization, the introduction of Western scientific learning, and the adoption of many customs and conveniences from the West. But many saw that the more important human formation of life, which was so deeply needed at the time, could not be supplied by Western science or political thought. These men were as conscious of the defects of scientism as the extreme Progressivists were conscious of the defects in 19th-century Confucianism.

World War I brought new developments in China's attitude toward the West. Before this war it was the belief of K'ang Yu-wei and of many others that the West was entering the "Age of Increasing Peace and Equality," [28] but increasing awareness of the universal afflictions that emerged from the war, particularly the mutual destruction of the Western nations, set into motion a current of anti-Western criticism in the immediate post-war years. In 1919, the year in which Dewey began his visit to China, Liang Ch'i-ch'ao, once the foremost advocate of Westernization, returned from his study tour through Europe. He was deeply disturbed by what he saw there, as can be seen from his book, *A Record of Impressions during Travel in Europe.* His conviction of the decadence of Western scientific society was further manifested in the parting address he gave to his classes at Tung-nan University in 1923. There he considers that the West has reached an extreme state of spiritual famine, relief from which must be found in China and in India rather than in the West, for "Eastern learning has spirit as its point of departure; Western learning has matter as its point of departure." [29] Earlier, in answer to Hu Shih's *History of Chinese Philosophy* (1919), another scholar, Liang Shu-ming, had written a book which attained a wide reading public, *The Civilizations of Orient and Occident and Their Philosophies* (1922). Liang Shu-ming was not content to point out the difficulties in Hu Shih's approach to philosophy. He took a more positive stand in presenting Chinese civilization as the central civilization of the world, the one which avoids the inherent evils associated with both Western and Indian civilizations, and also the one most likely to become the universal civilization of the future, As a remedy for the defects found in Western Positivism, Liang proposed the Confucian spirituality found in Wang Yang-ming (1472-1529).

Further opposition to Dewey's Pragmatism derived its power from the new currents of Western philosophy, based on the thought of Hegel and Bergson, that began to appear in the 1920's. Carsun Chang expressed this opposition to Dewey and to others founding their thought on the empirical sciences in a lecture delivered at Tsinghua University in Peking on February 14, 1923, dealing with philosophies of life. This led to a new controversy. Chang was at the time a young professor returned from studies in Japan and Germany. His study of Bergson had given him a vision of reality radically opposed to the positivistic philosophies of the period, particularly when he saw these philosophies imported into China and used by Chinese scholars against the classical thought of the Chinese themselves. He was among the few Chinese at this time who had a true insight into what constitutes philosophical thought in the Western sense and what makes it distinct from inductive scientific thought. He insisted that our acquaintance with reality obtained through philosophy, aesthetics and religion is a higher and more necessary type of knowledge than that obtained by science and that, consequently, we must go beyond the range of the empirical sciences, both in subject matter and in method.

Professor Ting Wen-chiang (1887-1935), replying to Chang, asserted the universal application of scientific procedures and the purely subjective character of all trans-scientific knowledge. Ting, as the most outstanding of modern Chinese geologists, was thoroughly attached to the natural sciences and shared the suspicion, so widely shared by scientific-minded Chinese, of all metaphysical and ethical teaching not founded on the natural sciences. These scientists feared a reassertion of the traditional attitudes that had stifled the mental development of China in the past. This explains some of the vehemence that appeared in the debate. Something more than intellectual objections are felt in the arguments presented. We feel a sense of anxiety in the arguments of Ting and his fellow-scientists lest their fields again come under the judgment of ethics, metaphysics or religion. The only alternatives to such an abomination were to bring these latter realms of knowledge under the dominion of the natural sciences or to discard them as not belonging to the universe of knowledge at all.

The main support for Chang came from Chang T'ung-sun, Liang Ch'i-ch'ao, and Liang Shu-ming. Chang T'ung-sun had been trained in Japan where he had absorbed the thought of Kant, Hegel, and Bergson and delved more deeply into epistemological questions as they occur in a Western context than other Chinese thinkers of the period. He would limit the work of science to the description of the world of reality and accord to metaphysics alone the role of giving the deeper meaning of things and explaining the inner structure of knowledge itself. Liang Ch'i-ch'ao and Liang Shu-ming supported Carsun Chang's position more from an ethical and humanist standpoint.

The main support for Ting Wen-chiang came from Ch'en Tu-hsiu, Wu Chih-hui and Hu Shih. Ch'en stated clearly, "We believe that only objective material causes can change society, can explain history, and can determine one's philosophy of life." [30] Wu Chih-hui proclaimed the naturalist view of the universe and of man in his essay entitled "A New

Concept of the Universe and Life, Based on a New Belief," a work considered by Hu Shih as the most significant and acceptable essay of the entire discussion because it "ruled out God, banished the soul, and punctured the metaphysical idea that man is the most spiritual of all things." [31] Of Hu Shih himself it can be said: "Dr. Hu definitely accepts Mr. Ting's proposition that a common measure for all life may be found in science. And with the zeal of a herald of a new gospel he says, 'We must earnestly proclaim our new faith, incessantly proclaim it.' " [32] The final result of the controversy was to indicate how extensively Positivism had come to dominate the mind of Chinese intellectuals. Hu Shih wrote later that "with the exception of a few conservative scholars trained in German philosophy through the Japanese school, the majority of those who took part in this debate were on the side of science, which they held to be capable of dealing with all problems of human life and conduct." [33]

The Marxist challenge to Dewey proved to be more effective than the Confucian or the Idealist. This story of the rise and development of dialectical materialism in China is among the most significant stories of our century, one that deserves more intensive study and more widespread understanding. It still has practical implications in the continuing conflict between Communist and non-Communist thought for the mind of Asia. Briefly, it can be said that from 1918 on, Marxism began to awaken in the Chinese a response of very great depth and enthusiasm, and that in the 1920's it was already winning the allegiance of many professors and students throughout the country. Positivism and Hegelian Idealism, with their insistence on the progressive stages of development in the mind of man, had prepared the way. Thus the philosophical preparation for Marxism was substantially the same in China as in Europe, though in China the process was telescoped into a shorter interval of time.

The first person to express any adequate understanding of the Bolshevik Revolution was Li Ta-chao who wrote in 1918: "Henceforth, all that one sees around him will be the triumphant banner of Bolshevism, and all that one hears around him will be Bolshevism's song of victory. The bell is rung for humanitarianism! The dawn of freedom has arrived! See the world of tomorrow; it assuredly will belong to the red flag! . . . Although the word 'Bolshevism' was created by the Russians, the spirit it embodies can be regarded as that of a common awakening in the heart of each individual among mankind of the twentieth century. The victory of Bolshevism, therefore, is the victory of the spirit of common awakening in the heart of each individual among mankind in the twentieth century." [34]

Although the early part of the 1920's was the period most influenced by Dewey's liberalism and scientific empiricism, it is surprising how much was accomplished by the Communists between 1920 and 1927, for it was during this period that the "groundwork for the later facile acceptance of Marxist-Leninist premises among the Chinese intelligentsia was laid." [35] Interest in the social sciences increased noticeably. It was reported that among 400 new books produced between the spring of 1928 and the summer of 1930 seventy per cent concerned the social sciences and close to three-fourths of these treated themes of a Marxist nature. [36]

Henceforth, the most popular currents of thought tended toward Marxist positions. Both problems and—more important—the methods of dealing with problems became Marxist. Social and economic determinism came into increasing prominence in thought and morality as well as in the arts and literature. But immediately discussion of the Marxist historical dialectic led to further controversy: "The polemic on the materialist interpretation of Chinese history, which took place in 1928-31, was a direct sequel to the polemic between science and philosophy and the revolution in the history of Chinese history. Now that materialism and empiricism had won over idealism and rationalism and that two millenniums of ancient history had been expurgated, the Chinese thinkers began to reinterpret the course of authentic history in the light of economic determinism." [37] Kuo Mo-jo, a writer of exceptional ability in many different fields of philosophy, science, history and literature, and one of the men responsible for the development of this controversy, published in 1932 an impressive study of Chinese history in the light of the Marxist dialectic and thus solidified his claim to be the foremost among Marxist students of the social history of China.

One difficulty, a domestic debate among the Marxists, concerned the method to be used in determining the periods of Chinese history as these must appear to satisfy the demands of Communist historical dogma. But as early as 1929, the controversy had changed into a dispute between the Marxists and anti-Marxists about the entire question of historical development. Again Chang T'ung-sun appeared as a prominent figure in the controversy, this time as an exponent of the anti-Marxist view. He kept this anti-Marxist position for some years but abandoned it after World War II, as the subject of his thought shifted from pure philosophy to the social sciences. A few years later he was himself defending the Marxist position. Hu Shih, traveling in Europe during the most important years of the controversy, was never able to provide an adequate counterposition to that of Marxism either in the field of social theory or in the explanation of historical development. Pragmatism was progressively absorbed rather than refuted by the flood of Marxist thought that now began to dominate the country.

At no time in the history of modern thought could it be said that the Chinese sought an understanding of things with the detached philosophical or scientific attitude that has characterized Western thought in its periods of outstanding achievement. The Chinese quest was for an effective program of thought and political action that would enable them to effectively administer, defend, and develop the country. The empiricism of Dewey offered a less dynamic program than that of the dialectical materialists.

Dewey's Achievement

The problem of China in the 20th century, as we have stated it earlier, has been that of making an adjustment to a divided world. Adjustment to the technological and political forces of a liberal democratic West was sufficiently arduous, and China did give some promise of bringing about this adjustment and of taking her part in the formation of a world society of independent, democratic nations. Suddenly, however, a counterforce arose within the West to challenge the supremacy of the liberal regimes established there. A total explanation of reality with total claims upon man, Communism was dedicated to the complete destruction of all rival forms of social structure and all rival expressions of basic human values. China, so long humiliated by European powers, was invited to enter alongside Russia in the new world-struggle and to assist in bringing to an end the economic exploitation of the capitalist democracies. Western liberals had taught China to bypass the earlier spiritual forces of the Western tradition. Marxists now taught China to bypass the imperfect developments of Liberalism in favor of the newest and most perfect form of life and to enter directly into the world society of the future.

A change was taking place in the life of mankind that could only be compared with the original transition of man from the neolithic period to that of the higher civilizations. These now, after some five thousand years of dominion over human life, were out-dated in both

East and West. Distinctive cultural development was also a thing of the past. The future would be a world of unity and equality, human life would be renewed in its most profound and most universal sense. A global civilization worthy of man was finally in the making. Marxism would replace everything, Confucianism and Christianity, along with Hinduism, Buddhism, Islam, and all the rest. Marxism would provide the new theology and philosophy, the new religion and morality, the new history, science, art and literature. All former things would now pass away. "Behold, I make all things new!" [38] Day was about to dawn upon a world of darkness. Man was about to be released from the cave world of Plato.

As yet only the aurora was visible. This new culture had been able to establish itself only on the margins of the older societies of the West, in an underdeveloped area of the world. Yet it was already setting forth to besiege the entire world both from within and from without. Liberal society also had its dreams, its vision, and was holding out its promises to bring about the final evolvement of man. It also laid claim to the final goal of historical development, to protect and develop most perfectly those rights on which depended man's proper dignity and nobility. The difficulty in the non-Western parts of the world was that this same Liberalism which stoutly asserted the personal rights of its citizens, was denying these very rights to citizens of other societies and was even being used to justify exploitation of Asians and Africans for the benefit of the West.

When Dewey arrived in China, Marxist thought was not widely known or understood there. Neither Dewey nor his followers realized how powerful an influence Marxist-Leninist Communism would become. During the two years of his venture in China, Dewey made the greatest single effort ever made to bring that country into the new age of Western liberalism in political life, of radical empiricism in philosophy, and of progressivism in education. Now as we look back upon this effort we can see quite clearly that the cause Dewey represented was from the beginning severely handicapped for several reasons.

First and most important was the philosophical weakness of his position. It offered no satisfactory alternative to the traditional Humanism that in former centuries had fashioned the Confucian virtues in the individual person and which had given inner vitality to the social structure. His educational program contained some excellent ideas which could be most beneficial in the training of the young, but only within a more adequate philosophical and religious context which his philosophy could not supply. Secondly, his cause was in trouble from the lack of strength in the existing Chinese government. Liberalism can grow and develop only within an ordered society. Liberalism supposes order, it does not create order. Thirdly, his cause was in trouble from the existing antagonism toward the West rising from resentment against the colonial systems that had been imposed on so many Asian peoples. If the United States was to some extent exempt from this antagonism it was only a partial exemption. The growing anti-foreignism included also Americans.

Despite these difficulties Dewey achieved very much during his stay. The extent to which he established a communication of mind between himself and the Chinese intelligentsia of the period is indeed remarkable. We do not appreciate the excellence of this achievement until we consider that throughout the preceding century religious teachers from the West had experienced great trouble in establishing any basic contact with the Chinese intellectuals, even though much of the modern schooling of China was under their control. There remained in the Chinese mind an area apart, which was never truly reached by these religious leaders. The Catholics failed completely to establish any basic contact with the leading thinkers of the period. They made no serious effort in this direction. Protestants had become, in the 19th century, the successors of Matteo Ricci and the Jesuits of the 17th century. Timothy Richard, Young Allen, W. A. P. Martin, these Protestant missionaries did recognize the problem faced by China at this time, and they worked for a modernization of China in accord with Western standards of scientific development. They were in close touch with the leaders of the Reform Movement, particularly with K'ang Yu-wei. Yet on the whole there were no outstanding philosophical thinkers among them and the higher intelligentsia of the 20th century grew up with the secular and materialistic bias typical of the West in that period. Effective East-West confrontations in the intellectual order were founded on contacts between professors and students, between professors, and between universities; and these were increasing in number as Chinese students on the university level were going abroad to complete their work.

Dewey's meeting with the Chinese was of this latter type, and it had a special human attractiveness of its own. He was, in the 20th century, a secularized Matteo Ricci present at the new court of Chinese scholars assembled at the National University of Peking where devotion to Western thought was as intense as was the devotion in earlier centuries to Confucian thought,

The second outstanding achievement of Dewey was his recognition that the Chinese had the ability to do their own thinking and to resolve their own problems in their own way. They needed Western help. But in line with his belief that the one learning must make his own adjustment to reality, Dewey constantly encouraged them to take the initiative in bringing their nation into its proper place in the modern world. Dewey's great confidence in the power of the human mind to find its own way and his opposition to indoctrination or imposition of thought upon the mind of other persons were embodied in his insistence that the Chinese should administer their own affairs. This confidence in the ability of the Chinese cannot be fully appreciated until we observe that political and ecclesiastical authorities had consistently refused to acknowledge the abilities of Asians in general and of the Chinese in particular to conduct their own affairs. A person has only to read the life of Vincent Lebbe to see how unyielding an attitude had developed within Catholic ecclesiastical circles, on the ground that the Chinese were not ready to assume responsibility for their ecclesiastical government.

A third achievement of Dewey was to strengthen the bonds of American-Chinese association. Undoubtedly, much of his influence derived from the feelings of friendship for the United States found among a considerable segment of the Chinese leaders, and by his teaching and example he nurtured these feelings to greater vitality. After his visit other professors from America, particularly educators, were invited to China to assist in establishing training centers for teachers and to develop a research program to guide and promote the new effort at the universal education of the Chinese people in accord with modern standards.

However, these three achievements of Dewey should be balanced against a consideration of the detrimental effects of his influence. 1) In accenting the positivistic approach in communication between China and America, Dewey created further difficulties in spiritual communication between the two countries. 2) In encouraging the Chinese people to an immediate and thorough adaptation to the modern age, he helped to turn them further against their own better humanist traditions and thus brought them into further dependence on the West. 3) In fostering a closer association between China and America on the philosophical basis of Pragmatism, he helped to alienate the more humanist forces of China and thereby created an area of antagonism as well as an area of agreement.

Conflict with Communism

Already by the 1930's many Chinese intellectuals were tending toward Marxism. In determining the causes of this trend, we assign first place to the messianic quality of Marxist Communism. 1) It offered an integral body of dogma concerning man and society where Dewey had only a program of constant adaptation to the multiple life situations in which man finds himself. 2) It offered a doctrine of historical inevitability in the fulfillment of its aims for the reconstruction of society. In this way it provided not only an objective but a sense of certainty in attaining that objective. This certainty, again, was not founded on empirical evidence but on belief in an historical process that transcended every contingent circumstance and every particular judgment of man concerning the course of events. 3) It gave a prophetic mission to the intellectuals. Whereas the prophets of the Old Testament had only projected the outlines of a new and ideal world that would come into existence by divine intervention in a later messianic period, the new social prophets were not content to propose the vision of a universal society of peace and justice. They actually began to set up the institutional framework of the new order and to lead mankind, nation by nation, into this new universal City of Man. Thus, its origin is in human effort associated with the immanent forces of social development rather than in divine intervention. The Guides, Builders, and Rulers of the new order of things in China were the intellectuals.

The change envisaged involved a total destruction of the old and a total construction of the new. This sense of total change, of a transformed world, is a thing of such unparalleled magnitude that it has always been difficult for those outside the ranks of Communism to understand. Yet this ideal of a total renewal of life is at the center of the entire movement, and it is the function of the intellectual leaders to hold forth this vision at all times. The real leadership, according to Marxist theory, is to be sought in the ranks of the proletariat rather than from among the bourgeoisie, but in this particular the development of Communism in China was not in strict accord with the theory. For the leadership of the intellectuals was joined to a base formed almost entirely from the peasantry. The role of the students in the Communist movement brings out the unique position they have traditionally held in modern China. In the New Democracy period, beginning in the mid-thirties, some seventy per cent of the Chinese Communist leaders, it was estimated, were students from fairly well-to-do families.[39] The fulfillment of Marxist purposes in China was possible only because the students assumed in China a role of greater importance than in Russia or in other countries.

There is about the entire Communist Movement in China as elsewhere a general mood that must be considered of a religious rather than of a purely social or political nature. Its intense preoccupation with the extinction of the more traditional religions of mankind is itself one of the surest indications of the religious nature of the movement. Much of its success in China—and elsewhere—is due precisely to this religious factor, which is not entirely absent from the positivist and liberal movements of our times. Dewey himself made a conscious effort to develop his Pragmatism into a new religion and a new spirituality, as is clear from the closing pages of *Reconstruction in Philosophy*. He recognized that "poetry, art, religion are precious things," but insisted that, in the commonly accepted sense they had come into existence by imaginative and emotional processes which had been discredited by scientific advances. The task for the modern world was to develop the "vital sources of a religion and art that are yet to be," [40] by hastening the interpenetration of science and emotion. When this should be achieved, "poetry and religious feeling will be the unforced flowers of life." Yet more, "When the emotional force, the mystic force one might say, of communication, of the miracle of the shared life and shared experience is spontaneously felt, the hardness and crudeness of contemporary life will be bathed in the light that never was on land or sea." [41] Thus Dewey looked for the creation of a new religious, artistic and moral order within the context of Pragmatism itself. His trend was the same as that of Comte, though he was incapable of the vast constructive effort that Comte brought to his work and thus could not explicate his ideas so fully.

We witness in China a conflict between Pragmatism as a religion and Communism as a religion. Both were born out of the post-Christian West. Both carried a large share of the original dynamism of Christianity. Both conceived themselves as fulfilling a work of universal redemption, as being historical forces that would bring all mankind from darkness into the light and would answer the question of Nicodemus which now is the question proper not only to China but to all the world: "Can an old, vast, peculiar, self-sufficing civilization be born again?" Both agreed and in this both show their prophetic and Christian backgrounds. "Made over again it must be or it cannot endure." [42]

That Dewey was conscious of the New Testament origin of this question is clear from another passage at the end of *Reconstruction in Philosophy* (though without quotation marks): "The wind of the spirit bloweth where it listeth and the kingdom of God in such things does not come with observation." [43] It is clear that Dewey's thought was founded on a post-Christian Positivism which developed in predominantly Protestant America in the 19th and 20th centuries and then passed to the shores of China where it took upon itself the task of remaking that country and of infusing into it a new life of the spirit.

Marxist Communism is also a post-Christian development founded on a materialist interpretation of the historical dialectic outlined by Hegel. This interpretation of the past was projected one more step into the future when the final and most decisive stage of human development would become a reality. The society of the future was envisaged in terms filled with apocalyptic significance. Entry into this final stage of man's historical transformation was to be brought about by the redemptive suffering of the proletariat.[44] This apocalyptic element in Marxism was strengthened considerably when the Communist movement came to external expression in Orthodox Russia, the country in which the exotic visions of St. John concerning the final transformation of this world into the heavenly city and his vision of the thousand years' reign of the saints on earth had their most extreme interpretation. Almost immediately after the October Revolution in Russia this vision was communicated to China. Li Ta-chao in 1918 first proclaimed this vision of the future and began the remaking of China, not according to any existing reality, but according to the prophecies of the messianic age as found in Isaias and Micheas—all translated into terrestrial terminology. The association of apocalyptic imagery with the theme of revolution belongs to the very essence of the Bolshevik Movement. For as Hans Mühlstein wrote in 1925: "Bolshevism as a Russian phenomenon is nothing other than the entire Christian ideology of Millenarism, which a few determined men have associated, as a cataract, with the turbine of their materialistic doctrine." [45] It was under such powerful religious drives that Communism offered to remake the ancient civilization of China.

What is particularly impressive is the manner in which the Chinese intelligentsia responded to this vision of messianic Marxism. Before the introduction of Communism into China, they had begun to stir from their state of cultural equilibrium. But suddenly they were caught up in the full impact of history. Few people have desired renewal so much as the Chinese, nor have many nations realized so clearly that this renewal could come about only by contact with forces from without. The long delay through the 19th century had increased this desire to a rare intensity, as can be seen particularly in the most sensitive of Chinese writers of this period, Liang Ch'i-ch'ao. His quest for the renovation of Chinese society is evident in all his works.

China's difficulty was rooted in both the perfection and the imperfection of her former way of life. China was caught in a balance of tensions and resultant harmony of life such as is uncommon to the greater civilizations of man. It had attained a satisfactory status so far as its own development was concerned. No people were ever so careful in dating their history and in keeping a written memory of the past. But, on the other hand, no people were so distant from a conception of historical development such as we find it in the West. This accounts for the tremendous difficulty and the extreme consequences of disturbing this equilibrium. The past suddenly was transformed from its privileged status as the most valuable possession of the present to the status of a humiliating memory to be utterly rejected and abandoned. The future opened on a world divided between Liberal Bourgeois Democracy and Marxist Proletarian Communism, between Dialectical Materialism and American Pragmatism. The recent history of China is the story of the struggle of these two forces to establish themselves in a position of control.

Military force brought a final decision in the political order, but only after a sufficient number of intellectuals had been won to the Communist cause and the remaking of China on the Marxist pattern had begun in the universities of China and in the publications that appeared in the years of decision. During the difficult years of revolutionary struggle the Communists were so sure of their superior standing with the intellectuals, particularly with professors and students, that they often claimed, in the years prior to their final conquest, that their first act on returning to Yenching University would be to have an alumni reunion. The Pragmatism of Dewey was engulfed in something greater than itself. Essentially this something greater was a more dynamic Christian-Millenarist force that survived in a strangely twisted form within the Communist Movement. This prophetic and Christian influence is found also in Dewey's thought, but there it had been flattened with its American bourgeois success. Hu Shih carried the prophetic temper of Pragmatism with a worthy dedication of mind that was the equal of Ch'en Tu-hsiu's dedication to Marxism. But the movement was already a thing of the past. Pragmatism on its own principles must be judged inadequate. The mind considered as a tool becomes unequal to its task.

It seems then that the liberal and pragmatic influences brought to China by Dewey were not so much destroyed as absorbed by the incoming tide of Communism. To the followers of Dewey "The Communist movement was represented as an integral part of the Western civilization they admired, a logical development of the democratic ideal, supplementing democracy's so-called earlier individualistic stage." [46] This was especially true of Hu Shih.[47] There was in Pragmatism no inner principle of sufficient vitality to withstand the difficulties that it faced, nor was it able to present any positive program for the reconstruction of a social order which it had shrilly denounced for many years. While working against the Confucian order of the past and the Nationalist order of the present, the Chinese Liberals failed to recognize the threat of Communism in the future. They suffered, indeed, from a fatal attraction for this movement so dramatically gathering strength throughout the country. Later it could be written: "The fact is that nearly every leading citizen among the modern Chinese intelligentsia, with the exception of a certain number who had become identified with the Nationalist government, appears to have given a degree of moral support to the new Peking regime." [48]

It is wrong to suppose that the conquest of China was primarily due to military strength. It was much more a thing of the mind. As one of the most informed students of the Chinese Communist Party has pointed out: "The Communist success with the scholar class is in part a genuine achievement of ideology, a victory for the Communist creed as outlined in the preceding documents. Not that Western-trained Chinese intellectuals have become fanatical converts to Marxism-Leninism. But they have in a great many cases seen merit in the practises of the CCP and have in large part subscribed to its theories and explanation of its programme. Increasingly they seem to have accepted the Party line as a valid picture of the modern world." [49] This statement, though subject to further explanation, underlines a truth which is of very great significance. For the struggle that took place in China is still going on in Asia and throughout the entire world.

NOTES

1. John Dewey, "Old China and New," *Asia,* 21 (May, 1921), 445.
2. "New Culture in China," *Asia,* 21 (July, 1921) 642.
3. *Letters from China and Japan,* 21 (New York: Dutton, 1920) 168

4. "Old China and New," *Op. cit.* 448.
5. Hu Shih, *The Chinese Renaissance* (Chicago: University of Chicago Press, 1934) 39.
6. Kiang Wen han, *The Chinese Student Movement* (New York: King's Crown Press, 1948) 27.
7. Chiang Monlin, *Tides from the West,* (New Haven: Yale, 1947) 129.
8. O. Briere, S.J., *Fifty Years of Chinese Philosophy,* trans. from the French by L. G. Thompson (London: Allen & Unwin, 1956) 26.
9. "The International Duel in China," *New Republic,* 20 (August 27, 1919) 112.
10. "New Culture in China," *op. cit.* 584.
11. Benjamin I. Schwartz, *Chinese Communism and the Rise of Mao* (Cambridge: Harvard, 1951) 19, 20.
12. Ssu-yu Teng, John K. Fairbank et al., *China's Response to the West* (Cambridge: Harvard, 1954) 232.
13. Schwartz, *op. cit.* 7.
14. Henri Bernard, *Sagesse Chinoise et Philosophie Chrétienne* (Tientsin: Institute des Hautes Etudes, 1935) 207.
15. *Reconstruction in Philosophy* (New York: Holt, 1920) 24.
16. Wing-tsit Chan, "Hu Shih and Chinese Philosophy," *Philosophy East and West* VI 1 (April, 1956) 3-12.
17. *Ibid.* 4.
18. Homer Dubs, "Recent Chinese Philosophy," *Journal of Philosophy* 35 (1938) 350.
19. "The Student Revolt in China," *New Republic* 20 (August 6, 1919) 18.
20. "New Leaven in Chinese Politics," *Asia* 20 (April, 1920) 272.
21. "America and Chinese Education," *New Republic* 30 (March 1, 1922) 14.
22. Ou Tsuin-chen, *La Doctrine Pédagogique de John Dewey,* 2nd ed. (Paris: Vrin, 1958) 252.
23. Cyrus H. Peake, *Nationalism and Education in Modern China* (New York: Columbia 1932) 85, 86.
24. E. R. Hughes, *The Invasion of China by the Western World* (New York: Macmillan, 1938) 185.
25. Ou Tsuin-chen, *op. cit.* 3.
26. Ibid. 251, 252.
27. Peake, *op. cit.* 90-96.
28. K'ang Yu-wei, *Ta T'ung Shu,* trans. by Laurence G. Thompson, *The One-World Philosophy of K'ang Yu-wei* (London: Allen & Unwin, 1958) 72.
29. Teng, Fairbank, et al. op. cit. 267.
30. *Ibid.* 250.
31. Wing-tsit Chan, *Religious Trends in Modern China* (New York: Columbia, 1953) 234.
32. Frank R. Millican, "Philosophical and Religious Thought in China," *China Christian Yearbook,* (Shanghai: Christian Literature Society for China, 1926) 430.
33. Hu Shih, *op. cit.* 38.
34. Teng, Fairbank, et al. *op. cit.* 248, 249.
35. Schwartz, *op. cit.* 85.
36. Kiang, *op. cit.* 97.

37. Lin Mousheng, "Recent Intellectual Movements in China," *China Institute Bulletin,* 3 (October 1938) 16.
38. St. John, *Apocalypse,* xxi 5.
39. Nym Wales, *Inside Red China* (New York: Doubleday, Doran, 1939) 335.
40. *Reconstruction in Philosophy* 212.
41. Ibid. 213, 211.
42. "New Culture in China," *op. cit.* 642.
43. *Reconstruction in Philosophy* 212.
44. Emanuel Sarkisyanz, *Russland und der Messianismus des Orients* (Tübingen: J. C. B. Mohr, 1955) 121-34.
45. Hans Mühlestein, *Russland und die Psychomachie Europas* (Munich: C. H. Beck, 1925) 41.
46. Franz H. Michael and George E. Taylor, *The Far East in the Modern World* (New York: Holt, 1956) 235.
47. Hu Shih, *op. cit.* 42, 43.
48. C. Brandt, et al., *A Documentary History of the Chinese Communist Party* (Cambridge: Harvard, 1952) 478.
49. *Ibid.* 476.

A CHRONOLOGICAL AND BIBLIOGRAPHICAL
NOTE

A CHRONOLOGICAL AND BIBLIOGRAPHICAL NOTE

Since John Dewey's career was one of the longest and most productive in the annals of philosophy it may be useful to indicate here some of its more significant chronological and bibliographical events and to provide thereby a frame of reference within which the particularized studies of this present volume may be read.

Dewey was born on October 20, 1859 in Burlington, Vermont in a house which is still standing according to the informative essay of George Dykhuizen, "John Dewey: The Vermont Years," *Journal of the History of Ideas,* 20 (October-December, 1959), 515-44. He was the third of the four sons of his parents, Archibald Sprague Dewey, a grocer in the town, and Lucina Rich Dewey. Three of these children grew to maturity and John's older brother, Davis Rich, a well-known economist, had like himself a distinguished academic life.

Burlington, which a century ago was a small city of some fourteen thousand people, is magnificently located on the eastern shore of Lake Champlain in the great valley between the Adirondacks and the Green Mountains. Dewey once indicated that his youth in this relatively democratic and somewhat rural New England environment had helped shape certain of his characteristic recommendations for elementary schooling. Although he had not found the instruction in the Burlington public schools especially nutritious, he did feel that the round of cooperative household and agricultural activities which engaged children in the community of his boyhood constituted the most rewarding part of his education until he entered college. Consequently, the curriculum he later designed for urban schools put considerable stress upon gardening and handicraft projects which provided city children with educational experiences analogous to those encountered by the young people of an earlier day outside the classroom. The distinctive manner in which Dewey's thought was throughout all his life strongly influenced in this fashion by the events of his personal history has been underscored in two essays in intellectual auto-biography. One of these was his own contribution, "From Absolutism to Experimentalism," in the collection of statements edited by George P. Adams and William Pepperell Montague, *Contemporary American Philosophy*, Vol. 2 (New York: Macmillan, 1930), 13-27 and the other is the sketch, "Biography of John Dewey," which introduces the symposium edited by Paul Arthur Schilpp, *The Philosophy of John Dewey* (Evanston: Northwestern University, 1939), 3-45. This sketch, though actually written by Dewey's daughters, used materials which he had himself supplied and according to an appended note it may be considered autobiographical in its "emphasis on varied influences and in the philosophical portions."

Dewey was graduated from high school at fifteen and went on to the University of Vermont in Burlington. The university was then very small with fewer than a hundred undergraduates and a faculty of eight. The classical languages and mathematics rather dominated its curriculum but Dewey was also introduced to Darwinism through a Huxley text used in the physiology course, to Comte in his library browsings and to the philosophical traditions of Scotch Realism and German Idealism through the lectures of Professor H. A. P. Torrey. He was graduated as a Phi Beta Kappa in 1879 and during the following two years taught such traditional subjects as Latin and algebra in the high school of South Oil City, Pennsylvania. The academic year 1881-82 found him back in Burlington studying philosophy privately under the guidance of Professor Torrey and doing some teaching, apparently with less than total success, in the village school of a nearby town. It was in 1882 also that the first of his published pieces appeared in the *Journal of Speculative Philosophy,* edited by W. T. Harris, the leader of the American Hegelian movement who seven years later became the U.S. Commissioner of Education. Both these youthful essays were on distinctly metaphysical topics: "The Metaphysical Assumptions of Materialism" and "The Pantheism of Spinoza." Encouraged by these successes, Dewey began the graduate study of philosophy at Johns Hopkins University in the autumn of 1882 and received the doctorate two years later with a dissertation on "The Psychology of Kant." A good many of his publications, especially in the following decade, were concerned with some of the psychological issues then current although these were approached from the side of philosophy rather than through the laboratory and would be described by Dewey in 1939 as "scattered, and of late years, unprofessional writings."

Through the good offices of George S. Morris who had been Visiting Professor at Johns Hopkins, Dewey was invited to join the philosophy staff at Michigan, Morris's own university. The next twenty years were spent in the North Central States and they were significant years in Dewey's life and in the development of his distinctive philosophical outlook. Save for a year spent at the University of Minnesota, he taught at Ann Arbor during the decade from 1884 to 1894 and then moved to the University of Chicago where he became Chairman of the Department of Philosophy, Psychology, and Pedagogy and established the celebrated University Elementary School, or "Laboratory School." He remained at Chicago until 1904 when he resigned because of his dissatisfaction with President Harper's policies regarding this Elementary School, and the following autumn found him in New York as Professor of Philosophy at Columbia. In 1886, Dewey had married Alice Chipman and during those mid-western years six children were born to the couple and two of these, gifted boys, were lost through their untimely deaths in early childhood. Many of the personal relationships which, according to Dewey's own testimony, moulded his thinking, were also formed at this time. In addition to the important influence exerted by his wife, Dewey particularly benefited intellectually from his friendship with George Herbert Mead, his colleague both at Michigan and Chicago. Summers spent in the Adirondacks brought him the acquaintance of such distinguished older educators and philosophers as Harris, William James and Felix Adler, a founder of the Ethical Culture Society. In Chicago, Dewey's practical educational ideas and his humanitarian interests were nourished by friendships with Mrs. Ella Flagg Young, a District Superintendent in the Chicago public school system and with Jane Addams of Hull House.

It was during these decades that Dewey's philosophical orientation was moving through its radical transit from T. H. Green's version of Hegelian Idealism to the Pragmatic outlook associated with the names of C. S. Peirce and William James. This evolution may be partially traced in a large number of articles and reviews and in such longer works as Dewey's *The Study of Ethics: A Syllabus* (Ann Arbor: Register Publishing Company, 1894) and the *Studies in Logical Theory* by himself and other members of the Chicago philosophy department (Chicago: University of Chicago Press, 1903). This was the era, moreover, of much of Dewey's most influential work on the problems both of the theory and the practice of education. Since he had young children of his own ready for school he was drawn into a reflection upon the basic issues of elementary education. One result was that small, experimental school associated with the University of Chicago which Dewey founded and with which Mrs. Dewey was also closely involved. Here Dewey's children and those of his colleagues were among the pupils and here his characteristic theories were tested, their rationale and their results afterwards to be described in that minor classic, *The School and Society* (Chicago: University of Chicago Press, 1900). This book, which grew out of talks to parents on the work of the experimental school, was translated into Bohemian, French, German, Russian, Japanese, Polish, Spanish, Turkish, Arabic, Dutch, Bulgarian and Servo-Croatian and had also a revised and enlarged edition in 1915.

Although the school itself had a relatively brief course as a distinctively "Dewey school," its influence was widespread and contributed to Dewey's reputation as a philosopher of education as did also a number of small tracts written by him at the turn of the century. These included "Interest as Related to Will," an essay which appeared in the *Second Supplement to the Herbart Year Book for 1895* and was largely incorporated in a later work, *Interest and Effort in Education* (Boston: Houghton Mifflin, 1913); "Ethical Principles Underlying Education," which appeared in the National Herbart Society's *Third Yearbook* (Chicago, 1897) and was subsequently expanded in *Moral Principles in Education* (Boston: Houghton Mifflin, 1909); a well-known manifesto, "My Pedagogic Creed," which was first published in 1897 and is most readily available in a collection of Dewey essays edited by Joseph Ratner, *Education Today* (New York: Putnam, 1940) and *The Child and the Curriculum* (Chicago: University of Chicago Press, 1902). This last work, together with *The School and Society,* has been reissued by the University of Chicago Press in its paperback series of Phoenix Books.

The second chief phase of Dewey's career as a full-time faculty person in the university world had the Eastern seaboard as its setting and lasted for the quarter century of his service at Columbia from 1904 until he assumed emeritus status in 1930. These were continually productive years marked by a steady flow of books and essays and important involvements in a variety of professional and social movements. In 1905-06, Dewey was President of the American Philosophical Society; in 1915 he was a founder and first President of the American Association of University Professors; the next year he became a charter member of the first Teachers Union in New York City from which he later withdrew when the union began to be "used for promoting a particular political opinion rather than for educational purposes." ("Biography of John Dewey," in Schilpp, *The Philosophy of John Dewey, op cit.,* 39). His most significant contributions to the philosophy of education during the period from his arrival in New York until American entry into the First World War, were *How We Think* (Boston: Heath, 1910), which appeared in a revised edition in 1933; *Schools of Tomorrow,* an account of some progressive institutions by Dewey and his daughter, Evelyn Dewey (New York: Dutton, 1915) and, what is perhaps his best-known work, *Democracy and Education* (New York: Macmillan, 1916). Among the books dealing with more technical philosophical questions were the *Ethics* which Dewey coauthored with James H. Tufts (New York: Holt, 1908), a revision of which was published in 1932; *The Influence of Darwin on Philosophy and Other Essays in Contemporary Thought* (New York: Holt, 1910) and *Essays in Experimental Logic* (Chicago: University of Chicago Press, 1916). It should be noted, however, that Dewey himself observed that *Democracy and Education* stood for many years as the fullest exposition of his general philosophical positions and this because for him philosophy itself is well defined as "the theory of education in its most general phases," since education is the supreme human interest in which a great many cosmological, moral and logical problems all come to a head.

During the academic year 1918-19, Dewey was on sabbatical leave and he and his wife went to the Orient for a stay that was to be prolonged for several years. This was the first of several notable trips abroad during which he had influential associations with the leaders in education in other countries. During the early winter of 1919, Dewey lectured at the Tokyo Imperial University and the substance of these lectures became one of his most popular works, *Reconstruction in Philosophy* (New York: Holt, 1920). A somewhat enlarged edition of this book appeared in 1948. From Japan the Deweys went to China where they stayed for two years. Their experiences were reflected in a volume which they coauthored, *Letters from China and Japan* (New York: Dutton, 1920).

After his return from the Far East, Dewey's major writings during the 1920's and 1930's were concerned with the ethical aspects of broader cultural problems and with formal philosophical questions rather than with explicitly educational issues. Most of these books took their rise from lecture courses which Dewey had been invited to give. They included, along with a quantity of articles and journalistic pieces, these volumes among others: *Human Nature and Conduct:* An Introduction to Social Psychology (New York: Holt, 1922); his chief study of a metaphysical sort, *Experience and Nature* (Chicago: Open Court, 1925) which was somewhat revised in 1929; *The Public and Its Problems* (New York: Holt, 1927); *The Quest for Certainty,* his Gifford lectures at Edinburgh (New York: Minton, Balch, 1929); *Individualism, Old and New* (New York: Minton, Balch, 1930), a collection of six articles that had originally appeared in the *New Republic; Philosophy and Civilization* (New York: Minton, Balch, 1931); the most complete statement of his aesthetic theory, *Art as Experience* (New York: Minton, Balch, 1934); his Terry Lectures at Yale which propounded a naturalistic piety to supersede religions, *A Common Faith* (New Haven: Yale, 1934); *Liberalism and Social Action* (New York: Putnam, 1935), a brief essay in political theory; the massive epistemological study published in his eightieth year, *Logic:* The Theory of Inquiry (New York: Holt, 1938) and the concise statement of a *Theory of Valuation* (Chicago: The University of Chicago Press, 1939), which was a contribution to the *International Encyclopedia of Unified Science.* Among his many essays is one written in 1930, "What I Believe," for a series in *Forum* 82 (March, 1930), 176-82. This popular version of his *credo* was later reprinted in A. Einstein *et al., Living Philosophies* (New York: Simon and Schuster, 1931), 21-35.

There are also two short books on education dating from these years: *Sources of a Science of Education* (New York: Liveright, 1929) and *Experience and Education* (New York: Macmillan, 1938). This last is an afterword on the "New Education" by the man who, although the most famous of the so-called "Progressivists," was by no means either the whole of Progressive Education nor fully in agreement with every position represented in that movement of many strands. In *Experience and Education,* therefore, Dewey reprehended certain progressive school people with whose extreme views he could not agree and at the same time he reasserted his own tenets. On the rather complex question of Dewey's true relationship to the currents of Progressive Education, the following studies are of great help: Robert H. Beck, "American Progressive Education, 1875-1930," *Curriculum Journal,* 14 (March, 1943), 115-18, an abstract of an unpublished Ph.D. dissertation of the same title, Department of Education, Yale University, 1942; Lawrence A. Cremin, "The Progressive Movement in American Education: A Perspective," *Harvard Educational Review,* 27 (Fall, 1957), 251-70; Oscar Handlin, *John Dewey's Challenge to Education:* Historical Perspectives on the Cultural Context (New York: Harper and Brothers, 1959). During the 1920's Dewey also travelled on several occasions in order to make first-hand studies of the educational scene in other parts of the world. He went to Turkey in 1924, to Mexico in 1926 and to Russia in 1928. In 1937 he returned to Mexico as Chairman of a Commission on Inquiry into the charges made against Leon Trotsky in the Moscow Trials. One of his companions on this trip, James T. Farrell, has published an interesting account of it in his *Reflections at Fifty* (New York: Vanguard, 1954), 97-123.

Dewey lived for more than twenty active years after his retirement from Columbia. His first wife had died in 1927 and in 1946 he married Mrs. Roberta L. Grant and they subsequently adopted two young children. Dewey continued to write occasional essays; various collections of his earlier pieces were made and in 1949, the year of his ninetieth birthday, he published with Arthur F. Bentley, *Knowing and the Known* (Boston: Beacon, 1949). John Dewey died in New York City on June 1, 1952. As yet no full-length biography of him has been published but there are some interesting memoirs by his former students including Max Eastman's "John Dewey," *The Atlantic Monthly,* 168 (December, 1941), 671-85, the material of which is also to be found in Eastman's book, *Great Companions* (New York: Farrar, Straus and Cudahy, 1959) and Sidney Hook's "Some Memories of John Dewey," *Commentary*, 14 (September, 1952), 245-53. The Dewey bibliography is enormously lengthy and only a portion of it has been indicated here. Although it is not yet so definitively compiled as to include every authentic item, two useful guides to it are *A Bibliography of John Dewey* which was prepared by Milton H. Thomas (New York: Columbia University Press, 1939) containing titles of works about Dewey as well as those by him, and the reissue of Paul Arthur Schilpp, editor, *The Philosophy of John Dewey,* second edition (New York: Tudor Publishing Company, 1951), which brought the listing of entries by Dewey himself closer to date.